1008278879

Speculative Satire in Contemporary Literature and Film

Since 1980, when neoliberal and neoconservative forces began th takeover of western culture, a new type of political satire has em works to unmask and deter those toxic doctrines. Literary and cul Kirk Combe calls this new form of satire *the Rant*. The Rant is gr imaginative, and complex in its blending of genres. It mixes facet science fiction, and monster tale to produce widely consumed s major studio movies, popular television/streaming series, bestsellin designed to disturb and to provoke. The Rant targets what Comb *Regime*. Simply put, the Regime is the sum of the dangerous social and political orthodoxies spurred on by neoliberal and neoconserv Such practices include free-market capitalism, corporatism, milita osity, imperialism, racism, patriarchy, and so on. In the Rant, then unique and wholly contemporary genre of political expression a *speculative satire*.

Kirk Combe is Professor of English at Denison University in Ohio and researches in satire and drama, cultural studies, and popular these topics, he has published numerous books and articles, includin *Satire: Essays in Literary Criticism* and *Masculinity and Mo Contemporary Hollywood Films*.

Speculative Satire in Contemporary Literature and Film
Rant Against the Regime

Kirk Combe

First published 2021
by Routledge
52 Vanderbilt Avenue, New York, NY 10017

and by Routledge
2 Park Square, Milton Park, Abingdon, Oxon OX14 4RN

Routledge is an imprint of the Taylor & Francis Group, an informa business

© 2021 Taylor & Francis

The right of Kirk Combe to be identified as author of this work has been asserted by him in accordance with sections 77 and 78 of the Copyright, Designs and Patents Act 1988.

With the exception of Chapters 1 and 5, no part of this book may be reprinted or reproduced or utilised in any form or by any electronic, mechanical, or other means, now known or hereafter invented, including photocopying and recording, or in any information storage or retrieval system, without permission in writing from the publishers.

Chapters 1 and 5 of this book is available for free in PDF format as Open Access at www.taylorfrancis.com. It has been made available under a Creative Commons Attribution-NonCommercial-NoDerivatives (CC-BY-NC-ND) 4.0 International license.

Trademark notice: Product or corporate names may be trademarks or registered trademarks, and are used only for identification and explanation without intent to infringe.

Library of Congress Cataloging-in-Publication Data
A catalog record for this title has been requested

ISBN: 978-0-367-62681-5 (hbk)
ISBN: 978-1-003-11049-1 (ebk)

DOI: 10.4324/9781003110491

Typeset in Sabon
by Newgen Publishing UK

The Open Access version of Chapters 1 and 5 was funded by Denison University.

For Bren
my partner in thoughtcrime

Contents

	Acknowledgments	viii
	The Briefest of Introductions: What, Why, How	1
1	The Rant	4
2	The Regime	41
3	Ranting Against the Regime	73
4	Living Under a Lousy Orthodoxy	98
5	Special Topic Rants	127
6	Neoliberal A.I.	153
	The Briefest of Conclusions: So What? Why Bother? How Does This Matter?	183
	Bibliography	186
	Index	195

Acknowledgments

I would like to thank all of the students who have been in my college classes through the years. Their ideas and input have certainly improved my scholarship. Likewise, I hope my scholarship has enriched their classroom experience. I would like to thank as well the many, many scholars and critics I've read over the years. The work of others is integral to one's own work. The following colleagues have had a special impact on my thinking about literature, culture, and satire: Brian Connery, Christopher Wheatley, Timothy Raylor, and Sangeet Kumar. Many thanks. In particular, I would like to thank my very good colleague, Dr. Brenda M. Boyle, for her expert advice as I wrote this book. One could not ask for a better partner. Equally, the love and support of our children, Clayton, Olivia, and Hannah, and now our grandson, Carter, is essential to my wellbeing. Finally, I would like to thank Denison University for granting me a Doane Faculty Fellowship and research leave to begin work on this project.

The Briefest of Introductions
What, Why, How

What

This book operates according to the conviction that the economic and social ideologies today known as neoliberalism and neoconservatism are destructive and oppressive creeds. To be clear, then, I express in this study a distinct political point of view. This is not an "objective" analysis of fictive texts. Just as such texts never have a neutral, nonculturally specific, "universal" meaning to them, analyzes of them are never carried out by perfectly detached scholars. Such an impartial critic is a chimera. What I offer instead is what all academics offer: an argument. Mine goes like this. Since roughly 1980, when neoliberal and neoconservative forces began their hostile takeover of western (and especially American and British) culture, a type of sophisticated protest has emerged and developed alongside them within the sphere of popular culture that seeks to comment upon and even deter those toxic doctrines. This type of protest is certainly not the only form of challenge popular entertainment levels against the mounting neoliberal/neoconservative hegemony. In recent decades, there has been a proliferation of oppositional political satire available on cable and broadcast TV, over new media, and in feature and documentary films.[1] Such satire can take many forms. The kind of dissent I point out in this book, though, is distinct and identifiable. I call it the Rant. The Rant is grim (even in its humor), highly imaginative, and complex in its blending of genres. It mixes facets of satire, science fiction, and monster tale to produce widely consumed spectacles designed to disturb and to provoke. Specifically, the Rant targets what I call the Regime. Simply put, the Regime is the sum of the dangerous social, economic, and political orthodoxies spurred on by neoliberal and neoconservative polity. Such practices include free-market capitalism, corporatism, militarism, religiosity, imperialism, racism, patriarchy, and so on. It is my contention that the Rant seeks to gut-punch audiences with an unmistakable warning against the Regime. That warning is this: we are astray; it's only getting worse; change course now or suffer the consequences—which are likely to be calamitous.

That is my argument in a nutshell.

DOI: 10.4324/9781003110491-1

2 *The Briefest of Introductions*

Why

Exercising oneself in the possible cultural- and power-related readings of a creative text is among the most stimulating educational experiences I know. This book attempts such an exercise. In it, I present neither Universal Truth nor Timeless Beauty; instead, I put forward turmoil and estimation that is, I hope, reasonably intelligent and capably argued. Removing a creative work from the complex social circumstances that produced it—and in which it is read—is to neuter that work of importance. More serious still, such contextually naïve reading has nothing to do with the education of a thinking citizen. The training of citizens requires study and understanding of the workings of culture and, more to the point, of power. I think it an understatement to say that, as we enter the third decade of the 21st century, nothing is wanted more than citizens capable of critical thinking. Thinking citizenship has become buried in an avalanche of social media consumerism, of dualistic political vitriol, of support-the-troops xenophobia, of neoliberal arts vocationalism—just to name a few of the loudest distractions. Taking a deeper look into things counteracts such superficialities, and taking a deeper look into the productions of popular culture can be especially rewarding—particularly works of satire, science fiction, and monster story. Read attentively, popular culture can tell us where we've been, where we are, and where we might be going. It can reveal to us the best and the worst, the smartest and the dumbest, the most innovative and the most conservative in our society. It can tell us who might be trying to influence whom, and toward what purposes. Delight and instruction, therefore, need not be mutually exclusive. Tales of notable imagination, featuring ostensibly superficial thrills, can also be plumbed as texts of substantial intelligence as well as real public significance.

For these reasons, I offer a cultural studies investigation of contemporary popular culture.

How

In Chapter 1, I outline in detail the Rant being proposed, that is, its function by way of its intricate mixing of satire, science fiction, and monstrosity. There is ample literary and cultural theorizing in this chapter. In Chapter 2, I describe the Regime railed against by the Rant, that is, the current-day neoliberal/neoconservative hegemony at work. There is ample economic and political explication in this chapter. Chapter 3, then, offers a series of concise examples of works ranting against the machinations of the hegemon. These brief illustrations, to include Margaret Atwood's novel *The Handmaid's Tale* and Terry Gilliam's film *Brazil*, entail an account of how and for what purposes the imaginative protests target modern power. Following these initial chapters of theoretical and historical grounding, three final chapters present close readings of particularly striking Rants against the Regime. Chapter 4 examines Joon-ho Bong's film *Snowpiercer* and Margaret Atwood's novels *The MaddAddam Trilogy* as works depicting in detail life lived miserably under the thumb of a neoliberal/neoconservative authority. Chapter 5 looks at a series of Rants that focus on a particular oppressive aspect of the Regime. Works studied are Jordan Peele's film *Get Out*, an episode from the Netflix series *Black Mirror*, and an episode from the Hulu series *The Handmaid's Tale*. Chapter 6 considers the crucial and intensifying role of Artificial Intelligence (A.I.) in this unholy mess. Considered from this perspective is the novel *The Circle* by Dave Eggers, the films *Her* by Spike Jonze, *Blade Runner* by Ridley Scott, *Ex Machina* by Alex Garland, and *Blade Runner 2049* by Denis Villeneuve, as well as the HBO series *Westworld* by Jonathan Nolan and Lisa Joy. A brief Conclusion asks and offers answers to the all-important "So what?" question. That is, why does any of this matter? Why should anyone care about the ideas advanced by this book?

Note

1 Popular television shows such as *The Daily Show* (hosted by Jon Stewart then Trevor Noah), *The Colbert Report* (hosted by Stephen Colbert), and *Last Week Tonight* (hosted by John Oliver) have been on the forefront of this movement. For academic studies of such satire, see, for example, Day; Gray, Jones, and Thompson; Kumar and Combe.

1 The Rant

The purpose of this chapter is to outline in detail the Rant being proposed. Distinctively, the Rant blends three fictive forms—satire, science fiction, monster tale—in the pursuit of exposing, and perhaps even starting to dismantle, the dominant ideologies of our time. First, I set the specific cultural stage in which the Rant operates. Next, I discuss in turn each component genre of the Rant. Finally, I delineate the kind of social and political critique at the core of such works. As the reader will see, there are a number of moving parts in play when it comes to understanding the Rant.

Modern State, Postmodern Critique

My fundamental premise is that the Rant is a subgenre of modern satire that has come into being in the last four decades or so; moreover, it is always a form of political satire. Although the Rant has certain roots and precursors in literary satiric practices stretching back to early modern Europe as well as to the ancient Romans and Greeks, my primary focus is not in situating the Rant within a broad historical and literary category. Instead, I put forward and investigate the Rant as a satiric creation of our contemporary moment. Such a view and approach to this new form of political commentary, then, necessarily involves the work of Michel Foucault.

Foucault theorizes the modern state to be a system of differentiations wherein a powerful minority, through various instrumental modes, forms of institutions, and degrees of rationalization, is able to act upon the actions of the majority of the population ("Subject" 140–141). Such disciplinary power creates a regimen of "truth"—a dominant and sanctioned worldview—that is a condition for the formation and development of capitalism ("Truth" 316–317). Foucault stresses, however, that although power relations are inevitable to society, those that are established are never everlasting or inescapable. Modern hegemony is particularly subject to alteration and renegotiation. Comments Foucault:

> I would say that the analysis, elaboration, and bringing into question of power relations and the "agonism" between power relations and the

intransitivity of freedom is an increasingly political task—even, the political task that is inherent in all social existence.

("Subject" 140)

Since the early modern era, much satire has come to serve, in my view, this function of challenging the "truth" formulated by power.[1] Specifically, modern satire is adept at, as Foucault characterizes the method, "detaching the power of truth from the forms of hegemony, social, economic, and cultural, within which it operates at the present time" ("Truth" 317–318). In the early 21st century, one needs only watch episodes of *The Daily Show*, *The Colbert Report*, or *Last Week Tonight*, for example, to witness the strategies and techniques of satire applied toward the debunking of powerful political and corporate bunk.

Other key ideas from Foucault's theories pertain to modern satire as well. For example, from *Discipline and Punish*: how the main effect of the panopticon on the prisoner is a permanent visibility that assures the automatic functioning of power (201–202); how the early modern transition from feudal monarchal spectacle to modern panoptic surveillance featured a new conception of power as a set of actions upon other actions (208–209); and how feudal power sought to form a single great cultural body, but modern power seeks to fabricate particular kinds of individuals that contribute to the productivity of the regulated state (216–217). All of these phenomena become distinct when comparing, say, the feudal and monarchal intimidation taking place in Dryden's political satire *Absalom and Achitophel* (1681) as opposed to the carceral control enacted by the modern state in Terry Gilliam's film *Brazil* (1985). Similarly, Foucault points out in "Truth and Power" that whereas feudal power was a repressive power that said "No," modern power is a productive power that produces goods, induces pleasure, forms knowledge, and constructs discourse (307, 311). Modern power, then, can seductively mask its control over a population. Oppression is not necessarily overt. In effect, this subtlety makes modern disciplinarity a form of virtually unseen war-like domination by the hegemonic group in a society. As Foucault memorably summarizes the situation, "Peace would then be a form of war, and the State a means of waging it" (310). As we will see later in this book, a satiric analysis of a film seemingly as whimsical as Spike Jonze's *Her* (2013) reveals extensive cultural combat at work. Additional concepts instrumental to investigations of modern satire occur in the relationship Foucault theorizes between the individual and the state. In "The Subject and Power," Foucault discusses the ways people resist being made subject to the modern state. These struggles generally are of three kinds: (1) against forms of domination, such as ethnic, social, and religious; (2) against forms of exploitation by the rich, which separate individuals from what they produce; (3) against that which ties the individual to forms of subjectivity and submission to authority (130). When we inspect, in a later chapter, Joon-ho Bong's film *Snowpiercer* (2013), all three types of struggle will be very much in evidence. Perhaps most important, as pointed out above, Foucault asserts that while power is an indispensable feature of society, any given manifestation of it should not be taken fatalistically. Modern hegemony is always under challenge and thereby subject to change. For this reason, Foucault advises us not to pursue "universal philosophy," but to inspect instead the historical here and now—that is, how the current hegemonic discourse came into power and what can be done to thwart its oppressive disciplining (134). Whether defending or attacking the status quo, modern satire is a clear-cut participant in this contemporary cultural battle. For its part, the Rant is a particularly sharp weapon of satiric resistance and attack against the dominant discourse.

What is more, in its critique of the modern state, the Rant employs postmodern analytical techniques. Along with this Foucauldian reading of modern satire, I've argued elsewhere that the form itself activates undecidability.[2] For this assertion, I draw on Derrida's concept of *différance* and Colbert's term "truthiness" to make a case for the postmodernity of satire. Whether advocating for conservative or radical positions, satire deals in the truthy, that is, in social constructions. As a cultural creation, satire undermines, as Derrida states it, the "coherence in contradiction" that characterizes any social desire for a Transcendental Signified (495). Like the thinking of the Sophists, satire runs as a counter-discourse to Platonic thought in western culture. Any "truth" structured by a satirist comes with the knowledge that she is decentering someone else's "truth," and that her center, in turn, likely will be decentered. Thus, in my view, satire partakes of and contributes to Derrida's "joyous affirmation of the freeplay of the world ... without truth, without origin, offered to an active interpretation." This "Nietzschean *affirmation*" of "*the non-center*" indicates, for Derrida, the activity of interpretation as a game played "without security" (509), where language criticizes *itself* and structure is ever provisional. That is to say, as meaning-making beings, we inevitably create a center, but another center is sure to come along to destroy that old machinery (500). Satire, then, embodies that "terrifying form of monstrosity" that is Derrida's concept of deconstruction (510).[3] What I mean by satire, then, and in particular the Rant as it carries out a postmodern critique of the modern state, is this combined Foucauldian–Derridean tenor of agonistic monstrosity. Turning now to a description of the tripartite Rant, I begin with a more detailed account of satire.

Satire

Attempting to define this genre is notoriously tricky. It's a bit like trying to put toothpaste back in its tube. You'll meet with some success, but the mess makes you wonder if the effort was really worth it. While some essential ingredients of the form can be identified, too many other aspects of it inevitably escape delineation. In the English tradition, John Dryden's "A Discourse Concerning the Original and Progress of Satire" (1692) marks the first comprehensive effort to explain the genre. Even at that point, more than three centuries ago, Dryden tries to summarize and concretize a satiric tradition stretching back at least to Archilochus, a Greek satirist of the 7th century BCE, and wending its way through classical Rome and then medieval and renaissance Europe. Dryden's pedantic decrees about satire (e.g., a work of satire ought mainly to condemn a single vice and recommend its opposite virtue) carried considerable critical weight well into the 20th century. Formalist critics, when bothering at all with this shambolic brand of writing, pursued a rhetorical theory of satire up into the 1950s. When postmodern critical practices emerged in the 1960s, satire was recontextualized into its various cultural settings. Although working without definitional absolutes, scholars at that point nonetheless felt the need to establish satiric common ground. In 1968, Leonard Feinberg writes: "we have no right to demand complete conformity to a particular variety of satire, and we should be willing to accept numerous deviations from customary procedure" (31). Nonetheless, as reasonable generic similarities, Feinberg declares of satire that "it always criticizes, it always distorts, it always entertains" (36). Two decades later, Don Nilsen outlines a more elaborate rubric for recognizing satire, postulating four necessary conditions—grounding in reality, distortion, negative tone, posture of attack—and three strongly correlative ones—irony, social bonding, humor (8). Many such helpful formulations for the cardinal traits of satire have been offered. Among them, a statement by Edward Rosenheim stands out for its acumen and efficiency; satire, he maintains, is an "attack by means of a manifest fiction upon discernible historical particulars" (31). Applying these simple guidelines for analysis allows a critic to explore, in nearly endless detail and combination, the disposition of the attack, the complexion of the fiction that is its vehicle, plus just how patent that work of imagination is. In the same vein, the critic must ask which historical particulars, precisely, are being brought into play, and exactly how visible are those local concerns. Intention, reception, rhetoric, cultural context, and the rich heritage of the genre are all subjects for scrutiny.[4]

Such operational guidelines make good sense. As discussed above, in the modern era satire has become as well an hegemonic device of discipline and subject formation within the struggle of modern power relations. By way of summarizing the key features of satire, I offer the following digest.

Satire is a polemic: a passionate argument against something and, thus, in favor of something else; key aspects of satiric discourse include:

- a combination of *laus et vituperatio* (praise and blame)
  o the negative behaviors being condemned are highlighted and predominant
  o the positive behaviors being recommended sometimes are clear, but sometimes are implied or even indistinct
- an exploration of important cultural issues of the day
  o social (e.g., religion, class, gender, race, literary matters, tastes, and fashions, etc.)
  o philosophical (e.g., ethical conduct, nature of The Good, human perception, etc.)
  o political (e.g., the best form of government, factional wrangling, Truth and Power, etc.)
  o often these types of issues are in combination
- a frequent and effective rhetorical tool of satire is distortion and exaggeration

Satiric persona is a key element: what kind of narrator is the satirist presenting to us—and why? That is, what rhetorical and polemical functions does that narrator serve? For example:

- the Horatian *vir bonus* (the good, honest man)
- the Juvenalian *vir iratus* (the irate, indignant man)
- the parodic narrator (pretending to be someone or something else)
- the self-damning narrator (a trap for the reader)
- the unreliable narrator (sometimes reasonable, sometimes ludicrous)
- any combination of the above; other types?

Satiric form needs to be evaluated: what structure or manner of communicating does the satirist construct—and why? For example:

- the *thesis-exempla satire*: basically, an essay with a main point followed by supporting argumentation and a loose series of examples
- the *situational satire*: basically, a semi-dramatic storyline presented through various scenes, characters, and voices (such as an *adversarius*)
- a mixture of both thesis-exempla and situational elements
- a fully realized longer work of fiction, whether in prose (such as a novel), in verse (such as a mock-epic poem), for the stage (such as a social comedy), or in audiovisual format (such as a feature film or a broadcast/cable/new media series)
- a thoroughgoing invasion of another genre or form—personal letter, philosophical dialog, newspaper editorial, travel narrative, scientific article, film documentary, musical, television news program, etc.

Important to keep in mind as well is that satire generates a particularly concerted transactive reader response dynamic. That is, if text + reader = meaning, then satirists are especially attuned to precipitating an exact kind of partnership with their contemporary readership. As much critical attention needs to be paid to the satiric narratee, then, as to the satiric narrator. Questions to be deliberated include: precisely who is the contemporary audience for a given satire? Exactly how is that current-day reader being manipulated into becoming the ideal reader of a piece—that is, to fall into complete agreement with the satirist? Is the reader being bullied, cajoled, having heartstrings tugged on, collective fears tapped into, empathy created, outrage fomented, shame provoked, or pride stimulated? Is the satirist preaching to a choir or making a broader appeal to the society? Has the satirist ventured into the lion's den of the oppositional camp? Who is listening has everything to do with how a satirist embeds a text with things for that reader to do. Obviously, with these readerly issues comes the all-important historical contextualization of each piece of satire we consider.

Another vital component to consider when recognizing and analyzing satiric works is that satire itself has origins as a genre of power. In the western tradition, satire very much tends to be works created by educated urban men of means—that is, the dominant social group. Thus, satire can be seen as a patriarchal genre, one produced by those participating in the hegemonic masculinity of the day. Is satire, then, merely infighting among the elite? Satire also tends to be located in the major city of its day: Athens, Rome, Paris, London, New York, Los Angeles. While such major urban centers obviously blend together a diverse population, they are nonetheless the focal points of political, economic, and cultural power. Given this privileged backdrop for satire, some interesting questions emerge regarding the form. Where do women fit in the satiric game—aside from being its constant targets? Where do non-white, non-European peoples fit in? What about lower-class voices? Can satire be an instrument of social justice? Or is satire an instrument of social disciplining and control? Clearly, when raising these issues and asking these questions, we enter the ambit of cultural power and the theories of Foucault.

In short, satire operates within a cultural context to enact a polemic mission. To accomplish its persuasive task of blame and praise, satire invades other genres, manipulates its narrative persona, specializes in exaggeration, and establishes an intense transactive relationship with its audience. The Rants examined in this book certainly partake of all of these satiric components outlined above. For our purposes, a final factor of satire to be considered is what mode of the genre best suits a late 20th-century, early 21st-century attack against neoliberal and neoconservative supremacy. If one wants to upend a socially constructed "truth" of the neoliberal/neoconservative power elite, which satiric methods effectively accomplish that aim?

Classicist Kirk Freudenburg points out that when Quintilian famously states *satura quidem tota nostra est* (*Institutes* 10.1.93-5), the Roman rhetorician does not claim that his society *invented* the form, that "satire is *totally* ours." Rather, Quintilian's inflection reads "satire *at least* is totally ours," meaning that the form, as it was then being *practiced* by the Romans, was unique and different, at any rate, from how their Greek predecessors had put satire to use (Freudenburg 1–4). The distinction is crucial. Within a given cultural context, satire is an investigative *action*. What that activity looks like, and what might result from it, depends chiefly on the locality determining the instrument, not the other way around. Thus, Freudenburg is able to remark: "For the most part Roman satire does not matter to us. It does not have to. And we are therefore justified in thinking that our satire is exactly that: entirely ours" (21). If the formal traditions and customary practices of the genre count for less than the local needs to which they are applied, then often we put the cart before the horse when conceptualizing satire. We focus overly on the vehicle at the cost of ignoring the more vital cause for its motion. Like the current critical term queer, then, perhaps satire is better used as a verb, not as a noun. Not as a clear-cut thing, but as a wider-ranging intellectual and social action, even something of a critical method.

Recently, Ashley Marshall has asserted with regard to the golden age of early modern English satire:

The two broadest truths about eighteenth-century satiric practice are that it is highly diverse at all times and that it changes with bewildering speed from decade to decade. Both of them stem from the fact that satire is largely generated in response to its immediate circumstances.

(302)

In her study, which she calls "an exercise in 'archaeo-historicism'" (37), Marshall surveys over 3,000 works of satire produced between 1658 and 1770 in order to debunk persistent New Critical myths about a unified "Augustan mode" of satire existing during this period. Marshall demonstrates that, because of such fanciful and simplistic metanarratives,

> we are misrepresenting the culture of satire in the eighteenth century. The scope and diversity of that culture is enormous, dauntingly complex, and until now largely unknown: scholars rightly proclaim that this is the great age of satire and then overlook much of what makes it so spectacular.
>
> (xi)

Integral to what makes that early modern satire so spectacular is its "chaotic but vibrant diversity" (xiv) propelled by its intense circumstantiality. Like Freudenburg, then, Marshall finds that satire *satires* in many different ways. As a result, her newfound literary history resituates "canonical masterpieces in the full complexity of their original setting," thereby transforming "the way we conceive of satire in this period" (xiv). I look to accomplish something similar with regard to current-day satirical output. I seek to emphasize and to examine more the cultural forces driving it. What steed (or nag) pulls the ornate (or shabby) cart of our satire? And just whither might this horse roam? Certainly, motivation alone is insufficient as a way to theorize satire; formal elements of the genre, such as the ones detailed above, need analysis as well. However, the construction of grand narratives about satire that remove it from its local settings and incentives is patently silly critical business. As both Freudenburg and Marshall note, individual satires are written less to take part in a grand satiric tradition and more to participate in the controversy of a here and now. The best satire doesn't transcend the moment. The best satire *reacts* to the moment—it *is* the moment. Like Marshall, then, I explore an "explanation-strategy" (302) for how satire functions within our social moment. Which satiric moves expose best the specific enormities of our times? What is the exact complexion of that satiric action? What does it mean nowadays, not to produce "a satire," but "to satire"?

Arguably, the best and most influential manner of satire currently at work is the fake news program. Pioneers such as Jon Stewart, using a thesis-exempla satiric format on *The Daily Show*, and Stephen Colbert, using the situational satire of pretending to be a conservative pundit on *The Colbert Report*, firmly established the practice in the early 2000s and set the bar high for biting political commentary. Their legacy continues with John Oliver and Trevor Noah as well as with many spin-off fake news programs around the globe.[5] When it comes to opposing the neoliberal/neoconservative hegemony, however, there is more than one way satirically to skin a cat. Since the 1980s, another means of invective likewise has registered a significant mark of social protest within our popular culture. That approach is Menippean satire. This brand of satire has a long, murky, and critically controversial past. It begins with the now lost writings of Menippus, a Greek philosopher and Cynic satirist of Gadara in Syria, who flourished about 250 BCE. His works greatly influenced the Roman scholar and satirist Marcus Terentius Varro (circa 116–27 BCE) and, subsequently, Lucian of Samosata (circa 125–180 CE), the enormously popular and influential rhetorician and satirist who wrote in ancient Greek. The writings of these men and others carried Menippean satire forward into medieval and renaissance Europe. In his "Discourse Concerning Satire," Dryden traces and theorizes satire "of the Varronian kind," offering an account of the form along with ancient and contemporary examples.[6] In the 20th century, Menippean satire is brought to the critical forefront first by Northrop Frye in his famous *Anatomy of Criticism* (1957) and then even more influentially by Mikhail Bakhtin in his *Problems of Dostoevsky's Poetics* (first translated into English in 1973 and then again in 1984). Frye characterizes the form as an unconventional, not really novelistic prose work that attacks intellectual foolishness and duplicity. Bakhtin weaves a far more intricate description of the genre, basing it in a carnivalesque, topsy-turvy prose landscape and assigning to it a great many fundamental characteristics. These include an extraordinary freedom of plot and philosophical invention, a bold use of the fantastic, a broadscale contemplation of the world and ultimate questions, violations of established norms of social behavior, dreams or journeys into unknown lands, mixed styles and tones, and an almost journalistic concern with current and topical issues. While Frye's and Bakhtin's observations and concepts are estimable and instructive, they also paint Menippean satire in such broad and, at times, implausible brushstrokes that almost any work—from, say, *The Anatomy of Melancholy* to *Moby Dick*—can be seen to fit its vast boundaries.[7] In his 2005 book, *Menippean Satire Reconsidered*, Howard Weinbrot clears the critical underbrush in order to correct the many confusions within the study of this genre, thereby effectively reducing the number of works that can be categorized as Menippean satire. The scope of Weinbrot's study is an updated account of the workings of this complex literary practice from antiquity up through 18th-century France and England. I use Weinbrot's streamlined definition of Menippean satire as the starting point for my own theorizing of its complex manifestation over the last four decades.

Weinbrot remarks that, "Genre is a necessarily uncertain but certainly necessary construct" (*Menippean* 4). It is a series of codes and systems used by an author, and understood by a reader, to interpret aspects of reality. Summarizes Weinbrot:

> Genre thus includes (1) historical process and movement in which (2) form and content reflect (3) variously used but essential coded traits within a literary world that comments on and shapes the external world

as (4) perceived by a specific author's temperament and strategy and (5) responded to by an appropriately aware reader. Mingled process and stasis allow us to recognize the stable and the dynamic, the family resemblance and the new offspring.

(4)

Like Freudenburg and Marshall, Weinbrot conceptualizes satire as an active combination of custom and locale, of literary form meeting social context, wherein the polemical needs of the cultural moment determine most the character of the composition. After examining the foundational texts to establish the roots of Menippean satire, then tracing how the form changes and adapts as it moves through time and space up to the early modern period, Weinbrot is able to offer the following definition:

> Menippean satire uses at least two other genres, languages, historical or cultural periods, or changes of voice to oppose a threatening false orthodoxy. In different exemplars, the satire may use either of two tones: the severe, in which the threatened angry satirist fails and becomes angrier still, or the muted, in which the threatened angry satirist offers an antidote to the poison he knows remains.
>
> (297)

With regard to 18th-century British practice, and mainly the satires of Swift and Pope, Weinbrot finds four different kinds of Menippean satire at work: that by addition (see 115ff.), by genre (see 230ff.), by annotation (see 251ff.), and by incursion (see 275ff.). While these strategies are not unknown in current Menippean works, they are not of primary importance for the present analyzes. Likewise, Weinbrot's stipulation that Menippean satire uses at least two other genres, languages, and so forth is a guideline time-bound to his investigation of the early modern period. As will be seen, current-day Menippean satires certainly mix and blend disparate storytelling elements in highly imaginative ways to pursue their confrontational goals, but not necessarily similar to the strategies observed by Weinbrot in 18th-century letters. Three traits of Menippean satire stressed by Weinbrot that do pertain, however, to the vituperation against neoliberal/neoconservative ideology that I propose are these. First, that the Menippean mode "is perhaps as much a collection of related devices as a formal genre" (xii). Second, that Menippean satire

> is a genre for serious people who see serious trouble and want to do something about it—whether to awake a somnolent nation, define the native in contrast to the foreign, protest the victory of darkness, or correct a careless reader.
>
> (xi)

Third, that the "dark satirists think the unthinkable, write the unthinkable with compelling concepts and language, and thereby help us to read the unthinkable"

(302). Attitude and purpose are thus more fundamental to Menippean satire than readily identifiable external features and structural ingredients.

In sum, the key satiric element of the Rant, as I theorize the practice, entails a bleak forewarning. This alert involves a postmodern critique of the modern state in the throes of the false and threatening orthodoxy of neoliberalism and neoconservatism. These works take the general form of a longer narrative. Sometimes this narrative is in novelistic prose (e.g., *The MaddAddam Trilogy*), sometimes it is a feature film (e.g., *District 9*), more recently it has begun to appear as a multiple-episode series on broadcast, cable, or new media video platforms (e.g., *Westworld*).[8] These narratives feature fantastical settings, situations, and characters, often of a dystopian quality. These agonistic tales also blend into their satire pronounced components of science fiction and monster story. In fact, the Rant tends to blend seamlessly these three kinds of expression.

Science Fiction

Turning now to a consideration of science fiction (hereafter sci-fi), as a genre it has a history and disposition remarkably similar to satire. Like satire, sci-fi proves to be difficult to define. Like satire, sci-fi has various roots and histories, but its most vital developments occur from the 17th century onward. Like satire, sci-fi is regularly a deconstructionist pursuit, offering critiques of the here and now by way of imagining an altered reality. Like satire, then, sci-fi often gives voice to nonhegemonic people and points of view. I explore all of these characteristics below.

A critical commonplace in sci-fi studies is that definitional consensus about the form does not exist. Notes Carl Freedman,

> There are narrow and broad definitions, eulogistic and dyslogistic definitions, definitions that position science fiction in a variety of ways with regard to its customary generic Others (notably fantasy, on the one hand, and 'mainstream' or realistic fiction on the other) and, finally, antidefinitions that proclaim the problem of definition to be insoluble.
> (Critical Theory 13–14)

Like satire, sci-fi is a protean and hybrid form (genre? mode? thought-experiment? pulp fiction trash?) that reduces critics to piecemeal classifications. Some identify key elements of sci-fi: an emphasis on science and reason; rich use of the imagination; the creation of alternative worlds and societies; the relationship between the imagined world and our own. Others identify an abundance of subgenres: time-travel story, initial encounter with aliens, robot story, space opera, utopia/dystopia story, end-of-world scenario, scientist story, future-war story, and so on. Very often, as with satire, sci-fi is not regarded by literary scholars as a "legitimate" or "worthwhile" form of writing to study. It is mere popular ephemera. With the coming of structuralist and poststructuralist literary analysis, however, focus shifted from the surface attributes of the sci-fi text to its reception among readers. As Brian Baker states, such reader-oriented approaches to sci-fi "attempt to locate the specific textual operation of the genre upon its readers, and the function it might play culturally or ideologically in relation to its time and space of production" (9). That is, what kinds of things—ideas and emotions—is the text giving contemporary readers to do, and how are readers reacting to them?[9] Among scholars who approach sci-fi in this way, something of a consensus does exist about who has formulated the most influential critical insight into the form. That critic is Darko Suvin, and his theory of sci-fi is that of the *novum*.

Suvin regards sci-fi to have much in common with realistic literature. Both are culturally specific and ideologically driven forms that treat human relations as mutable and subject to historical forces. What sci-fi can bring especially to readers, though, is the *novum*, what Suvin terms "a strange newness" (4). What he means by this term is that although sci-fi creates and depicts other possible worlds, no matter how extraordinary those other worlds seem to us, they in fact reflect our own. Explains Suvin:

> The aliens—utopias, monsters, or simply differing strangers—are a mirror to man just as the differing country is a mirror of his world. But the mirror is not only a reflecting one, it is a transforming one, virgin womb and alchemical dynamo: the mirror is a crucible.
>
> (5)

No matter how outlandish, sci-fi participates in the social and political moment of its production; moreover, that strange newness of sci-fi enables us to see better our own here and now. According to Suvin, the *novum* works to strip away the naturalizing processes of ideology, myth, and convention. By having the familiar made unfamiliar to us, we are given the chance to recognize the constructedness—and thereby the strangeness—of our own social order. For example, ten pages into Huxley's *Brave New World* a reader is likely to be thinking: *This is the most bizarre society I've ever encountered.* Twenty or thirty pages in, though, the awful realization dawns on that same reader: *Oh my God, this is us! This is modern consumer culture gone ballistic!* Suvin uses Berthold Brecht's well-known dramatic device of *verfremdungseffekt*, "estrangement," as a basis for his theory of the *novum* (6). Brecht stages representations that estrange theater audiences from their own cultural norms, demonstrating for spectators just how unnormal and unfamiliar their conventions actually are. As a result, audiences have the opportunity to rethink "normal" and to see the world anew. Louis Althusser similarly argues that if ideology signifies the imaginary ways in which people experience the world, art has the capacity to do more than just passively reflect that experience. Certain art can manage to distance itself from ideology to the point where it permits us to "perceive" and "feel" more acutely our own ideological convictions (222). Art can supply us with an objective correlative for ideology that allows us to see and understand better the qualities of our own belief system. The work of art will not put into scientific language for us an exact analysis of our cultural mythology, but it will pack an emotional punch that begins to move us in the direction of that fuller intellectual comprehension of the powers that shape us. Pierre Macherey pursues this idea further. He maintains that by giving ideology a determinate form, by fixing it within certain fictional conventions, art is also able to reveal to us the limits and faults of that ideology. Art can in fact contribute to our deliverance from the ideological illusion.[10] These ideas are precisely those of Suvin with regard to the functioning of sci-fi:

> Science fiction is, then, a literary genre whose necessary and sufficient conditions are the presence and interaction of estrangement and cognition, and whose main formal device is an imaginative framework alternative to the author's empirical environment.
>
> (7–8; emphasis deleted)

Sci-fi gives us something strange to contemplate so that we can understand how strange we are.

Freedman points out how *all* fiction—even the most "realistic"—constructs an alternative world for us to consider in relation to our own (*Critical Theory* 21). Building on Suvin's theories, Freedman emphasizes in particular, though, how sci-fi puts into dialectic those crucial principles of *estrangement* and *cognition*. Says Freedman:

> The first term refers to the creation of an alternative fictional world that, by refusing to take our mundane environment for granted, implicitly or explicitly performs an estranging critical interrogation of the latter. But the *critical* character of the interrogation is guaranteed by the operation of cognition, which enables the science-fictional text to account rationally for its imagined world and for the connections as well as the disconnections of the latter to our own empirical world.
>
> (16–17)

That is to say, a dynamic tension and balance needs to exist between giving readers an alien world and giving readers a recognizable world. If the fictional world is *too* recognizable, if that tension flattens out to mere cognition, the result is merely realistic fiction that performs no estrangement. If, on the other hand, the fictional world is *too* bizarre, too disconnected from the reader's world, that tension flattens out to mere estrangement, and the result is merely fantasy fiction that performs no cognition. For Freedman, then, what he terms "cognitive estrangement" and the "cognition effect" are definitional to the genre of sci-fi. The sci-fi text must produce the indispensable outcome of readers rethinking their current reality, not simply being further immersed in it or altogether escaping it. Freedman acknowledges how such a view of sci-fi seemingly eliminates from the genre countless works in the pulp-fiction tradition, where new gadgetry, space flight, and hero saga dominate. Even the extremely popular sci-fi franchises of *Star Wars* and *Star Trek*, he notes, become suspect, since neither story line performs much in the way of stimulating in viewers a more profound cultural understandings of themselves. As we've seen previously with Freudenburg, Marshall, and Weinbrot, however, Freedman advocates for a looser way to look at genre, where "a text is not filed under a generic category; instead, a generic tendency is something that happens within a text." By this measure, Freedman widens the scope of texts that can be regarded as sci-fi by not judging them on outward appearance and formulistic considerations; instead, "cognitive estrangement is the dominant generic tendency" (*Critical Theory* 20).[11] This emphasis on critical thinking and the reexamination of social order dovetails perfectly with the account of satire discussed above. A Menippean polemic mounted against the threatening false orthodoxy of neoliberal/neoconservative hegemony triggers the selfsame cognitive estrangement of sci-fi. The estrangement comes from satire's penchant for exaggeration and the invasion of other genres—both strategies for pointedly making the familiar unfamiliar. The cognition comes from satire's transactive aim of condemning certain behaviors and recommending others in their place—thereby bringing readers to a different and broader understanding of their social moment. Like Suvin's and Freedman's concept of sci-fi, Menippean satire is recognizable more by its mindset than by a strict generic formula. Furthermore, both modes invent amazing and peculiar narratives as vehicles for their cultural exposé. So similar nowadays are certain manifestations of satire and sci-fi that it begs a few questions. Is satire invading the genre of sci-fi? Or is sci-fi, in fact, part of the genre of satire? Does differentiating really matter?

Satire and sci-fi share parallel historical developments as well. Although satire has a distinct and well-studied presence in the ancient Greek and, especially, Roman worlds, what can be taken as early sci-fi exists in those Hellenic and Roman periods as well. Some scholars see Greek myths and epics as prototypes of sci-fi. Many point to fantastic voyage narratives, such as Lucian's *A True Story* or *Icaromenippus*, as early forms of sci-fi. Such narratives are often of a Menippean satiric ilk (see Weinbrot, *Menippean* Chapters 1–3). Most critics, though, argue that modern sci-fi begins in the Renaissance through Baroque eras with works such as Thomas More's *Utopia* (1516), François Rabelais's *Gargantua and Pantagruel* (1532), Cyrano de Bergerac's *Journey to the Moon* (1657), and Jonathan Swift's *Gulliver's Travels* (1726).[12] All of these works are also satirical, fanciful adventure narratives with Menippean roots. It seems that the incredible journey functions integrally to both genres. Where satire and sci-fi clearly cross paths, however, is from the 17th century onward. Modern satire, as I characterize it above in terms of Foucauldian agonism, and sci-fi are both cultural developments of the rising modern state. As capitalism replaces feudalism, as republicanism replaces aristocracy, as science replaces magic and, to a lesser degree, religious faith, and as aggressive European colonialism begins and rapidly expands, satire and sci-fi—whether working separately or in tandem—become fictional ways to process and to inspect this shifting social reality. As H. Bruce Franklin notes when reviewing the history of sci-fi:

> During the seventeenth century, technological and social change were accelerating so rapidly that they could be experienced within a person's lifetime. Thus some people began to imagine a future qualitatively different

from the past or present. ... As capitalism and modern science continued to develop each other, SF [science fiction] extrapolated from both the tremendous changes and their disturbing consequences.

(28)

Sci-fi has antecedents going back at least 2000 years, but as a distinct genre it is a phenomenon of the modern world. Before there was science, frequent and widespread technological innovations, worldwide exploration, new theories of time and space, new visions of the future and of human macrohistory, and society based in reason as opposed to superstition, sci-fi as we know it simply could not exist. Similarly, although satire was a well-established and thriving genre prior to the modern era, like all fictive expressions—and certainly as one dealing so vitally in contemporaneity—it transformed and adapted to these radically new cultural circumstances. Modern satire clearly inherits traits from earlier satiric traditions, but as a creative, intellectual, and ideological construct, modern satire carries out different polemical missions than its predecessors. Both our sci-fi and our satire, then, are genres forged in the blast furnaces of Capitalism, Scientific Revolution, Enlightenment, Industrial Revolution, and Empire.

For example, consider briefly two well-known early modern works, Jonathan Swift's *Gulliver's Travels* (1726) and Mary Shelley's *Frankenstein* (1818). In 1951, Isaac Asimov famously stated that, "science fiction is that branch of literature which is concerned with the impact of scientific advance on human beings" (qtd. in Anders). Arguably, in both Swift's faux-travel narrative and Shelley's horror story, we see evidence that science had advanced sufficiently for western writers to contemplate its impact on society in more than merely fanciful ways. For Swift, advances in navigation had made far-flung voyaging an actuality. Swift does not so much concoct a ludicrous journey, as did Lucian, as he invades the authentic form of early modern exploration journals. In this way, due to its scientific authenticity, Swift's satire against 18th-century British society is that much more incisive and biting: its initial believability works to heighten its ultimate satiric impact. Similarly, for Shelley's novel, by the early 19th century the notion of better (or worse) living through chemistry (or any other branch of science) had become a real possibility. The element of Gothic horror in her chilling tale is not supplied by the supernatural, but by current-day scientific knowledge. Many critics, in fact, name *Frankenstein* as the starting point of modern sci-fi. What's interesting to note as well is the mixing of sci-fi and satire in these two works. *Gulliver's Travels* is ubiquitously studied as satire and only occasionally named as a possible work of sci-fi. Yet real science drives much of Swift's fiction, particularly in Book 3 where Swift attacks aspects of the new science practiced by the Royal Academy (see Lynall; Chalmers). *Frankenstein* reverses this critical judgment, being studied frequently as science fiction but rarely associated with satire. If read with the guiding principle in mind of a polemic combining blame and praise, however, Shelley's book can be seen as delivering quite the satiric punch in several areas. Discernible historical particulars attacked by this manifest (science) fiction plausibly include the exploitation of the new industrial proletariat (in the form of the stitched-together and maltreated Creature), the navel-gazing obtuseness of the bourgeois oppressor (in the form of nabob Victor), the new science run amok (chemistry and electricity in the hands of selfish and socially irresponsible nabobs), as well as the destructive privilege of patriarchy (symbolized graphically by the She-Creature that never gets up off the laboratory table). At the moment when the European bourgeois was hard at work to secure its command over the modern state, Shelley's novel plausibly speaks counter-truth to power (see Montag).

Suvin observes how subsequent historical periods brought new traits to sci-fi. The Romantic era added Faustian overreach and political apocalypse. The Victorian era blended in late-Gothic visions of anxiety, pathology, and terror as well as stories of new technology striving for utopia but causing, instead, social and imperialistic blowback. The 20th century establishes sci-fi as the literature of cognitive estrangement.[13] For the purpose of identifying recent Menippean fictions targeting neoliberal/neoconservative authority, I focus on sci-fi of the later 20th century that looks to disrupt the status quo. Two common categories of sci-fi are "hard" and "soft." Hard sci-fi tends to emphasize impending gadgetry and pay careful attention to known actualities of the natural sciences when depicting future or alternative worlds. Isaac Asimov and Arthur C. Clarke are often named as master practitioners of this type. Soft sci-fi, on the other hand, underscores issues from the social sciences—politics, economics, sociology, psychology—and tends to focus on how well or, more usually, poorly human society might deal with technological advances. Ray Bradbury, Ursula K. Le Guin, and Philip K. Dick are often cited as masters of this kind, also sometimes known as "sociological" sci-fi. A related and maybe better term for this manner of sci-fi is "speculative fiction," a designation first coined by Robert Heinlein in the 1940s and recently refined by Margaret Atwood as a no-alien brand of sci-fi about things that might actually happen.[14] These more culturally attentive works of sci-fi blend readily with the social commentary of satire and thus pertain best to the Rant being proposed. In particular, such works dominate post-1960 sci-fi production and feature themes and issues from cultural theories such as Marxism, feminism, queer theory, and postcolonialism.

Fundamental to an understanding of sci-fi is its relationship to stories of utopia and dystopia. Suvin regards such tales of alternative history to be integral to his theory of cognitive estrangement: "Strictly and precisely speaking, utopia is not a genre but the *sociopolitical subgenre of science fiction*" (61, original emphasis). Utopia theorist Lyman Tower Sargent constructs an impressive taxonomy of utopias, which he sees coming in many forms (191). These include not only a number of what he identifies as standard sci-fi storylines (e.g., tales of the future, extraordinary voyages), but also broader categories such as "Utopian satire" and "Critical utopia" (188). These are sociopolitical tales that provoke the contemporary reader to inspect her own society in comparison to the fictional one presented. Overall, Sargent conceptualizes utopias as "social dreaming" reflecting "that essential need to dream of a better life" (189).

Fictive challenges that stimulate critical rethinking of the modern status quo necessarily entail Marxist thought. Indeed, the Marxist vein in sci-fi scholarship runs deep and rich, and it begins with critics linking utopian/dystopian visions with the genre.[15] Raymond Williams sees sci-fi as the new platform for the old impulse of imagining a better world, asserting: "it is where, within a capitalist dominance, and within the crisis of power and affluence which is also the crisis of war and waste, the utopian impulse now warily, self-questioningly, and setting its own limits, renews itself" (66). Fredric Jameson maintains that sci-fi succeeds because it inevitably fails at any utopian society it sets before us. That is, because sci-fi can never depict for us an actual future, never close its own narrative at the endpoint of an actual perfect social order, it forces readers into an ideological evaluation of their own social order. Jameson writes that such stories "serve as unwitting and even unwilling vehicles for a meditation, which, setting forth for the unknown, finds itself irrevocably mired in the all-too-familiar, and thereby becomes unexpectedly transformed into a contemplation of our own absolute limits" (*Archaeologies* 289). While not strictly equating utopian stories with sci-fi, as does Suvin, Jameson does set them on parallel ideological paths. Both have the effect of mirroring and neutralizing our historical world. As Baker puts it:

> the conception of utopia is of a simulation, the map of which conforms in all points to that of its referent but is paradoxically entirely different: its reverse, or inverse, image. It confronts the 'real' of history by providing a negating space, one which exists (through utopic imagining) as a product of that history and an alternate to it.
>
> (110)

Another influential critic of utopia/dystopia and its intersection with sci-fi, Tom Moylan conceives of both a "critical utopia" and a "critical dystopia" that carry out the same function of questioning and upsetting the current-day state of affairs. Using Althusser's well-known cultural theories positing that ideology is an imaginary social reality into which individuals are forced via the process of interpellation (see 127–186), Moylan suggests that utopias are not blueprints but rather usefully disruptive social dreams: "There can be no *Utopia*, but there *can* be utopian expressions that constantly shatter the present achievements and compromises of society and point to that which is not yet experienced in the human project of fulfillment and creation" (*Demand* 28). In a subsequent work, Moylan argues that the "dystopian turn" in sci-fi of the 1980s eventually outgrows the fashionable nihilism of Cyberpunk (such as William Gibson's *Neuromancer*, 1984) to revive "the most progressive possibilities inherent in dystopian narrative." Such dystopian texts (e.g., Atwood's *The Handmaid's Tale*) are "emancipator, militant, open, and 'critical' " of the status quo rather than resigned to it (*Scraps* 188). These critical dystopias emphasize what's amiss *now* in our society that will lead to future disaster. Significantly for our purposes, Moylan characterizes this new wave of dystopian sci-fi as being a product of an "era of economic restructuring, political opportunism, and cultural implosion" (*Scraps* 186). In other words, this movement comes at the outset of the neoliberal and neoconservative ascendancy post-Reagan. To return to the ideas of Suvin, he insists that noteworthy sci-fi always offers a roundabout commentary on its author's cultural context. The ostensible escape from current reality is but "an optical illusion and epistemological trick" of sci-fi that, in fact, provides the reader "a better vantage point from which to comprehend the human relations around the author." In the end, then, the actual escape provided by utopian/dystopian sci-fi is one "from constrictive old norms into a different and alternative timestream, a device for historical estrangement, and an at least initial readiness for new norms of reality, for the novum of dealienating human history" (84). As discussed above, such new seeing is the stock and trade of modern satire as well. And, not surprisingly, utopian and dystopian tales are a common and particularly powerful vehicle for satire. As a manifest fiction of distortion and exaggeration, locations such as More's remote island nation, Swift's Land of the Houyhnhnms, or Huxley's World State carry out the same manner of cognitive estrangement as sci-fi, proffering sociopolitical commentary in the form of blame and praise.

When reviewing the history of sci-fi studies, Mark Bould remarks that while there is no necessary relationship between Marxism and sci-fi, the link has always been close. In particular, "from the emergence of SF studies as an academic discipline in the 1970s, Marxism has provided a major critical-theoretical lens through with to understand the genre" (17). During the radicalizing period of the 1960s and 1970s, a great deal of counter-culture and popular culture studies entered academia. Among them was the study of sci-fi as an estimable form. With the establishment of the theoretically sophisticated journal, *Science Fiction Studies* in 1973 and Suvin's instrumental theory of the *novum* finding its full articulation in his *Metamorphoses of Science Fiction* in 1979, leftist and postmodernist approaches to sci-fi became standard, with Marxism all but wedded to the genre (18–19). While of course scholars since then wrestle in various ways with "the Suvin event" (19), looking to challenge or to hone Suvin's approach (see Bould and Miéville), Marxism as a method to open up sci-fi texts for cultural analysis is patently useful and stimulating. Freedman, for example, makes a compelling case for these two pursuits being motivated by the same intellectual and critical impulses. Just as Marx didn't want merely to contemplate the world but to change it, pushing gnosis into praxis, and just as Gramsci saw the need to create a robust revolutionary culture, sci-fi likewise participates in radical social change. Asserts Freedman of utopian sci-fi works in particular: "they do call, as clearly and eloquently as Marx and Engels's *Manifesto*, for the world to be not only interpreted but also changed; and changed with a far-reaching radicalism in many ways comparable to Marx's own" ("Marxism" 122). Dystopian sci-fi as well is mainly Marxist in its warnings against evil social systems. Freedman points out that such warnings

> are generally launched not out of any satisfied embrace of the status quo but, on the contrary, out of a sense that the tendencies represented as

having reached a logically and terrifyingly extreme culmination in fiction are already present in actuality to an alarming degree.

(123)

This "transformative, anti-conservative thrust" forms "the most basic affinity between Marxism and SF" in Freedman's view (124). More than sharing an ardent desire for social change, however, Marxism and sci-fi possess "a deeply formal—almost, in some ways, a *generic*—affinity" (125). The structural resemblance manifests in at least two distinct ways, according to Freedman.

First, both Marxism and sci-fi, as discursive forms, are predominantly *materialist* in character. Marx accepts Hegel's understanding of the world as a dialectical and historical construction, but rejects Hegel's essentialist and spiritualist conception of *Geist* (a kind of world spirit or spirit/mind inhabiting all humans) as the driving force of history. Instead, for Marx, material production determines human affairs. In a similar way, materialism defines sci-fi as a genre. Unlike fantasy, sci-fi takes us to other worlds but explains, in at least some degree of detail, what that world is and how we got there. Not magic, but rationalist, scientific, technological—that is to say, material—explanations and concepts account for the strange new world of the narrative. For Freedman, "this materialist rationality is … closely allied to that practical transformative spirit integral to SF and generally much weaker or altogether nonexistent in fantasy" ("Marxism" 126). Second, *historicism* is a strong structural affinity between Marxism and sci-fi. The Marxist concept of historical materialism considers "material reality not as a passive unchanging essence but as an active historical unfolding that is never quite the same in one particular time and place as in any other" (128). In this way, the make-believe of human "universals" is set aside. The always-changing material world determines our consciousness, and we are perpetually in the process of constructing our social order. Sci-fi implements this perspective of history. Just as the historical novel "deals with the dynamic continuity of present and past," sci-fi "deals with the dynamic continuity of present and future" (128). That is, no matter where the sci-fi text imaginatively may take us, its starting point is in the historical here and now of its cultural moment of production. Ray Bradbury's *The Martian Chronicles* tells us far more about America in 1950 than it does about any future colonization on Mars. Sci-fi, then, whether extrapolating a history-to-come or imagining an alternative history, exercises an understanding that history is *not* caused by supernatural beings or forces exerting their will on society. Instead, culture is a human-made construct and, thus, history—even a "future history" as Heinlein termed sci-fi—is a chronicle of struggle between different social classes rooted in the underlying economic base. As Bould notes: "SF worldbuilding is typically distinguished from other fictional world-building, whether fantastic or not, by the manner in which it offers, however unintentionally, a snapshot of the structures of capital" (4). Being a cultural product of the modern world, sci-fi cannot help but use capitalism as the launch pad of its fiction. In the judgment of many critics of the genre, the best and highest-flying sci-fi rocket ships are those looking to land the reader in a destination where the primitive and exploitative oppression of capitalism is exposed, challenged, and, with hope, eventually transformed.

Finally with regard to the connection sci-fi has with Marxism, Freedman points out that indispensable to Marxism is a destructive critique of capitalistic practice. At the same time, however, that critique is incomplete if a constructive alternative to the status quo is not offered as well. In this way, Marxism has its utopian side in that "the social relations peculiar to capitalism would be replaced by relations more humane and just" ("Marxism" 130). While Marx and Engels were always scornful of the term "utopia" used in ways that were merely wishful thinking, the transformative project of their socioeconomic criticism certainly aimed for a better day. Freedman contends that among literary genres "the utopian imagination crucial to Marxism is the special province of SF." In fact, not only is sci-fi today "the privileged but almost the exclusive genre for the utopian literary imagination." The Marxist dialectical tension between critique and utopia, then, is embodied seamlessly in the combination of Marxism and sci-fi. Marxist analysis tends to emphasize the critical and sci-fi storytelling the utopic in a "dialectical complementarity" that indicates, according to Freedman, that the "two modes not only *can* be paired ... They must be" (131). Such a combination of blame and praise is, likewise, the indispensable component of satire. Like Marxist sci-fi, modern satire routinely targets the functioning of the capitalistic state. When separating "Truth" from modern power, satire carries out the same mission of rebuke-and-replace, the same gnosis–praxis project of exposing for our consideration the oppressive socioeconomic practices of capitalism and recommending instead a pathway toward increased social justice. In effect, then, sci-fi and modern satire can conjoin in their radical excoriation of modern discipline and subject formation.

With its Marxist underpinnings, sci-fi struggles against forms of exploitation by the rich that separate individuals from what they produce. Similarly, post-1960 works of sci-fi often participate in the two other ways, according to Foucault, that people resist being made subject to the modern state: against forms of subjectivity that submit individuals to authority; against forms of ethnic, social, and religious domination ("Subject" 130). With regard to resisting imposed subject status, patriarchy became a particular target of sci-fi as new works by women overlapped with second-wave feminism. In the 1960s, the French feminist critiques of Simone de Beauvoir, Julia Kristeva, Hélène Cixous, and Luce Irigaray became influential among American activists and academics. During the 1970s, a new wave of women writers—Marge Piercy, Joanna Russ, Sally Miller Gearheart, Ursula K. Le Guin—began to use sci-fi as a way to interrogate and challenge constructions of gender, in particular "femininity" (Baker 120). Many of these works involve the creation of a feminist utopia that stands in obvious criticism of the author's current-day patriarchal society. Le Guin, for example, saw traditional male sci-fi as sexist and racist "Techno-Heroic" stories that were regressive in their politics and featured masculinist principles of domination and repression. In contrast, she viewed the "female principle" as being "basically anarchic. It values order, without restraint, rule by custom not force" ("Is Gender" 163). Looking to transform the genre of sci-fi, Le Guin called for the addition of "a little human idealism, and some serious consideration of such deeply radical, futuristic concepts as Liberty, Equality, and Fraternity"—to include, of course, "Sisterhood" ("American" 99). In the same vein, Russ declared sci-fi to be a problem-solving genre for women writers in that it could break them out of the two storylines traditionally available to women: the marriage plot or the madness plot. Within the imaginative freedom of sci-fi, narratives can be created that are not "about men *qua* Man and women *qua* Woman; they are myths of human intelligence and adaptability." These stories "ignore gender roles" and "are not culture-bound" (18). Since the 1970s, numerous works of fiction and films inspired by such precepts have enriched and expanded the genre of sci-fi. Thus, along with Marxism, feminist approaches to sci-fi are instrumental to the genre and its study. A leading critic in this area is Marleen Barr with her theory of "feminist fabulation."

Barr asserts that where most "male SF writers imagine men controlling a universe once dominated by nature; most female SF writers imagine women controlling a world once dominated by men" (*Feminist* 4). In this way, feminist sci-fi disrupts the hegemonic discourse of capitalistic patriarchy by creating "literature whose alien ingredients are concocted by the female imagination" (31). Barr characterizes fabulation as an exercise in acute social critique that operates via Suvin's principle of cognitive estrangement. Profoundly different alternative worlds and futures are deployed as a way to displace and disrupt the contemporary familiar. Writes Barr: "Feminist fabulation is feminist fiction that offers us a world clearly and radically discontinuous from the patriarchal world we know" (10). Such speculative fictions estrange readers from conventional reality so that they may question the dominant worldview. Via a range of postmodern demolitions of the patriarchal "normal," this kind of feminist sci-fi depicts women characters doing the presently impossible, in various ways frees women from reproductive slavery, and overall subverts traditional conceptions of gendered behavior by demonstrating how the very notion of gender is a social construct. Novels such as Le Guin's *The Left Hand of Darkness* (1969) and Russ' *The Female Man* (1975) are exemplary to this manner of fabulation. Of course, not all works conveying feminist perspectives create women-run worlds. Atwood's *The Handmaid's Tale* (1985) performs quite the opposite as a means to deliver her anti-patriarchal message, and Denis Villeneuve's recent film *Arrival* (2016) gives us a woman protagonist who steadily works to undermine the dominant masculine bluster with her intelligence and empathy.[16]

In due course, gender theory as an expansion of feminist theory came into play in the writing and analysis of sci-fi. The male/female gender binary can be blurred and problematized in any number of ways by sci-fi works involving weird or horrific scientific experimentation, space or time travel, aliens, cyborgs, A.I., or any other alternative or otherworldly scenario that can be imagined. In her well-known essay "A Manifesto for Cyborgs" (1985), Donna Haraway calls for reconstructed gender roles by way of women modeling themselves on cyborgs—monstrous hybrid machine–humans. Such a disturbance of the normal man/woman and human/machine binaries would bring about a "postgender world" (67), where identities could be constructed for pleasurable and utopian purposes. Humans, then, would possess "permanently partial identities" (72) that disobey the oppressive gender positions currently assigned and enforced by the ideologies of capitalism and patriarchy. For Haraway, sci-fi is the realm where such stories of possibility best occur, that is, tales featuring gender deconstruction and radical defiance to modern subject formation. Haraway's declaration anticipated the influential gender theories of Judith Butler, in particular Butler's notion of gender performativity as outlined in *Gender Trouble* (1990). Queer theory, as it formulated and escalated from the theories of Butler and others, proved a readily applicable tool for sci-fi studies. Butler's foremost contention that gender and subjectivity is not a natural essence manifesting from within but a social varnish ideologically applied from without matches entirely with a genre dedicated to upending the familiar here and now. Baker remarks how Butler's concept of performativity "deeply informed the critiques of subjectivity and gender that have been central to the discourses that surround SF, and to the development of a strand of SF criticism that has 'queered' the genre" (127).[17] Feminist, gender, and queer theories alike figure prominently in the disruption and resistance sci-fi can mount against the techniques of modern discipline.

With regard to struggles against forms of ethnic, social, and religious domination, increasingly issues of race and colonialism are patent in works of sci-fi. In his opinion piece "Black to the Future," novelist Walter Mosley points out that only "within the last thirty years have positive images of blackness begun appearing in even the slightest way in the media, in history books, and in America's sense of the globe" (203). Even this small acknowledgment, though, has produced an outpouring of accomplishments for African-Americans in any number of professional fields. Notes Mosley:

> The last hurdle is science fiction. The power of science fiction is that it can tear down the walls and windows, the artifice and laws by changing the logic, empowering the disenfranchised, or simply by asking, What if? This bold logic is not easy to attain. The destroyer-creator must first be able to imagine a world beyond his mental prison.
>
> (203–204)

Mosley predicts a coming explosion of sci-fi from the black community, new works "created out of the desire to scrap five hundred years of intellectual imperialism" (204). Signs of this innovation are found, for example, in the novels of Nigerian-American author Nnedi Okorafor. In a talk at the TEDGlobal 2017 conference, she describes her *Binti* trilogy (2015–2018) as a work of Afrofuturism, a fresh strain of sci-fi that functions differently from traditional western sci-fi. Okorafor describes the narrative arc of her three novels as: "African girl leaves home. African girl comes home. African girl becomes home. ... This idea of leaving but bringing and then becoming more is at one of the hearts of Afrofuturism." Her approach to the genre, then, is altogether not through a European perspective. Explains Okorafor: "Growing up, I didn't read much science fiction. I couldn't relate to these stories preoccupied with xenophobia, colonization and seeing aliens as others. And I saw no reflection of anyone who looked like me in those narratives." Instead, Okorafor writes her *Binti* novella trilogy not

> following a line of classic space opera narratives, but because of blood that runs deep, family, cultural conflict and the need to see an African girl leave the planet on her own terms. My science fiction had different ancestors, African ones.

Like Mosley, Okorafor sees this new bloodline of sci-fi as a way to break out of white supremacist and Eurocentric chains:

> African science fiction's blood runs deep and it's old, and it's ready to come forth, and when it does, imagine the new technologies, ideas and sociopolitical changes it'll inspire. For Africans, homegrown science fiction can be a will to power.

In the 21st century, sci-fi is expanding as a form of nonwestern counter-hegemonic discourse. The genre has become an emerging world literature and expression that challenges British and American literary and, far more important, cultural–economic domination.[18] Unsurprisingly, themes of colonization are frequently pertinent, if not central, to the production and the study of sci-fi these days.

As Matthew Candelaria points out, "science and industrialism are themselves thickly intertwined with the successive waves of colonialism/imperialism emanating from the powers of Europe" (133). Since western sci-fi sees its very development as a way to respond to the emerging modern world, it makes good sense "to read and analyze SF texts in terms of their explicit or implicit commentary on historical episodes in European imperialism" (134). Needless to say, some works of sci-fi support the imperialistic project (consciously or not), while other works question, problematize, or outright challenge the aggressive spread of modern power. In *The War of the Worlds* (1897), H. G. Wells famously turns the tables on British imperialism, imagining England invaded by a rapacious and militarily superior civilization. Steven Spielberg's 2005 remake, *War of the Worlds*, similarly asks American audiences fictively to experience the terror and powerlessness of being subjugated by an overwhelming and callous foreign force—that is to say, to feel what it might be like to be invaded by the American military-economic machine. In *District 9*, Neill Blomkamp explores issues of South African apartheid with a unique, strangely inverted alien-invasion plotline. To date, a top-grossing film worldwide remains James Cameron's *Avatar* (2009), a sci-fi blockbuster premised in the brutality of colonial expansion.[19] Of course, one could say that all of these works are themselves imperialistic acts, given that they enjoy the support and clout of the western publishing and filmmaking industries. As Cyberpunk novelist Bruce Sterling once remarked, "Trying to conquer the American publishing industry would be the same as trying to conquer the US

Air Force" (qtd. in Sousa Causo 153). From any number of angles, sci-fi is rife with the concepts of postcolonial theory. Candelaria, for example, emphasizes ideas such as civilized metropolitan center/savage wilderness periphery, imperial Self/colonized Other, and a "progress discourse" advocated by the colonizer but, in fact, denied to the colonized (135–138).[20]

I have reviewed carefully not just sci-fi but how that genre parallels the history and function of satire. In particular, post-1960 sociological sci-fi and Foucauldian–Derridean modern satire pair remarkably well. So well, in fact, that at this point I am ready to coin a literary term: *speculative satire*. At the core of the Rant against the Regime is the anti-establishment speculative fiction of sci-fi blended with the warning against false orthodoxy distinctive of the Menippean cautionary tale. While satire and sci-fi form the baseline of this Rant, a third ingredient of monsters, or at the very least issues of monstrosity, is powerfully at work as well in speculative satire.

Monster Tale

The word "monster" comes from the Latin *monstrum*, "a portent"; its root word is *monere*, "to warn." Right from the start, then, the very concept of a monster has something to do with upsetting the applecart of the social norm. A belief in monsters of all kinds is a global, historical phenomenon of culture. Studying their variety or theorizing about the psychology behind them are interesting ways to approach the bestiary of human imagination. My purpose here, though, is to consider monsters as symbols, as constructs of specific societies, as terrifying signifiers linked, usually, with even more disturbing signifieds.[21] A leading critic in this approach to monsters is Jeffrey Jerome Cohen, who proposes Monster Theory as "a method of reading cultures from the monsters they engender" (3). Asserts Cohen: "The monstrous body is pure culture. A construct and a projection, the monster exists only to be read. ... Like a letter on the page, the monster signifies something other than itself; it is always a displacement" (4). In particular, Cohen regards monsters as cultural signifiers that subvert the current normal. Monsters act, in effect, as binary busters, as disturbing hybrids whose externally incoherent bodies resist attempts to include them in any systematic cultural structuration. Calling such creatures "the Harbinger of Category Crisis," Cohen sees the monster as "a form suspended between forms that threatens to smash distinctions." Monsters are therefore dangerous because "by refusing an easy compartmentalization of their monstrous contents, they demand a radical rethinking of boundary and normality" (6). In the epic of *Beowulf*, for example, the monster Grendel seems but a brute beast gathering up, killing, and eating Danish thanes. Yet, at the same time, Grendel pursues a political agenda as he targets and disrupts, for 12 winters, King Hrothgar's seat of power, the great mead-hall, Heorot. Is Grendel, then, just a mindless and bloodthirsty creature? Or is he a thinking being, a rebel in fact (or terrorist, depending on one's point of view) with a sophisticated take on the world? Answers are murky. In this way, monsters expose the provisionality of the present; they act as agents of deconstruction. Cohen calls them "the living embodiment of the phenomenon Derrida has famously labeled the 'supplement' (*ce dangereux supplément*)" because, like supplementarity, monsters erase the either/or logic of binary opposition (7). Grendel upsets such neat pairings as human/animal, culture/nature, hero/enemy. Part of its terror, then, is the monster's ability to decenter our carefully constructed and much desired totalization of existence, thereby dragging us, kicking and screaming, into Nietzschean freeplay. Monsters are inexplicable yet, suddenly, there they are, forcing us to rethink what we formerly thought of as reality.

What is more, the monster often embodies the social Other, dwelling at what Cohen terms "the Gates of Difference." A monster is constructed to appear aberrant and from beyond the cultural normality, yet actually it originates from *within* the culture as a representation of those who are excluded by the dominant discourse, that is to say, as those who must be exiled or destroyed. King Hrothgar, after all, oversees an invading and colonizing force, one that took possession of Grendel's native lands. No wonder Grendel becomes—in the Danish telling of the story—an evildoer that must be obliterated. Monsterization, then, can be an act of social power, a means of segregation and marginalization. Remarks Cohen: "Any kind of alterity can be inscribed across (constructed through) the monstrous body, but for the most part monstrous difference tends to be cultural, political, racial, economic, sexual" (7). Clearly, Grendel can be read as a political opponent of the Danes expediently reduced to slathering horror. Similar acts of monstrous exclusion in western culture include those against strong women (e.g., Grendel's nameless mother), against racial difference (e.g., King Kong), against ethnic-religious difference (e.g., Xerxes and the Persians in the graphic novel and film *300*), against sexual deviation (e.g., Lilith). In Cohen's view, monsterized Others serve as scapegoats for the problems of a society. Creating then blaming victims (e.g., Jews, Muslims, immigrants, the poor) seems a special proclivity of modern discipline. At the same time, however, Cohen points out how the "political-cultural monster, the embodiment of radical difference, paradoxically threatens to *erase* difference in the world of its creators" (11). If pondered thoughtfully, monsters have the potential to reveal the contrived workings of the society. Once Grendel can *also* be seen as a freedom fighter challenging colonial domination, Hrothgar can *also* be seen as an old, drunken, feeble chieftain who must hire a glory-seeking thug, Beowulf, to reestablish oppression. Suddenly vanished is the national feel-good of epic grandeur and heroism. As René Girard notes about the scapegoat:

> Difference that exists outside the system is terrifying because it reveals the truth of the system, its relativity, its fragility, and its mortality. ... persecutors are never obsessed with difference but rather by its unutterable contrary, the lack of difference.
>
> (qtd. in Cohen 12)

Monsters imperil not just individual members of a society, then, but, as Cohen remarks, "the very cultural apparatus through which individuality is constituted and allowed" (12). Monsters derail the mechanisms of modern subject-formation.

A further paradox of the monster theorized by Cohen is its ability simultaneously to enforce social borders and to invite their dissolution. The monster both "Polices the Borders of the Possible" (12) and our "Fear of the Monster is Really a Kind of Desire" (16). As extreme examples of what *not* to be, monsters administer modern panoptic discipline. These strange creatures warn us:

> that one is better off safely contained within one's own domestic sphere than abroad, away from the watchful eyes of the state. The monster prevents mobility (intellectual, geographic, or sexual), delimiting the social spaces through which private bodies may move. To step outside this official geography is to risk attack by some monstrous border patrol or (worse) to become monstrous oneself.
>
> (12)

More specifically, monsters act as herdsmen to control the traffic in women and to establish male homosocial bonds "that keep patriarchal society functional" (13). As constructs of the dominant discourse, monsters are created to keep us in our social place. As discussed above, however, such controls can backfire. Cohen affirms that, under scrutiny, "The monster's destructiveness is really a deconstructiveness: it threatens to reveal that difference originates in process, rather than in fact (and that 'fact' is subject to constant reconstruction and change)" (14–15). What can trigger this insight into the mutability of culture is our uncanny attraction to the monster. As transgressors and lawbreakers, these "same creatures who terrify and interdict can evoke potent escapist fantasies; the linking of monstrosity with the forbidden makes the monster all the more appealing as a temporary egress from constraint" (16–17). Perhaps this is why Mary Shelley tells us, in the introduction to the 1831 edition of *Frankenstein*, that her ghost story will "speak to the mysterious fears of our nature, and awaken thrilling horror" (23). Monsters may be embodiments of the culturally abject, of that which the general society wants to shun, but unlike us, who are so carefully disciplined in our behaviors and attitudes, monsters enjoy a terrible freedom as border-walkers. Their despair as outsiders can be enticingly sublime. In his novel *Grendel* (1971), John Gardner takes us inside the thinking, emotions, and backstory of the monster, very much humanizing that beast. In her novel, Shelley allows us to feel the confusion, loneliness, and betrayal experienced by Frankenstein's creature, arguably making it a far more sympathetic character than Victor. The moment we empathize in any way with the monster is the moment we realize that we have created it through careful exclusion and as an act of power. Concludes Cohen:

> These monsters ask us how we perceive the world, and how we have misrepresented what we have attempted to place. They ask us to reevaluate

our cultural assumptions about race, gender, sexuality, our perception of difference, our tolerance toward its expression.

(20)

Monsters can be unnerving and penetrating symbols that demystify the "reality" formulated by a society.

Cohen's notions of monstrosity augment and blend well with the disruptive genres of satire and sci-fi. As a component of an attack by means of a manifest fiction upon discernible historical particulars, the device of a monster can serve the satiric polemic admirably. In its attack on knavery and folly, satire ever has been in the business of monsterizing its victims. Swift in *Gulliver's Travels* and Rabelais in *The Life of Gargantua and of Pantagruel* (five volumes c. 1532–1564), for example, give us all manner of giants, little people, sea monsters, rational horses, winged pigs, giant wasps and monkeys and eagles, magicians, ghosts, immortals, deformed and savage humanoids, and so on. All such creatures are used to make satiric points, none better, perhaps, than Swift's Yahoos as a caustic portrait of rapacious, vainglorious, and brutish Europeans. Nor does monsterization necessarily entail the representation of strange creatures. The behaviors, attributes, and attitudes of specific individuals or groups of people often are exaggerated and vilified in satire to the point of monstrosity. Political adversaries routinely come in for this kind of rough treatment, and the satiric tradition is rife with the monsterization of women.[22] Of course, satire can be cunning in its use of monsters as well. Looks, after all, can be deceiving, and satire is adept at setting traps for the unwary reader. With Swift's "A Modest Proposal" (1729), we seem to be reading the treatise of a highly educated and well-intended social engineer tackling the problem of poverty in Ireland—until that narrator recommends, by way of solution, that poor Irish start selling their babies for food to wealthy gentlemen and ladies.

> A young healthy child well nursed, is, at a year old, a most delicious nourishing and wholesome food, whether stewed, roasted, baked, or boiled; and I make no doubt that it will equally serve in a fricassee, or a ragout.
>
> (Swift 490)

This monstrous political economist then sets out a detailed and rational scheme for treating human beings as commodities. In a satiric flash, Swift reverses our understanding of social order: poor Irish are not the problem; rich British are. A similar occurrence of monster-inverting satire comes with the so-called "Prawns" in *District 9*. These aliens, as monsterized racial Others excluded and oppressed by the hegemonic social order, function poignantly as standins for victims of actual South African apartheid. These marooned, insect-like beings have been ghettoized into shanty towns by hysterical public opinion and draconian governmental policy; meanwhile, an avaricious and underhanded multinational corporation hopes to exploit their advanced weapons technology. By way of this unexpected scenario, the film mounts a pointed argument against the neoliberal state, highlighting for blame the bigoted, corrupt, and violent collusion between political and corporate institutions ruthlessly pursuing abusive objectives. Held up for praise, on the other hand, is the longsuffering communitarianism of these erstwhile monsters. While as viewers we are given no details at all about these space aliens, and while when provoked these aliens can act unpredictably and sometimes violently themselves, we nonetheless witness how they possess more "humanity" than do the humans in the film. This application of monstrosity, then, like Swift's, explores important social, economic, political, and philosophical issues of the day via two frequent and effective rhetorical tools of satire: distortion and exaggeration. *District 9* readily can be read as a monster-driven Menippean warning against a threatening false orthodoxy.

If my suggestion of monsters functioning as a strategy of satire is somewhat surprising, the idea of monsters being a commonplace and integral feature of sci-fi certainly is not. Monsters, aliens, and strange beings of all sorts have populated fantastic voyage, utopia/dystopia, and sci-fi stories from their earliest iterations. As confounding triggers of what Cohen terms "category crisis" (6), monsters operate perfectly within the strange newness of Suvin's *novum*. In fact, the necessary and sufficient conditions for sci-fi specified by Suvin—that is, "the presence and interaction of estrangement and cognition" (7–8)—match exactly the impact of monsters as theorized by Cohen. Both the alternative reality of sci-fi and the horror of the monster first estrange the reader from her empirical environment and conventional social order. Second, sci-fi and monster then spark in the reader, by way of that estrangement, a recognition that her *own* reality is not a "natural" one but likewise artificial and the product of cultural construction. Sci-fi and monsters (and, yes, satire) hold up a strange mirror to our own world that works to undermine and denaturalize current ideologies and customs. By way of another quick example, consider the Na'vi in the film *Avatar*. At first, they seem to be a combination of exotic space alien and colonized savage, both bizarre and inferior to the humans establishing an industrialized foothold on the planet Pandora. During the course of the film, however, it becomes clear that the real monsters in this story are not the eccentric indigenous beings of Pandora, but the invaders from Earth. Specifically, corporate greed and military machoism—as we will see in the next chapter, trademarks of neoliberalism and neoconservatism—emerge as the rampaging beasts of the narrative. As viewers, then, we come to recognize our own cultural practices as being violently acquisitive and intolerant. Startlingly, a further bit of cognitive estrangement we undergo is realizing our *technological* inferiority to the Na'vi as well. Not only is their communal society superior to our individualistic one, but their biotechnology is far advanced to our crude mechanized technology. The Na'vi mesh and thrive alongside the environment of Pandora, while we primitive and exploitative humans have devastated and exhausted our own planet. These sci-fi Others thus begin the film as monsters but end the film as ideals.

Post-Marxism versus The Man

Now that the cultural stage has been set and the component parts of the Rant have been explained, I end this chapter by characterizing the type of social critique driving these works. While the issues of Marxism certainly animate much modern sci-fi, the best way to understand all the kinds of resistance to modern power available in speculative satire—against social domination, against subject-formation, against economic exploitation—is through the lens of post-Marxist theory. As argued above, at the core of the Rant is a postmodern dissection of the modern nation-state as it is currently being controlled by neoliberal and neoconservative doctrines. By putting into operation the fundamentals of post-Marxist theory, Rants are able to tackle the full range of abuses suffered at the hands of the present-day hegemon.

Post-Marxist theory came into existence contemporaneously with the rise of neoliberalism and neoconservatism. As will be discussed in Chapter 2, when Keynesian embedded liberalism began to sputter in the late 1960s and through the 1970s, responses to that economic crisis polarized between neoliberalists looking to detach business and the market from state regulation and social democrats looking to extend central planning and state regulation of the economy. In the advanced capitalist world, labor unions and urban social movements began to converge to form a realistic socialist alternative to economic liberalism. As a response to this social democratic threat to the ruling elite, the forces of neoliberalism began their gradual march to power (Harvey 15). In the academic activist world, the socialist resistance to these neoliberal forces became theorized as post-Marxism. The term itself means *beyond* Marxism, that is, taking Marxist theories as a basic starting point, but adding to them and moving forward with their social implications. Basically, what has been added to Marx's 19th-century struggle for economic fairness (e.g., labor unionism) is a range of 20th- and 21st-century struggles for social justice (e.g., feminism and racial equality). As a theory, post-Marxist stems from the works of Louis Althusser (1918–1990) and Michel Foucault (1926–1984). Althusser laid the groundwork for post-Marxist theory by successfully undermining the Hegelian universalism of traditional Marxism, thereby opening up a variety of social critiques beyond economic determinism. Foucault augmented these developments by demonstrating how discourse and the episteme are hegemonic constructs always under the stress and possibility of change; that is, the creation of a dominant discourse is not the sole purview of the owner class (as implied by Marx's concept of ideology) nor does it always serve the interests of the elite (as implied by Althusser's concept of interpellation).[23] Emerging from the influence of these two thinkers is a great variety of social enquiry pursued by many critics looking into philosophical, economic, historical, feminist, racial, literary, and cultural matters in ways that broaden traditional Marxism. Asserts Philip Goldstein of this new approach:

> The work of all these scholars suggests ... that, unlike traditional Marxism, which defends the priority of class struggle and the common humanity of oppressed groups, post-Marxism reveals the sexual, racial, class, and ethnic divisions of social life and promotes its progressive transformation.
> (21)

No longer is a Marxist analysis concerned only with a generic oppressed "worker" (meaning, really, a toiling white man being exploited by a wealthy white man). Subject to scrutiny now are a variety of identity positions as they are formed and regimented by various and competing power discourses within the modern state.

A key early text in this social and intellectual movement is *Hegemony and Socialist Strategy: Towards a Radical Democratic Politics*, first published in 1985 by political theorists Ernesto Laclau and Chantal Mouffe. In their call for a new socialist strategy, Laclau and Mouffe dismiss the notion from traditional Marxism of the worker being a transcendental ideal, a homogeneous group that someday will set right all the wrongs of capitalism. They argue that the "ontological centrality of the working class" must be set aside because the "plural and multifarious character of contemporary social struggles has finally dissolved the last foundation for that political imaginary" (2). The manifold social struggles of the day necessitating this theoretical reconsideration of Marxism include:

> the rise of the new feminism, the protest movements of ethnic, national and sexual minorities, the anti-institutional ecology struggles waged by marginalized layers of the population, the anti-nuclear movement, the atypical forms of social struggle in countries on the capitalist periphery.

Social conflict, then, extends far beyond the clash of capital and labor. Hegemonic contest exists in a wide range of areas, the exploration of which "creates the potential ... for an advance towards more free, democratic and egalitarian societies" (1). Needing to be tackled are both issues of "redistribution" (meaning wealth inequity) and issues of "recognition" (meaning social identity). In this way, "struggles against sexism, racism, sexual discrimination, and in the defence of the environment" can be "articulated with those of the workers in a new left-wing hegemonic project" (xviii).[24] Central to Laclau and Mouffe's new leftist politics is Gramsci's concept of hegemony—but rethought and radicalized by postmodernism. That is to say, as a political articulation, hegemony is no longer considered to possess a stable, "universal" meaning as it might within the rationalism and essentialism of classical Marxism. Instead, applying the poststructural theories of Derrida and Lacan, Laclau and Mouffe regard hegemonic discourse as a time- and location-bound, evershifting articulation of modern power. They declare:

> At this point we should state quite plainly that we are now situated in a post-Marxist terrain. It is no longer possible to maintain the conception

of subjectivity and classes elaborated by Marxism, nor its vision of the historical course of capitalist development, nor, of course, the conception of communism as a transparent society from which antagonisms have disappeared.

(4)

Given the rise of a globalized, information-based form of capitalism, the collapse of the Soviet Union, and the radically altered intellectual landscape of postmodern thought, Laclau and Mouffe assert the need to reject 19th-century Marxist essentialist thinking as well as Leninist and Stalinist communist dogma that grew out of the cultural specificity of 20th-century Russia. Older forms of Marxism simply were not relevant to the new political and economic circumstances of the day. Marxist theory needed reinvention.

At the core of this reinvention are Derrida's deconstructive principle of "undecidability" as well as Lacan's notion of a "nodal point" in the formation of the subject. From these ideas, Laclau and Mouffe formulate two key concepts: hegemonic subjectivity and social antagonism (xi–xiv). By hegemonic subjectivity, they mean that social structure and one's position within it are not matters determined by "nature" or any kind of universal "truth," but instead are cultural constructs determined by the actions and articulations of powerful groups. Here of course, the strong influence of Foucault's cultural theory of "truth and power" is evident in their thinking. Like Foucault, Laclau and Mouffe propose that "the privileged discursive points" of the powerful act as "privileged signifiers that fix the meaning of a signifying chain," thereby creating a social order that masquerades as fixed, stable, natural, and timeless. At the level of the individual psyche, these "partial fixations" are what Lacan calls *points de capiton*, that is, a means by which we can make sense of the world by imposing an order upon it. At the political level, these *nodal points*, to use Laclau and Mouffe's term for this concept, structure a social center, a political–economic transcendental signified, along with a dominant discourse to support it (112). However, because of linguistic undecidability, any given social construct and center cannot hold. Derrida's idea of freeplay maintains that every signifier is a floating signifier, never becoming fixed forever to a single, unchangeable signified. Laclau and Mouffe apply this precept politically, remarking that "this floating character" of all signifiers "finally penetrates every discursive (i.e. social) identity" to render it a contingent and impermanent state of affairs. They elaborate:

> It is not the poverty of signifieds but, on the contrary, polysemy that disarticulates a discursive structure. ... *The practice of articulation, therefore, consists in the construction of nodal points which partially fix meaning; and the partial character of this fixation proceeds from the openness of the social, a result, in its turn, of the constant overflowing of every discourse by the infinitude of the field of discursivity.*
>
> (113, emphasis original)

34 *The Rant*

Any given social moment, then, is just that: a moment. Culture is no more everlasting than language. There can certainly seem to be stability and longevity to both, but, as Derrida posits, that is fond wish, not existential circumstance.

Because linguistic freeplay ceaselessly creates then undermines nodal points of partially fixed meaning, Laclau and Mouffe put forward their second key concept: social antagonism. This idea is the central argument of their book and asserts the inevitable clash of contending forces and groups in society, *not* as part of a cultural superstructure but as the *base* of social organization itself. They state:

> Our thesis is that antagonisms are not *objective* relations, but relations which reveal the limits of all objectivity. Society is constituted around these limits, and they are antagonistic limits. … This is why we conceive of the political not as a superstructure but as having the status of an *ontology of the social*.
>
> (xiii–xiv)

Society is rivalries, with competing factions ever vying to fashion and impose a nodal point of cultural "reality" upon the population. To turn to specifics, the cultural moment and nodal point troubling Laclau and Mouffe in the mid-1980s and thereafter is that of the left wing not adequately revitalizing itself in order to combat the takeover of right-wing neoliberalism. In the 2000 preface to the second edition of *Hegemony and Socialist Strategy*, they write:

> Instead of a recasting of the socialist project, what we have witnessed in the last decade has been the triumph of neo-liberalism, whose hegemony has become so pervasive that it has had a profound effect on the very identity of the Left. It can even be argued that the left-wing project is in an even deeper crisis today than at the time in which we were writing, at the beginning of the 1980s.

That crisis, for Laclau and Mouffe, is the development of the so-called "centre-left" and a "third-way" politics premised on the misconception that "with the demise of communism and the socio-economic transformations linked to the advent of the information society and the process of globalization, antagonisms have disappeared" (xiv). While they are certainly not calling for a return to Nikita Khrushchev banging his shoe on the table at the 1960 United Nations General Assembly, Laclau and Mouffe are concerned that, during the 1990s, social–democratic parties abandoned their leftist identities (think of Clinton in the U.S. and Blair in the U.K.) to capitulate to neoliberal pressures. They are pleased that the Left has acknowledged "the importance of pluralism and of liberal-democratic institutions," but they are concerned that, in doing so, the Left mistakenly has abandoned any attempt to transform the current neo-liberal hegemonic order. They comment:

> In our view, the problem with "actually existing" liberal democracies is not with their constitutive values crystallized in the principles of liberty and equality for all, but with the system of power which redefines and limits the operation of those values.
>
> (xv)

In other words, Laclau and Mouffe favor liberal democracy so much that they want to *extend* its benefits to all—not limit its benefits, as does the neoliberal hegemony, to the privileged few. They conclude:

> This is why our project of "radical and plural democracy" was conceived as a new stage in the deepening of the "democratic revolution", as the extension of the democratic struggles for equality and liberty to a wider range of social relations.
>
> (xv)

To pretend that social antagonism no longer exists, that humanity has somehow magically arrived at an endpoint to the political, is nothing more than a neoliberal nodal point, an act of power to partially fix meaning at a place beneficial to the neoliberal elite. Laclau and Mouffe expose and debunk this political maneuver of the bourgeoisie.

A specific strategy of liberal discourse is to fix a new definition of reality to replace the feudal, aristocratic world order it overthrew.[25] For Laclau and Mouffe, such beliefs are not only delusions but carefully crafted lies propagated by the plutocratic elite in order to secure and cement a social arrangement advantageous to themselves. Capitalists, then, are forever in the process of contriving and disseminating "hegemonic articulations" (187)—that is, *their* ideology; *their* interpretation of the world—informed by liberal ideology and masquerading as universal truths and timeless values.[26] As will be discussed in the following chapter, neoliberal ideology in particular pushes the idea of the individual needing liberation from the state. Laclau and Mouffe note, for example, how: "the new conservatism has succeeded in presenting its programme of dismantling the Welfare State as a defence of individual liberty against the oppressor state." Yet the very idea is self-contradictory. If the state is seeing to the well-being of the citizen, how is that despotic? Conservatives and Libertarians argue that social welfare programs create a debilitating dependence in people as well as welfare-cheaters, for example, the mythical figure of the "welfare queen" so heavily promulgated by Republicans in the 1990s. In fact, dismantling welfare programs only serves to create the legions of cheap, desperate laborers neoliberalism preys upon (see Chang, Thing 21). Bulldozing welfare, then, is an act of hegemonic articulation, not sound social–economic policy. Laclau and Mouffe point out how neoliberal articulations above all else work to establish a dominant discourse of "possessive individualism," which "constructs the rights of individuals as existing before society, and often in opposition to it." However, it is inevitable that as more and more people come to demand this formulation as a right of the democratic revolution, "the matrix of possessive individualism would be broken, as the rights of some came into collision with the rights of others" (175). That is, possessive individualism is a self-defeating doctrine in that it forces a choice between liberal capitalism *or* democracy. This stark choice Laclau and Mouffe term a "crisis of democratic liberalism": at some (nodal) point, the partnership of capitalism and democracy (a bond that ousted aristocratic rule) must be dissolved in order to preserve and protect the wealth and power of the new capitalistic elites (creating, in effect, a new bourgeois aristocracy). Such a discursive project is the entire focus and purpose of neoliberalism: to obstruct democracy from spreading any further than itself. Note Laclau and Mouffe:

> This is why the liberals increasingly resort to a set of themes from conservative philosophy, in which they find the necessary ingredients to justify inequality. We are thus witnessing the emergence of a new hegemonic project, that of liberal-conservative discourse, which seeks to articulate the neo-liberal defence of the free market economy with the profoundly anti-egalitarian cultural and social traditionalism of conservatism.
>
> (175)

This "liberal-conservative discourse" is what I have named the Regime of hegemonic neoliberalism and neoconservatism. Its enemies—the enemies of the free market and of western primacy—are, not strangely, all the old enemies of European aristocracy: the worker, the poor, women, non-white people, non-Christian people, non-native-born people, non-heterosexual people, non-able-bodied people, and so on. Like feudalism, liberal/neoliberal capitalism does not function without people to exclude and a great many people to exploit.

Traditional Marxism and Soviet Communism propagate their own nodal point of an inexorable and marvelous Workers Revolution that, in Laclau and Mouffe's view, is every bit as fictitious as the possessive individualism of neoliberalism. Both are the articulations of powerful groups attempting to fix a hegemonic subjectivity and, as a result, put a stop to the process of social antagonism. Post-Marxism looks instead to embrace the freeplay of social antagonism and to continue the modern political–economic innovation of capitalism joined with democracy. Proclaim Laclau and Mouffe: "*The task of the Left therefore cannot be to renounce liberal-democratic ideology, but on the contrary, to deepen and expand it in the direction of a radical and plural democracy*" (emphasis original); moreover, their "extension of the field of democratic struggles" covers "the whole of civil society and the state" (176). All peoples, not just wealthy white men, deserve the benefits of modern democracy. As political deconstructionists, similar to Foucault, Laclau and Mouffe see incessant hegemonic struggle as the guarantor of democracy itself:

> The central role that the notion of antagonism plays in our work forecloses any possibility of a final reconciliation, of any kind of rational consensus,

of a fully inclusive "we". ... Indeed, we maintain that without conflict and division, a pluralist democratic politics would be impossible.

(xvii)

What this means is that democracy never reaches an endpoint; it is never wholly complete; circumstances always will demand adjustment; politics is a perpetual conversation—if not shouting match. Writing in 2000, Laclau and Mouffe see democracy in serious danger. Around the globe, disaffection with the democratic process "is reaching worrying proportions, and cynicism about the political class is so widespread that it is undermining citizens' basic trust in the parliamentary system." In some countries, this situation "is being cleverly exploited by right-wing populist demagogues, and the success of people like Haider and Berlusconi is there to testify that such rhetorics can attract a very significant following" (xix). Given the subsequent right-wing populism of Putin, Trump, neo-Nazi groups in Europe and the U.S., and emerging hardline conservative leaders around the world such as Bolsonaro in Brazil and Johnson in the U.K., this analysis by Laclau and Mouffe is nothing short of chilling. They warn that as long as the left wing fails to engage in hegemonic struggle, as long as it chooses to languish in "the centre ground," there is little hope of combating such right-wing demagoguery. They say:

> To be sure, we have begun to see the emergence of a series of resistances to the transnational corporations' attempt to impose their power over the entire planet. But without a vision about what could be a different way of organizing social relations, one which restores the centrality of politics over the tyranny of market forces, those movements will remain of a defensive nature.
>
> (xix)

What the left wing needs to do is both "define an adversary" and "know for what one is fighting, what kind of society one wants to establish." That undertaking will require from "the Left an adequate grasp of the nature of power relations, and the dynamics of politics. What is at stake is the building of a new hegemony" (xix). The Rant is part of this left-wing pushback prescribed by Laclau and Mouffe. The Rant is capable of defining the current hegemonic adversary, of indicating the better kind of society for which it fights, of putting to use the freeplay of political power, and of working to construct a new hegemony to replace that of the oppressive neoliberal–neoconservative Regime.

To Sum Up

Satire, sci-fi, and monsters all stimulate perplexity then critical thinking then reexamination of social order. When blended into a single tale, they form the potent cocktail of an outlandish world or an incredible journey that shocks our understanding. Post/Human theorist Elaine Graham, working from Foucault's archeological/genealogical method of disinterring social and intellectual lineages as a way to queer what is currently taken as "normal," "natural," and "universal," contends that the "realization of alternatives for the future can only be made possible by apprehending the strangeness of what we now take for granted, thereby subverting its inevitability." Cultural activities that open up this kind of "critical space within which social critique and political action might emerge" include, for Graham, journalists, satirists, and political radicals using devices such as "fantastic, speculative and utopian literature" (55). Such works emphasize "the provisionality of the present, and the indeterminacy of likely futures, the better to disrupt the stability of a monolithic interpretation of reality" (56). In particular, Graham situates sociological science fiction and monster stories squarely within this kind of production.

> Science fiction, too, shares these preoccupations, creating alternative worlds primarily in order to refract our own back to us. By invoking the paradigm shift of estrangement, the suspension of reality, or the creation of incongruous speculations, science fiction as 'fabulation' is designed to break the hold of the *status quo*. Science fiction is also the genre, arguably, in which contemporary equivalents of teratology flourish.
>
> (59)

By stirring in satire with this sci-fi/monster mix, I've theorized speculative satire as a subgenre of modern political satire. At the turn of the 20th/21st century, a creative/critical/societal perfect storm has amalgamated three renegade genres in opposition to the enormities of the neoliberal/neoconservative hegemon. In the next chapter, I examine that dominant political–economic formation.

Notes

1 In my own attempts to theorize satire, I've argued that, emerging at the cusp of modernity, 17th- and 18th-century British satire became factionalized within the politics of the developing modern state. What we can recognize as modern political satire emerges around the English Civil War first in the vitriol of Parliamentarian versus Royalist, then after the Restoration in the paper scuffles of Whig versus Tory. See Combe, "The New Voice of Political Dissent"; *A Martyr for Sin*; "Making Monkeys of Important Men." See also Lord.
2 In "Stephen Colbert: Great Satirist, or Greatest Satirist Ever?" I make the case that satire problematizes notions of certainty, stable reality, and absolute truth. A satirist does not traffic in certitude but rather is a polemicist making an interim case for better versus worse in the here and now. Thus, even satiric claims of Truth are based in cultural relativism. My article points out as well how many current media critics misapprehend this postmodern satiric project to operate instead with a modernist view of the genre. Such an approach to satire is inadequate and fails to notice the significance of the form. See Combe, "Stephen Colbert."
3 These views on satire obviously run counter to Fredric Jameson's pronouncement about our postmodern condition, namely, that critique is now impossible because there is no "outside" position from which to criticize the viewpoints of another. Remarks Jameson on the unattainable prospect of "moralising judgments" within

the postmodernist space: "the luxury of the old-fashioned ideological critique, the indignant moral denunciation of the other, becomes unavailable" (*Postmodernism* 46). One hardly requires, however, the chimera of an essentialist, timeless, a priori reality existing independent of human perception—but somehow "objectively" assessable by humans—in order to disagree with someone else about the best version of polity, economics, society at large, or anything else for that matter. Postmodernity does not negate debate; it renders debate inexorable. Thus, postmodernity does not invalidate satire; it makes satire all the more keenly robust. For an example of a critic following Jameson's edict about the incompatibility of satire and postmodernism, see Neeper 295. For a close reading and critical appraisal of Jameson's position, see Robert Samuels' "After Frederic Jameson: A Practical Critique of Pure Theory and Postmodernity" (Samuels 51–68). There, Samuels argues for a critical and progressive mode of postmodern political action that runs contrary to Jameson's regressive cultural order.

4 For accounts of the various ways that satire has been theorized, see Griffin Chapter 1; Connery and Combe; Marshall 1–8.
5 See Amarasingam; Geoffrey Baym; Borden and Tew; Gray, Jones, and Thompson; Jones; Jones and Baym.
6 See Combe, "Shadwell as Lord of Misrule."
7 For a succinct summary of the Menippean theories of Frye and Bakhtin, see Weinbrot, *Menippean* 11–16. For an excellent overview of Menippean satire, see Weinbrot's introduction, "Clearing the Ground: The Genre That Ate the World."
8 Originally, I assumed that certain graphic novels and manga would fit easily into the manner of Rant I'm proposing. For example, Alan Moore's *V for Vendetta* and *Watchmen*, Shirow Masamune's cyperpunk *The Ghost in the Shell*, or Jacques Lob and Jean-Marc Rochette's *Le Transperceneige* ostensibly seem a perfect match as highly imaginative protests against modern power. All of these graphic novels have been turned into feature films as well. Two of them, James McTeigue's *V for Vendetta* and Joon-ho Bong's *Snowpiercer*, I see as excellent specimens of contemporary Menippean satire. However, I find that many graphic novels and manga, perhaps due to their being targeted mainly at young-adult readers, offer as a worldview a simplistic binary of white/black, good/evil and, as a result of that unsophisticated conception of the world, partake too heavily either in adolescent libertarianism or schmaltzy sentimentality. That is, these works do not bring with them the intellectual complexity and seriousness required for meaningful satiric exposé.
9 For the debate on how to define sci-fi, see in particular Baker 1–24 and Freedman 13–23; see also Anders; Rabkin. For an intriguing essay arguing that sci-fi is *always* in the process of being defined by its local conditions, see Vint and Bould.
10 See in particular Macherey's Chapter 10, "Illusion and Fiction."
11 For Freedman's fuller discussion, see *Critical Theory* 19–22. For critics voicing opposition to Suvin's and Freedman's dismissal of Fantasy and other imaginative works that are somehow deficient for, supposedly, not possessing enough "cognitive estrangement," see Milner; Miéville.
12 For informative overviews of the history of sci-fi, see Baker, Chapter 2; Franklin.
13 In *Metamorphoses of Science Fiction*, Suvin dedicates four chapters to a review of "Older SF History" and four chapters to a review of "Newer SF History." For an overview of Suvin's theory of historical "clusters" of sci-fi development, see Baker 26–28.
14 See Atwood's "Introduction" to *In Other Worlds*.

15 See Baker's Chapter 6, "Utopias and Dystopias"; see also Freedman, *Critical Theory* 62–86. For a consideration of Utopia as a literary genre, a study acknowledged by both Fredric Jameson and Ursula LeGuin as an influence, see Elliott.
16 For excellent overviews of feminist issues in sci-fi, see Donawerth; Baker, Chapter 7.
17 For examples of queer criticism of sci-fi, see Piercy; Braidotti; and particularly Pearson.
18 For a good introduction to sci-fi as a modern international genre, see Sousa Causo; see also Baker's Conclusion, "Science Fiction as a World Literature." For a collection of essays examining the practice of sci-fi in countries around the world, see Hoagland.
19 For a reading of Spielberg's film as anti-colonial, see Combe, "Spielberg's Tale"; for readings of *District 9* and *Avatar* as counter-hegemonic films, see Combe and Boyle, Chapter 5.
20 For the commercial domination of Anglo-American sci-fi, see Gwyneth Jones. For examples of scholarly studies of colonial issues in sci-fi, see Kerslake; Rieder.
21 For an historical account of monsters, see Asma. For a Freudian reading of monsters, see Gilmore. For readings of monsters as representational of social issues, see Cohen; Combe and Boyle; Graham; Levina and Bui. For a study of the figure of the monster in Latin-American literature and popular culture, see Moraña.
22 Dryden attacking the Earl of Shaftesbury in *Absalom and Achitophel* or Pope and Swift attacking Sir Robert Walpole in any number of their satires are good examples of political figures being depicted as beyond the pale. A more recent example of this kind of attack is Alec Baldwin's impersonation of Donald Trump on *Saturday Night Live* where the president is rendered as a monster of narcissism and ignorance. For women satirically depicted as illogical, frivolous, deceitful, hypersexual, or otherwise "unnatural" beasts, see Juvenal's infamous *Satire VI* (late first, early second century CE), often translated or imitated through the centuries as "Against Women." For scholarly studies of the abundant early modern British satire against women, see, for example, Gubar or Nussbaum.
23 For detailed analyses of Althusser's and Foucault's influences on post-Marxist theory, see respectively Chapter 1 and Chapter 2 of Philip Goldstein's *Post-Marxist Theory: An Introduction*. See that book in general for an overview of this cultural theory.
24 As Goldstein points out: "What exposes the fissures within hegemonic ideological practices is not, then, the conflict of classes but the antagonisms of women, minorities, gays, and others. The conflicts and struggles of these social movements undermine hegemonic literal meanings and conservative identities and justify those movements' assertion of democratic ideals" (55).
25 As Claude Lefort points out, a key difference between the theological–political logic of aristocratic society and the rule of law of democratic society is that while the former is founded on the transcendental signified of God, which imposes a hierarchical and unconditional order, the latter has as its power site an empty space subject to constant negotiation. No law is final and not subject to contest; no classification of citizenry is ever wholly closed and indisputable (173). However, this situation does not mean that within democratic society there are no totalitarian efforts to reimpose the kind of imaginary unity and hierarchy that democracy shatters.
26 Examples of these grand-sounding falsehoods include Manifest Destiny, the American Dream, Pulling Yourself Up By Your Bootstraps, Capitalism = Democracy, The Free Market, A Rising Tide Lifts All Boats (i.e., wealth trickles down), and, most recently, Make America Great Again.

2 The Regime

In this chapter, I describe the Regime railed against by the Rant, that is, the current-day neoliberal/neoconservative hegemony at work. I want to make clear from the start that I don't write as an economist, as a political scientist, or as a thoroughgoing expert in such specialty areas. At best, I am (or strive to be) an enlightened amateur in certain socioeconomic and political matters that pertain importantly to the textual and societal issues I pursue as a cultural materialist critic. In this way, I follow the advice of Cambridge University economist Ha-Joon Chang, who urges us all to be "active economic citizens." With regard to the economy in particular, Chang points out how most people throw up their hands in frustration over the many complex, technical matters involved. We believe that only experts can deal with such convoluted questions and concerns. Chang wants us to think differently: "95 per cent of economics is common sense made complicated, and even for the remaining 5 per cent, the essential reasoning, if not all the technical details, can be explained in plain terms" (xviii). We don't need to be auto mechanics to know that the oil needs changing in our cars. Chang assures us, "Making judgements about economics is no different: once you know the key principles and basic facts, you can make some robust judgements without knowing the technical details" (xvi). The purpose of this chapter is exactly that: to elucidate key principles and basic facts about neoliberalism and neoconservatism so that robust social judgements can be made. The reasons for pursuing such active citizenship, whether economic or political, are vital. As Chang states them:

> we need to ask whether the decisions that the rich and the powerful take are based on sound reasoning and robust evidence. Only when we do that can we demand right actions from corporations, governments and international organizations. Without our active economic citizenship, we will always be the victims of people who have greater ability to make decisions, who tell us that things happen because they have to and therefore that there is nothing we can do to alter them, however unpleasant and unjust they may appear.
>
> (xvii)

DOI: 10.4324/9781003110491-3

In other words, ignorance in civil matters guarantees an inability to defend our own interests and effectively negates our working for the greater good.

With this explicatory and civic goal in mind, I've consulted any number of specialists and thinkers in sociological fields for basic information as well as their many opinions about the current circumstances of our world—both where we stand and how we got here. What I present below, however, is more than just an explanation of political–economic theories and historical events. It is my own take on neoliberalism and neoconservatism as intellectual movements shaping our current circumstances. As I make clear in the Introduction and Chapter 1 of this book, I see the world currently under the grave threat of a combined neoliberal and neoconservative ascendancy. Moreover, this threat has been building for roughly four decades. While neither ideology—neoliberalism nor neoconservatism—is by any means a monolithic belief system, and while these two orientations toward reality are by no means necessarily tied to one another, I nonetheless see the two working significantly enough in conjunction to characterize them as the Regime—that is, the hegemonic forces and discourses of the day that, to a great degree, dictate our cultural moment. In outlining their development and tenets below, I pursue the following proposition. Neoliberalism, as an economic theory and practice, generates—indeed, requires—what amounts to dystopia. Neoconservatism, as a political viewpoint and exercise, wages war against that result. I will inspect each ideology separately and then discuss how they mesh. As I do, please keep in mind the characteristics of the Rant theorized in Chapter 1, that is to say, a warning against a dangerous false orthodoxy carried out by a creative mixing of satire, sci-fi, and monstrosity for the purpose of promoting, instead, a radical and plural democracy. Remember as well that substantial demonstrations of the Rant taking on the Regime will follow in Chapter 3.

Neoconservatism

We'll begin with neoconservatism. Though no less important than neoliberalism, this ideology will not take nearly as long to explain. The name itself has an early meaning of a former liberal espousing political conservatism—that is, someone newly coming to more conservative political viewpoints. As the movement evolved, the term "neoconservative" has come to denote, generally, someone who advocates the assertive promotion of democracy and U.S. national interest in international affairs, particularly through military means. Historically, neoconservatism is an American Jewish movement starting in the 1960s with a group of New York public intellectuals and liberals who turned right wing when it came to the defense of Israel. During the 1970s, neoconservatism had something of a second wave as these Jewish intellectuals reacted negatively to George McGovern as the Democratic candidate for president. Not only did they disapprove of his domestic policies involving what they considered to be government overreach, but his foreign policy stances of withdrawal from Vietnam and cuts to defense spending worried them as well. Nor did these neoconservatives like anything about the New Left of the era, that is, student anti-war protest, the counter-culture movement, black nationalism, feminism, environmentalism, and the like. Although still considering themselves liberals, "they stressed the limits of social engineering (through transfers of wealth or affirmative action programs) and pointed out the dangers that the boundless egalitarian dreams of the New Left had created for stability, meritocracy and democracy" (Vaïsse, "Why Neoconservatism" 1). Fundamentally, these early neoconservatives wanted to steer the Democratic Party back toward the center, meaning toward reasonable progressive policies at home and muscular anti-communism abroad.[1]

In the mid-1990s, a third wave of neoconservatism came together. At this point, the movement had migrated fully over to the Republican party and included a younger generation of adherents who had never been liberals or centrist Democrats. With the Soviet Union gone and America standing as the lone superpower in the world, as well as the most powerful economy, the focus of these latter-day neocons shifted as well. No longer having to battle the worldwide threat of Soviet communism, they decided it an opportune moment, instead, to project American might around the globe. Whereas earlier neoconservatives had urged the U.S. to defend democracy and human rights in the world, third-wave neocons actively looked to shape the world politically and economically into one safer for and more in line with American interests and values. This shaping involved the bold use of military action where needed. The signature organization for this undertaking was the Project for the New American Century (1997–2006), and its members held high positions in and crucially fashioned the policies of the George W. Bush administration (2001–2009). Two other major neocon advocacy projects forming at this time (and still operational) were the think tank The American Enterprise Institute and the publication *The Weekly Standard*.[2] Despite the intervening Obama presidency, and despite the strangeness of the Trump presidency, this third-wave manifestation of neoconservatism persists and works in conjunction with neoliberalism.

With regard to the basic tenets of neoconservatism, analysts of the movement are quick to point out that there is no single leader or core group exerting tight control over its ideas. While neocons often coordinate their messaging to create effective echo chambers, there are substantial differences of opinions and tactics among them, too. Notes Justin Vaïsse, "No two neoconservatives think the same on all issues, and many object to being called neoconservatives in the first place" ("Why Neoconservatism" 3). Similarly, while this worldview began as an American Jewish concern for the security of Israel, from the outset many neocons have been (and currently are) non-Jewish. Jim Lobe stresses as well "that the very large majority of Jews in this country are neither neoconservative nor Republican—a source of considerable frustration to Jewish Republicans over the last 30 years" (2). What this means is that neoconservatism is not, and never has been, a popular movement of any kind; instead, it is an elite school of thought practiced by political insiders sharing certain intellectual tendencies and outlooks. Vaïsse asserts, "Neoconservatism has no religious, regional or economic base. It is in no way an organized force with a central authority" ("Why Neoconservatism" 3). Third-wave neocons, then, tend to be Washington D.C. movers-and-shakers or prominent national journalists/pundits or, in effect, think tank lobbyists who share an agenda of influencing American foreign policy in certain directions. Although amorphous as a group, however, neocons push for policies that can be articulated with clarity. Summarizing a wealth of neoconservative statements since 1995, Vaïsse offers what he calls "The Five Pillars of Neoconservatism" embraced by those who keep to this ideology. These mainstay beliefs are as follows:[3]

1 *Internationalism.* The most basic tenet of neoconservatism is the firm conviction that America must be active in world affairs, that is, "to preserve and extend an international order that is in accord with both our material interests and our principles" (4). Isolationist tendencies of any kind, therefore, upset neocons. Above all else, America should never do too little in the world, and it would be difficult for neocons to imagine America doing too much internationally.

2 *Primacy.* According to neocons, America is "the indispensable nation," "the benevolent empire," and represents "the unipolar moment" when an all-good superpower dominates the planet. No rival superpower, then, should be allowed to rise because "American primacy in the international system is a stroke of good fortune for the rest of the world, since America does not seek to conquer and oppress, but rather to liberate and democratize, and offers public goods to all" (4). Such beliefs obviously stem from a creed of American exceptionalism as well as a self-righteous Manichean view that morally pure America represents Good on earth, and thus acts as the deterrent to all Evil.

3 *Unilateralism.* Unsurprisingly, neocons also maintain that only America can provide peace and security to the world. No other nation—and particularly not the multinational United Nations—is up to this sacred task. "The United States, therefore, should not be restrained in its capacity to act, neither by multilateral institutions nor by treaties" (5). Being the first among no-equals, America must have unconditional free reign around the globe.

4 *Militarism.* In order to sustain its worldwide preeminence and ability to act singly, America must retain massive military capabilities as well as the political will to use them. Such readiness compels sustained high levels of defense spending, and indeed "no year passes by without neoconservatives calling for a major increase of the Pentagon budget and the number of U.S. troops." Neocons tend to engage in a use-it-or-lose-it alarmism, too, when it comes to the military. Remarks Vaïsse: "This love affair with the American military machine has another aspect to it: the tendency to inflate threats to national security, either out of genuine concern or as a way to mobilize public opinion" (5). In other words, to justify all this military spending, neocons believe it best that our forces be put to use.

5 *Democracy.* For neocons (and many Americans) the United States and democracy are one and the same thing. Our national identity is wholly

tied to the democratic ideal, so much so that America must aggressively spread it around the world. Only then will we (and, by extension, the rest of the world) be safe. Dealing with nondemocratic states, then, is not something neocons like to do. To their way of thinking, tyrannical regimes are the source of most conflicts on the world stage. Therefore, "it is utterly unrealistic, in the long term, to accommodate autocracies rather than try to achieve regime change—whether in the USSR, Iraq, Iran or North Korea" (6). Neocons have a missionary zeal for democracy, believing it a universal good that must be imposed on all nations.

When the hype is peeled away, one can see that neoconservatism is at heart a narcissistic and belligerent approach to the world. The "peace" it seeks to install is a global Pax Americana. Its doctrine of "peace through strength" means, really, constant unilateral intervention abroad—to include preemptive military strikes and engagements. Stemming from its Jewish origins comes the belief that Israel, like the U.S., is also a morally exceptional nation, and therefore not bound by international norms or agreements. Thus, neocons fixate on the security of Israel. They are convinced as well that the primary lesson we need to learn from history is never to allow another Hitler to rise to power. That is to say, had Hitler been met with strength right from the start, as opposed to appeasement, World War II and the Nazi Holocaust could have been avoided. Lobe points out, then, how the importance of maintaining and using overwhelming military power "cannot be overstated" as a neoconservative imperative. Neocons engage in a consistent pattern of threat-inflation and fear-mongering because "a new Hitler is always just around the corner, and we must be in a permanent state of mobilization against him" (3). For the first two waves of the neoconservative movement, communism served as that external threat. For the neocon third-wave, Islam has been designated the nemesis of Good. A vague, never-ending, threats-from-all-sides "War on Terror" is an ideal contrivance for the neoconservative agenda. Nor is the neoconservative commitment to democracy—a problematic floating signifier—wholly noble. Former National Security Advisor to Jimmy Carter, Zbigniew Brzezinski, observed that when neoconservatives talk about "democratization," they usually mean destabilization (Lobe 4). Upsetting the inner workings of rival nations is a higher priority than planting saplings of democracy around the world. Moreover, historically neocons have always had a soft spot for "friendly authoritarians," that is, dictators and strongmen who support U.S. political, military, and economic objectives. Lobe notes that the neoconservative "record over the past 40 years suggests that their devotion to democracy depends entirely on the circumstances" (5). Neocons never advocate for the civil and human rights of Palestinians, for example. And if a democratically held election brings to power a party that is seen as too Marxist or too Islamist, that nation remains earmarked for regime change.

Thus, you have neoconservatism in a nutshell: a militarily aggressive, religiously self-righteous, unapologetically brash strain of America First.

Neoliberalism

I turn now to the doctrine of neoliberalism. The term itself is thorny. As a descriptor, it can mean various things to various people; as a label, it runs the gamut from affirming to pejorative (Iber 51). The foundation for neoliberalism is, of course, capitalism and, even more specifically, the concept of economic liberalism. That Enlightenment innovation was first analyzed by Adam Smith in *The Wealth of Nations* (1776) as it developed in opposition to feudalism and mercantilism. A liberal economy features free markets and private property with a minimum of government intervention, which is seen to inhibit open trade and competition. At its base, then, *neo*-liberalism is a reassertion of such an approach to capitalism. In theory, the self-interest of individual owners of private property, subject to contract law and participating within unhindered markets, will lead to the best social results for everyone. This formula for the common good is Smith's famous concept of "the invisible hand."[4] Nowadays, a few centuries later, economic liberalism is the prevailing arrangement and set against noncapitalistic systems such as socialism, planned economies, and to a degree protectionism. Even more particularly, however, neoliberalism is a 20th-century movement that resurrects aspects of 19th-century laissez-faire economic liberalism, an aggressive brand of capitalism that emphasizes principles such as deregulation, privatization, austerity, and reductions in government spending in order to enlarge the role of the private sector in social matters. Laissez-faire (translatable as "let do") economics takes the individual to be the basic unit in society, and that individual's "natural" right to freedom will lead to a harmonious and self-regulating social order. Government is to steer clear of commerce, allowing "free" trade and competition. The supposed laws of nature are to oversee the economic sphere. Historically, separating neoliberalism from its 19th-century predecessor are the two World Wars, with the 1929 Crash and Great Depression coming in between those conflicts. Emerging after World War II was an era of state-regulated compromise between capital and labor—quite the reverse of laissez-faire theory—and such policies guided European and American economics up through the 1970s. Thus, in its most intense and influential manifestation, neoliberalism didn't find its feet as a reaction against this postwar settlement until around 1980. What this all means is that the second half of the 20th-century is marked by the clash of contending economic models—basically forms of capitalism versus forms of socialism—out of which neoliberalism has arisen, to date, victorious.

David Harvey's 2005 study, *A Brief History of Neoliberalism*, provides an excellent overview of just that—the course of this economic theory since the second world war. As just alluded to above, coming out of the war, the macroeconomic theories of the British economist John Maynard Keynes guided the policies of the leading western economies. In a political–economic organization now referred to as "embedded liberalism," market practices and business activities were circumscribed by a variety of state-controlled constraints and regulations. (Such practices had already formed the basis of Roosevelt's New Deal before the war.) Harvey sums up the postwar economic environment thus:

> What all of these various state forms had in common was an acceptance that the state should focus on full employment, economic growth, and the welfare of its citizens, and that state power should be freely deployed, alongside of or, if necessary, intervening in or even substituting for market processes to achieve these ends. Fiscal and monetary policies usually dubbed "Keynesian" were widely deployed to dampen business cycles and to ensure reasonably full employment. A "class compromise" between capital and labour was generally advocated as the key guarantor of domestic peace and tranquillity.
>
> (10)

In effect, points out David Graeber, "the white working class of the North American countries, from the United States to West Germany, were offered a deal." If they abandoned any socialist dreams of overthrowing capitalism,

> then they would be allowed to keep their unions, enjoy a wide variety of social benefits (pensions, vacations, health care ...), and, perhaps most important, through generously funded and ever-expanding public educational institutions, know that their children had a reasonable chance of leaving the working class entirely.
>
> (373)

The result of this "Keynesian era" arrangement was both rising productivity and wages that lasted into the late 1970s, setting the stage for our consumer economy of today. When this longstanding economic trend started to sour, the neoliberal project arose with its goal being to *dis*embed capital from state controls—that is, to dismantle the Keynesian policies that had been put into place. By the late 1960s and through the mid-1970s, liberal states were facing serious difficulties with regard to economic growth and capital accumulation. The result of this economic crisis was "to polarize debate between those ranged behind social democracy and central planning on the one hand ... and the interests of all those concerned with liberating corporate and business power and re-establishing market freedoms on the other" (Harvey 13). In particular, the converging of labor and urban social movements in the advanced capitalist states signaled the emergence of a viable socialist alternative to economic liberalism. That possibility—what in Chapter 1 I outlined as post-Marxism—was seen by the economic elites as a clear political danger. As Harvey puts it, "To have a stable share of an increasing pie is one thing. But when growth collapsed in the 1970s, when real interest rates went negative and paltry dividends and profits were the norm, then upper classes everywhere felt threatened" (15). In short, rich and powerful people wanted to stay rich and powerful. In order to ensure their privilege, something needed to be done to combat this encroaching democratic socialism. Neoliberalism was that something.

Harvey points to the years 1978–1980 as potentially a watershed period where the world order changed. This is when an early neoliberal agenda took shape "to curb the power of labour, deregulate industry, agriculture, and resource extraction, and liberate the powers of finance both internally and on the world stage" (Harvey 1). The elections of Margaret Thatcher as Prime Minister of Great Britain in 1979 and Ronald Reagan as President of the United States in 1980 brought such socioeconomic policies to the fore. Key neoliberal theorists in the movement were Friedrich von Hayek and Milton Friedman, along with the many members of the Mont Pelerin Society that had formed in Switzerland in 1947. This group was an early neoliberal gathering of western essentialist thinkers who worshiped private property and the free market—and who saw western civilization (meaning white, Eurocentric, capitalistic patriarchy) in peril as a result of communism and FDR's New Deal thinking. Subsequent and influential neoliberal think tanks grew out of this movement, such as The Institute of Economic Affairs (founded 1955) in the U.K. and The Heritage Foundation (founded 1973) in the U.S. These organizations continue their efforts to sway public opinion and government policy in favor of free-range capitalism. During the 1980s, union-busting, dismantling of the welfare state, and the "trickle-down economics" of Reagan became well established in America and Great Britain. At the same time, U.S. imperialism helped spread neoliberalism globally by propping up political strongmen (e.g., in Chile, Iran, and Iraq) who allowed western corporate investment in their countries. Moreover, under pressure from the Reagan administration, the International Monetary Fund and World Bank were soon purged of any Keynesian influences.[5] By the 1990s, neoliberal theory and policy had become economic orthodoxy in the Economics Departments of American colleges and universities, with the department at the University of Chicago, since the mid-1970s, being the leading bastion of neoliberal thought. The so-called "Washington Consensus" of the mid-1990s consolidated neoliberal control and dominance. The political and economic actions and compromises of President Bill Clinton and Prime Minister Tony Blair—ironically both center-leftists—did the most to ensconce, finally, neoliberal doctrine. Bodies such as the World Trade Organization (founded 1995) and accords such as the North American Free Trade Agreement (signed 1994) pursued the primary neoliberal goal of opening up the globe to unhindered capital flow (Harvey 90–93). Wealth, and thus political power, had begun its steady flow back up the class ladder.

Often neoliberalism is characterized as aiming to establish a free-floating, self-regulating market completely detached from the state. Recently, historian Quinn Slobodian has offered a corrective to that view, arguing that the real neoliberal objective always has been to insulate markets and capital from the intervention of individual democratic states by way of "a specific institution-building project" involving the creation of a superseding global economic order (4–5). While neoliberal thinkers unquestionably sought to free commerce from governmental control, they accomplished this ambition not so much by pushing for market fundamentalism as by "redesigning states, laws, and other institutions to protect the market." That is to say, the "invisible hand" of market competition needed to be accompanied by the "visible hand" of the law by way of the "legalization" and "juridicization" of world trade (6–7). If Keynesians had embedded liberalism in the state to work for the benefit of all citizens, the Mont Pelerin Society embedded neoliberalism in the multinational accord to work for the enrichment of the already wealthy. What this arrangement recalls are the nondemocratic origins of capitalism. Capitalism developed under monarchies, mixed-monarchies, or, at best, republics with a very limited political franchise (normally only male property holders above a certain level of wealth had the right to vote). It is an economic system unambiguously designed to favor those possessing the most capital (see Chang 140–142). What is more, capitalism is joined at the hip with imperialism. The global spread of European empire and economic liberalism more or less coincide. It should be unsurprising, then, when Slobodian places neoliberalism in history as a 20th-century reaction to the fall of 19th-century empires. As the world decolonized and democratic nation-states became the new reality, neoliberals looked for ways to protect *dominium* (the rule of property) from *imperium* (the rule of states), thereby keeping capital "safe from mass demands for social justice and redistributive equality" (16). Not only does neoliberalism seek a return to laissez-faire economic practices, but to the unfettered, undemocratic political powers of plutocracy and empire. Slobodian describes the neoliberal perspective on the 20th century as a time when increasing democracy and equality threatened wealth. As a result, the neoliberal project became

> about the development of a planet linked by money, information, and goods where the signature achievement of the century was not an international community, a global civil society, or the deepening of democracy, but an ever-integrating object called the world economy and the institutions designated to encase it.
>
> (16–17)

The neoliberal backlash to the post-World War II economic settlement, therefore, can be seen as little more than a grand scheme to install a global economic order devoted to optimizing profits—that is to say, to enabling the rich to get richer. Notes Slobodian of this process, "The fix was found, time and again, in a scale shift for governance, including in the League of Nations, international investment law, blueprints for supranational federation, systems of weighted franchise, European competition law, and ultimately the WTO itself" (20). With the protections of 19th-century empire gone, capital required a new way to be safeguarded. Such security came in the form of markets legally protected, under the law for a "world economy," from the 20th-century democratic state. For neoliberals, the added prefix "neo" signifies this new and different way to configure the noneconomic conditions enabling a liberal economic system (6).

Finally in this thumbnail sketch of the history of neoliberalism, for all the bluster about its being the *ne plus ultra* of capitalistic achievement, neoliberal policy did not yield high levels of economic performance in the United States or Great Britain during the 1980s. Harvey points out that the "overall result was an awkward mix of low growth and increasing income inequality" (88). As the world economy moved into the 1990s, wide-open, deregulated, innovative financial markets along with the increasing global mobility of capital and goods became increasingly the means to make and to concentrate wealth into the hands of the privileged few (90–93). Capital was free to roam the globe in search of the cheapest labor, with predictable results. Since 1980, the link between productivity and wages has been severed. As Graeber notes, "productivity rates have continued to rise, but wages have stagnated or even atrophied" (375). The inevitable results of this trend in lower wages has been increased job insecurity, the loss of benefits and job protections, diminished or absent state safety nets for workers, a significant decrease in personal savings coupled with a dramatic increase in household debt, and—as is to be expected—larger and larger segments of the population falling into poverty. At the same time, wages flattened, workers were guided, if not forced, to turn to financial markets in an effort to create their own economic security, such as with 401(k) retirement accounts. Such a state of affairs amounts to a gigantic swindle. In effect, regular people now hope to cash in on profits created by their own exploitation. Under neoliberalism, a tremendous amount of market wealth is created on the back of consumer debt. Participating in financial markets fueled substantially by one's own financial liabilities is indeed a mug's game. As Graeber characterizes the situation: "for many, 'buying a piece of capitalism' slithered undetectably into something indistinguishable from those familiar scourges of the working poor: the loan shark and the pawnbroker" (376). Prior to the COVID-19 pandemic, the most egregious neoliberal scam came in the form of the mortgage-refinancing schemes of the 1990s and 2000s that led to the market crash and resulting recession of 2008. The subprime mortgage crisis demonstrated fully—yet again—how capitalism is not a formation of democracy but ultimately a system of power and exclusion (see Graeber 381). The resulting taxpayer bailout of banks considered to be "too big to fail" has been seen as not only the consolidation of the capitalist class, especially its financial wing, but as something of a neoliberal coup against the U.S. republic and its citizens (see Dienst 23–32). Although the causes of the 2008 crash are clear (the basic culprit is the financial instrument of the derivative, discussed below), those in power remain unwilling to do anything meaningful to correct the problems. As Dienst describes the situation: "It is as if the system itself wants to be seen as 'too big to fail,' it being understood that bigness is the best defense against government regulation and popular unrest alike" (31). Dienst sees us, therefore, as currently being locked into what he terms a "regime of indebtedness" (28). Under these neoliberal circumstances, one is hard-pressed to spot economic or social justice on the horizon.[6] As of this writing (July 2020), the economic handling of the pandemic by the Trump administration certainly signals more neoliberal business as usual.

Now that the broad strokes of neoliberal history have been reviewed, I move to a closer consideration of the basic tenets as well as the most destructive practices of this economic formation. Harvey defines neoliberalism thus:

Neoliberalism is in the first instance a theory of political economic practices that proposes that human well-being can best be advanced by liberating individual entrepreneurial freedoms and skills within an institutional framework characterized by strong private property rights, free markets, and free trade. The role of the state is to create and preserve an institutional framework appropriate to such practices.

(2)

Furthermore, neoliberalism "holds that the social good will be maximized by maximizing the reach and frequency of market transactions, and it seeks to bring all human action into the domain of the market" (3). If markets don't exist in certain sectors—for example, social security, health care, education, environmental pollution—then they should be created, by the state if necessary. Much beyond the preservation and creation of markets, however, the state must not go. Neoliberal theory claims that the state is incapable of reading markets effectively or intervening in them without bias (2). Only the private sector can deal properly with markets. Another key element Harvey stresses about neoliberalism is its predilection and dependence on what he terms a "time–space compression." Neoliberal economics thrive on a global range and short-term market contracts—the shorter the better (3–4). Increasingly, then, information technologies, instantaneous trading, and Big Data all have enabled a worldwide economy operating at the speed of light and favoring those with the most computational power. As for a motivating philosophy behind these economic praxes, the founding neoliberal thinkers claimed human dignity and individual freedom to be the central values of civilization, and the best way to guarantee those wonderful-sounding political ideals was by the freedom of the market and of trade (5–7). Notes Harvey: "These values, they held, were threatened not only by fascism, dictatorships, and communism, but by all forms of state intervention that substituted collective judgements for those of individuals free to choose" (5).

Freedom, of course, is a beguiling call-to-action for any number of political philosophies and movements. Once a political–economic theory is put into operation, however, a different reality often emerges. Such is the case with neoliberalism. Harvey demonstrates how the apparatus of a functioning neoliberal state is one that reflects only "the interests of private property owners, businesses, multinational corporations, and financial capital" (7).[7] When set in motion, a worldview of *Market über alles* favors money and property over democracy and people. Slobodian lists 15 points that summarize a basic consensus shared by the neoliberal intellectuals at the core of his study. The common thread among them is the protection of global profit-making versus the citizenry of democratic states. For example:

> "World economic order depends on the protection of … the rule of property … against the overreach of … the rule of states" and "Democracy's danger is its legitimation of demands for redistribution. All world economic problems are rooted in domestic distribution struggles."
>
> (271–272)

52   *The Regime*

The upshot of these 15 core principles is one of prohibition, of neoliberal laws functioning as a kind of worldwide fiscal police: "Thus, the role of international institutions is primarily negative" (272). Paradoxically, then, the individual freedoms of laissez-faire economics are to be imposed by a decidedly unfree, undemocratic system of global economic regulation—one aimed primarily, moreover, at curbing the emerging postcolonial democratic states of the Global South. Writes Slobodian:

> In the neoliberal vision of world order, the world economy exercises discipline on individual nations through the perpetual threat of crisis, the flight of investment that punishes expansion in social policy, and speculative attacks on currencies in reaction to increases in government spending.
> (270–271)

A market economy, it seems, is like a dictatorship: the single-minded objectives of one group trample the self-determination, human rights, and social justice of everyone else (see also Iber 52–53).

About the neoliberal project, Harvey proposes for us a choice. Either we can see it "as a *utopian* project" to reorganize international capitalism, or we can see it as "a *political* project" to restore money and power to economic elites. Harvey opts for the latter: "Neoliberalization has not been very effective in revitalizing global capital accumulation, but it has succeeded remarkably well in restoring, or in some instances (as in Russia and China) creating, the power of an economic elite" (19). Neoliberal happy talk about individual freedom is but a mask to justify and legitimate whatever needs to be done to achieve this goal. Without regard for an accurate description of socioeconomic reality, neoliberal advocates steadfastly champion the pipedream of capitalistic business practices and financial marketplaces serving humanity as the benevolent pathway to individual freedom, self-actualization, and monetary security for all. Such a tale is palpable utopian nonsense told to suit the purpose of continuing to channel insane amounts of wealth into the possession of an advantaged coterie. As of May 2018, Iber reports:

> Eight men, it is calculated, hold as much wealth as the poorest half of the planet: 3.6 billion people. A global system underlies this vastly unequal distribution of wealth and power. ... [Economists] call it "neoliberalism."
> (51)

In 2017, a Credit Suisse report highlighted the increasing gap between the superwealthy and the rest of the global population. Reports Rupert Neate of *The Guardian*:

> The world's richest people have seen their share of the globe's total wealth increase from 42.5% at the height of the 2008 financial crisis to 50.1% in 2017, or $140tn (£106tn), according to Credit Suisse's global wealth report published on Tuesday.

Neate notes as well,

> At the other end of the spectrum, the world's 3.5 billion poorest adults each have assets of less than $10,000 (£7,600). Collectively these people, who account for 70% of the world's working age population, account for just 2.7% of global wealth.

The Credit Suisse report refers to this situation as the "global wealth pyramid," and advocacy groups such as Oxfam point out how "one of the main drivers of inequality" is "tax-dodging by rich individuals and multinationals" (Neate).[8] With regard to tax evasion by the rich, the 2017 scandal known as the Paradise Papers has revealed how, according to Juliette Garside, the "world's biggest businesses, heads of state and global figures in politics, entertainment and sport … have sheltered their wealth in secretive tax havens" in places like the British Virgin Islands and the Cayman Islands in the Caribbean. Such tax abuses thrive in a complex, artificial, and global financial environment where the superrich legally can protect their wealth.

During the neoliberal era, the rich have avoided taxes by more direct means, as well, in the form of tax cuts to the wealthy predicated on the trickle-down mythology that such a move stimulates job growth, thereby benefiting everyone. History shows us that this is not the case (see Chang, Thing 13). The Reagan tax cuts (the Economic Recovery Tax Act of 1981) and the Bush tax cuts (the Economic Growth and Tax Relief Reconciliation Act of 2001) put more money into the hands of the wealthiest Americans, but they also added substantially to the national deficit by way of decreased revenues. The boost in job and economic growth that these cuts were supposed to stimulate, thereby offsetting the deficit increase, never materialized. Despite these failures in neoliberal tax policies, Trump and the Republican Congress have enacted another so-called "supplyside" tax cut for the rich and for corporations, this one optimistically/cynically named the Tax Cuts and Jobs Act of 2017. Early expert projections for this tax bill show it performing little differently than its forerunners.[9] Considering the bad track record of such tax cuts since the 1980s, one would think that politicians interested in social benefit would avoid going down this road once more. Given how members of Trump's cabinet as well as several Republican (as well as Democratic) superdonors were named in the Paradise Papers as those taking advantage of offshore tax shelters, one begins to grasp how good governance likely is not the goal here. Funneling wealth upward is.

Writing in 2005, Harvey describes how the phenomenal concentration of money and power that "now exist in the upper echelons of capitalism have not been seen since the 1920s." He comments: "It has been part of the genius of neoliberal theory to provide a benevolent mask full of wonderful-sounding words like freedom, liberty, choice, and rights, to hide the grim realities of the restoration or reconstitution of naked class power" (119). Obviously, the banking meltdown of 2008 has had no effect on slowing this flow of capital to the top. Even though that financial crash and deep recession demonstrated clearly the dangers of neoliberalism as a system, its practice continues undeterred as does a widespread devotion to its philosophies by global plutocrats. In fact, in his study of the phenomenon of debt, Dienst finds that under the regime of neoliberalism the concept of being poor has experienced a fundamental shift in meaning. Whereas once it meant sheer scarcity external to social organization, poverty "is now permanently installed in the global functioning of the system, as the price a certain portion of the population must pay for the enrichment of the rest" (35). Neoliberal thinkers explain away poverty in a number of ways, from seeing it as a disease or deficiency that only the market can cure (as opposed to the market being its cause), to seeing poverty as nothing more than a part of "nature" (as in the oft-spoken platitude "there are always going to be poor people"), to seeing it as the result of "bad government," or to simply not seeing any kind of equitable distribution of prosperity as a worthwhile social goal (33–39). After reviewing some extremely grim global wealth inequity numbers (44–48), Dienst remarks, "For thirty years or more, the mantra has been 'a rising tide lifts all boats.' As a description of what has happened through globalization, this is clearly untrue." Wealth polarization under neoliberal policies has proven to be detrimental to economic growth, so much so that Dienst wonders, "Now the real question has become: Does an ebbing tide sink all boats? Will the global downswing bring about a more equal distribution of wealth?" (48–49). The answer, of course, will be no. The wealthy and the powerful do not willingly relinquish their wealth and power. What the world will see instead—what we are already seeing—is the antagonism between haves and have-nots as humanity contests for—rather than shares fairly—shrinking assets of all kinds. As Dienst characterizes this split, the poor are seen in terms of how little they can consume in order to survive, while the rich are seen in terms of how much they can splendidly accumulate; moreover, "Between these extremes there can be no equal exchange and no common ground, but only the confrontation between the command structures of credit on one side and the webs of indebtedness on the other" (49). How grimly apparent this lopsided war of rich versus poor is now during the coronavirus pandemic. Trump and the Republicans blithely ignore scientific reality (e.g., drink bleach) as they cajole/coerce workers to risk death by returning to unsafe working environments. Right wing gun-thugs demand "liberation" in front of Statehouses while big corporations rake in more taxpayer "bailouts" and arrange for immunity from lawsuits while millions of Americans put out of work fight their way through byzantine bureaucracy in an effort to get inadequate unemployment benefits.

In short, behold the neoliberal dystopia—a slow-moving, economically caused apocalypse. How has this catastrophe, decades-long in the making, been taking place? I will explore three spheres: corporations and the workplace; financial markets; ideology. In various ways, Rants work to expose all three.

Sphere 1: Corporations and the Workplace

Amid many diverse practices among neoliberal states, Harvey points to two core principles common to them all. First is the need to create a good business climate for capitalistic endeavors. Second is the need to create an equally good investment climate. In doing both, labor and the environment are treated as mere commodities, the former allowed few or no collective rights while the latter is given little or no time to regenerate (70). In this section, I focus on the neoliberal business environment; the following section considers the neoliberal investment sphere.

Although neoliberal theory touts its business environment as one of freely negotiated contractual obligations between juridical and rationally acting individuals in an open marketplace, in practice, as just discussed above, we see it leading instead to the concentration of wealth into fewer and fewer hands. At the heart of this trend is the modern corporation. Law professor and legal theorist Joel Bakan regards the large, Anglo-American, publicly traded business corporation as currently the world's dominant economic institution. We are surrounded by corporate culture, iconography, and ideology as these entities posture themselves, similar to the medieval Catholic Church, as infallible and omnipotent. Says Bakan: "Increasingly, corporations dictate the decisions of their supposed overseers in government and control domains of society once firmly embedded within the public sphere" (5). In the neoliberal era, corporations have been set loose to pursue their single-minded goal of maximizing profits within a commercial setting that promotes the privatization of anything that can be bought and sold on a market, the deregulation of everything from state oversight, and the supposedly equal competition among individuals, firms, and territorial units (e.g., cities, states, nations). This situation has led to enormities. To assume a level playing field of competition among all business players is obvious nonsense and runs contrary to all experience of capitalism. Asymmetric power always exists in a market and grows worse over time, leading eventually to monopoly and oligopoly. Without the state to regulate in some manner of fair practices, players with less capital and limited access to key information will not be able to compete. The absence of effective state regulations leads to other problems as well. New technologies can be manipulated and positioned in ways detrimental to the public good but advantageous to private gain—such as pharmaceutical products or the internet. Corporations also routinely externalize liabilities, that is, avoid paying the full cost of doing business by shedding responsibilities outside the market. A common example is the dumping of noxious waste into the environment rather than spending the money to treat it safely. Another is not providing workers with sufficient health-care benefits or a living wage, thereby throwing those responsibilities onto state welfare programs—which, by the way, neoliberals always look to dismantle.[10] As a driving engine of neoliberal economics, corporations—possessing the legal status but not the ethical potential of an individual person—routinely apply less than civic-minded business habits. Bakan argues, in fact, that corporations have become amoral and socially destructive organizations. He goes so far as to liken the modern corporation to a psychopath. Pointing out a striking resemblance of personality traits, Bakan notes that "the corporation is *singularly* self-interested and unable to feel genuine concern for others in any context" (56). Other shared characteristics between the corporation and the psychopathic personality include a sense of irresponsibility, the manipulation of others, grandiosity, a lack of empathy and asocial tendencies, the refusal to accept responsibility for their own actions, the inability to feel remorse, and finally, a superficiality when dealing with others (56–57). Not surprisingly, all of these traits are defining characteristics of Donald J. Trump. In Chapter 4, the behaviors of corporations will be considered in more detail. For the moment, it is enough to recognize the tilted and cut-throat business climate fostered by neoliberalism.

Within this hostile neoliberal environment, people find themselves on their own, held responsible and accountable for their own actions and well-being in such a way that any shortcomings are attributed to their own failures and inadequacies rather than the result of systemic malfunction. At the macro level, while capital is free to hunt the globe for cheap labor, labor is not free to cross international borders in search of the best job situation. Although such issues always are pitched in political and cultural terms of immigration policy, in effect workers find themselves corralled and thereby exploitable by multinational corporations (Harvey 65–66; Chang 26–28). Unsurprisingly, immigration conflicts typically pertain to rich, predominantly white, northern countries barring the entrance of people of color from poorer, southern countries. It seems that, generally, not only do well-off white people not like to mingle with impoverished non-whites, but they enjoy as well the less-expensive commodities produced by "disposable workers" toiling in despotic and appalling conditions in foreign sweatshops (see Harvey 168–170). At the micro level, the neoliberal workplace is a precarious place to be even in wealthier countries. As mentioned above, the trend for a few decades now has been toward insecure, lower-wage jobs that bring little to no benefits. At the same time, more and more state welfare provisions—health care, public education, social services—have been withdrawn. Victims of these changes—in effect, discarded workers—are blamed for bad individual behavior, marginalized socially and politically, and increasingly jailed. This situation has come about, however, from the measureable and dismal failure of neoliberalism as an economic policy to stimulate worldwide growth and capital accumulation. An illusion of success exists due to the tremendous and ostentatious wealth of the elite. In fact, as Harvey shows, "The main substantive achievement of neoliberalization … has been to redistribute, rather than to generate, wealth and income" (159). As we've seen, this redistribution has been upward. The accumulation practices used by neoliberals are largely those Marx observed during the rise of capitalism when populations were expropriated of land and resources in the process of being transformed into wage-laborers. Added to these techniques have been efforts to reverse worker gains won during the postwar Keynesian era, things such as state pensions, paid vacations, access to education and health care, and the like. Harvey calls the overall neoliberal strategy "accumulation by dispossession"; that is, the rich gain because everyone else suffers loss. The process has four main techniques. First, privatize hitherto public assets of all kinds—from utilities to military service to prisons—so that they become money making activities for corporations.[11] Second, deregulate financial systems in ways that promote speculative and predatory behavior and that favor rich insiders (discussed below). Third, manage and manipulate global financial and debt "crises" as a means to extract money from developing countries. Fourth, use the state—once it has been neoliberalized—as an instrument of redistribution via lawmaking, cutbacks to public programs, subsidies and tax breaks for corporations, unfair tax codes and practices that favor the wealthy, and, whenever needed, state violence in the form of police action and incarceration against the poor and against civic protest.[12] Each of these neoliberal mechanisms has been operating in high-gear for several decades.

Mid-20th-century economic historian and social philosopher, Karl Polanyi, famously points to a fundamental misstep of capitalism: the insistence on treating land, labor, and money as commodities, as items to be bought and sold on the market. Polanyi counters that these things are not innately articles of trade, that "the commodity description of labour, land, and money is entirely fictitious." More to the point, subjecting these things to the marketplace is hugely destructive to the social fabric. With regard to workers in particular, Polanyi writes:

> For the alleged commodity "labour power" cannot be shoved about, used indiscriminately, or even left unused, without affecting also the human individual who happens to be the bearer of this peculiar commodity. In disposing of a man's labour power the system would, incidentally, dispose of the physical, psychological, and moral entity "man" attached to that tag.
>
> (73)

Humans downgraded to laborers and nature reduced to assets are fundamental practices of liberal capitalism. The neoliberal practice of capitalism ratchets up this dehumanization and environmental ruin markedly.[13] What Polanyi warned against is increasingly coming to pass: "human beings would perish from the effects of social exposure; they would die as victims of acute social dislocation through vice, perversion, crime and starvation." As a result of overuse, industrial pollution, and competition for dwindling resources, the natural world would become less and less fit for human habitation, with "neighborhoods and landscapes defiled, rivers polluted, military safety jeopardized, the power to produce food and raw materials destroyed" (73). In this neoliberal hellscape, the common person, meaning anyone outside of the top 10% of wealth-owners, scrambles for decent shelter, employment, education, health care, retirement security, and so forth while frantically attempting to avoid burdensome debt. Workers are not only turned into captive labor forces globally by draconian immigration policies, but they are made vulnerable within individual nations by the zealous, oftentimes violent anti-union activities of companies and neoliberal authorities. As a result, observes Harvey, "The individualized and relatively powerless worker then confronts a labour market in which only short-term contracts are offered on a customized basis" (168). Job security—and the long-term benefits that come with it—thus become largely a thing of the past. In the United States currently, such worker isolation can pertain equally to agricultural workers, factory-line workers, service-industry workers, office workers of all kinds, adjunct faculty in academia, even contract-workers for fabulously rich companies like Google. The embedded liberalism of the postwar economic settlement built and enabled the American middle class. Since 1980, neoliberalism slowly has been wringing the life out of it. In sum, neoliberalism is hyper-efficient at abusing labor.

Sphere 2: Financial Markets

As stated above, the second technique of "accumulation by dispossession" common among neoliberal states is that they favor the integrity and solvency of financial systems and institutions over the well-being of citizens or the environment (Harvey 70–71). This precept ignores Polanyi's warning about not imagining and then treating money as a commodity and, accordingly, centers around the practice of finance capitalism. Whereas industrial capitalism makes money from the production and sale of things, finance capitalism makes money from money. Basically, this happens by the channeling of money held in savings into various investment mechanisms. The process is termed intermediation and generally is carried out by banks or other financial intermediaries that bring together people who have money to invest with professional investment firms. Those professional investors then pursue profit via the purchase and sale of financial products such as stocks, bonds, futures, and other derivatives; currencies are also investment options, as can be the lending of money at interest. To state it mildly, the markets and instruments of finance capitalism tend to be convoluted and readily can turn into altogether mystifying contraptions. Since the early 18th century, for example, stocks have been a financial arena rife with foolish decisions by investors and subject to deceptive if not outright fraudulent behavior by brokers. Historically, finance capitalism started out as subordinate to industrial capitalism as an engine of growth, that is, the money a company could muster from the sale of its stocks enabled that company to expand its physical business. Toward the end of the 19th century, however, finance capitalism began to grow in importance as a source of profit in its own right. People already possessing a good deal of money (i.e., mainly the industrial capitalists) began to make even more money through investment schemes. In the 20th century, financial markets grew to play a central role in economic developments and political affairs. In the final chapter of his monumental 1936 study, *The General Theory of Employment, Interest, and Money*, Keynes advocates for "the euthanasia of the rentier"—that is, a call for the end of what he considers the damaging practice of rich people holding and increasing their liquid assets through market investments rather than that money being used to finance the employment-creating investments of industrial capitalism. As a proponent of full employment, Keynes proposes policies for the socialization of investment as well as for low and stable interest rates, putting a stop to nonlaborers exploiting capital toward no public good. In the wake of the 1929 Crash and during the post-World War II settlement, financial markets were regulated in an effort to prevent misuse. Legislation such as the Glass-Steagall Act (1933) kept separate commercial and investment banking, and programs such as the Federal Deposit Insurance Corporation (FDIC) guaranteed a specific amount of checking and savings deposits for its member banks. Since the early 1980s, however, financial markets have been pushed in just the opposite direction. Neoliberals have worked steadily to deregulate markets, their biggest revision, perhaps, coming with the repeal of Glass-Steagall in 1999. As a result of such deregulations, currently more profits are to be made in the financial sector than through manufacturing (see Chang 234–237). As one might expect, money has followed the money. Since the late 20th century, finance capitalism has become the dominant force in the global economy. Obviously, this volte face has had much to do with the tremendous accumulation of wealth by the elite over the past several decades.

I think it no exaggeration to characterize the financial sector these days as the wild west. Not only is federal oversight weak (there's no real sheriff in town), but those running the financial markets—central bankers, fund managers, insurance brokers, traders and fixers of all kinds—play only for the quick-draw kill of profit. There is no long game, no plan, no thought of a common good. As Margaret Thatcher opined, there is no such thing as society—only money to be had. Dienst describes these financial gunslingers thus:

> They are generally indifferent, even ignorant, about the global system they help to animate. Their sense of history is calibrated by the split seconds of arbitrage, the volatile turnover of portfolios, the slipstreams of interest, the fitful jockeying over exchange rates, and the implacable arithmetic of the actuarial tables. In striking their deals and hedging their bets, they aspire to achieve a kind of bootstrap transcendence, suspended for as long as possible between "too soon" and "too late," long enough to seize a good chance but not long enough to face the fallout or the blowback.
>
> (3)

This situation raises critical questions. Is there anyone in charge of the global economy? Or are there only its most powerful players? Can anyone maintain meaningful oversight, let alone real management, of instantaneously linked worldwide financial markets swarming with abstract instruments? Or is such comprehension, and thus the possibility of purposeful guiding, an illusion? For that matter, in our current unsupervised, split-second, deregulated financial free-for-all, is even basic information illusory? Who—or, more to the point, what computer—can possibly track all the variables? When describing the dizzying array of derivatives being bundled, sold, and resold leading to the subprime mortgage meltdown, Chang (a Cambridge economist) remarks, "By now even I am getting confused (and, as it turns out, so were the people dealing with them)" (238). The 2015 film *The Big Short* aptly portrays the fog of greed and markets run amok that created the 2008 crash. It also offers a clear answer to the question of who is in charge of the neoliberal financial world: no one. Dienst pushes this point a step further, calling the link between financial markets and the media reporting on them a misleading blend of "scientific discourse and showbiz hucksterism" (4). The "science" isn't firm and the showbiz is extreme. The two bounce off one another to the point of being difficult to distinguish. Cautions Dienst: "This sloppy feedback loop instills quick decision-making and permanent uncertainty at the same stroke" (5). The global economy, then, seems to be creating us more than we are creating it. The finance capital cowboys galloping amid this stampede of profit-taking—driving it on with their six-shooters in the air blazing away—are dealing just fine, so far, with the clouds of dust. Meantime, everybody else is getting trampled.

Alex Preda has explored the boundaries mediating the relationship between financial markets and society. He shows how from the mid-19th century onward financial writers in New York, London, and Paris (authors who were also active brokers and speculators) sought to create the myth of a market that behaves rationally and of brokers who are like scientists engaged reasonably in market transactions. By the beginning of the 20th century, this promotional campaign was able "to contain criticism, doubts, and ethical questions" about financial markets (22). Today, Americans both believe in this myth and are exhorted constantly to trade and to invest. One's economic well-being—one's very survival, runs the message—depends on engagement with the market. Leading this harangue is the figure of the "expert broker" who can guide the common investor to stock market riches. The problem with this myth about the market, however, is that it obscures the fact that financial markets are "a double game, in which rational and irrational features coexist and feed on each other." Moreover, most people are woefully undereducated about how markets work, and markets now are sophisticated technological systems of high-speed transactions. Preda's study demonstrates "how this system opens up new possibilities and avenues for the reproduction and proliferation of fraud, deception, and manipulation" (23). Possibly, the single most damaging financial swindle at present is the derivative. Writing shortly before the 2008 crash, Edward LiPuma and Benjamin Lee explain these perplexing financial instruments as appearing to be simply mechanisms of market profit without social or political bearing. In reality, however, "derivatives represent a new means of objectifying economic reality because they seek to capture and mediate the entire ensemble of relations that create the social through the concept of quantifiable abstract risk" (30). Their infernal complexity and obscure mathematics make derivatives the ideal device for evading government regulations as well as popular understanding. Those same attributes qualify them perfectly as a method for high-risk, high-stakes, high-speed speculative investment. Note LiPuma and Lee: "Derivatives have come to the foreground because they are the chosen instruments of a speculative and opportunistic capital that circulates globally, with worldwide implications, but is controlled by a rather small coterie of socially interconnected, mutually aware Euroamerican agents and institutions" (33). In other words, derivatives have become the financial plaything of the rich, and it is impossible to comprehend the global flow of money without knowing how these instruments operate.

I will not pretend here to explain fully the many ins-and-outs of derivatives.[14] Instead, I will supply some basic concepts and, more important, characterize the destructive financial hucksterism at work. A derivative is fundamentally a form of gambling, that is, a bet on the outcome of a future action. It is a transactable contract that: (1) exchanges no money until its settlement; (2) has a value determined by the change in the price of the underlying asset; and (3) has a specified expiration date in the future. The instrument has its origins in early modern maritime-trade insurance practices and, more directly, 19th-century commodity markets (particularly in Chicago). The maritime insurance derivative involved the calculation and monetization of risk. The commodity trade derivative innovated the concept of "futures," that is, separating the *future* price of a commodity (such as pork bellies) from the *current* price for that commodity. These early financial instruments were relatively straightforward because the underlying asset of such futures contracts were tangible commodities—the cargo of a merchant ship or an agrarian product. However, through the neoliberal deregulation of financial markets, the underlying assets of derivative contracts today have become separated from real commodities. This alteration means that virtually anything upon which a bet can be placed can become the underlying asset of a futures contract. Explain LiPuma and Lee: "Anything from currencies and interest rates to broadband and electricity can serve as underliers so long as they are volatile, produce risk, and can be given a price" (36). Such a market environment is anything but straightforward. Moreover, while many now common derivatives are traded on public and regulated exchanges, banks and other financial institutions also engage in devising and marketing more complex, sometimes even one-of-a-kind derivatives for clients. This practice is referred to as "the over-the-counter or OTC market" and is the "larger and more rapidly expanding derivatives market" that also happens to be "private and unregulated" (34–35). Huge amounts of money (a transaction under ten million dollars is called a "skinny" trade) are changing hands hidden from regulatory oversight and in ways that exert extraordinary influence on the global economy (30). The most damaging amplification of derivatives since the 19th-century commodity markets, though, is that currently the underlying asset of a derivative contract can *itself be a derivative*. That is, instead of actual pork bellies being the underlier of a derivative contract, a derivative contract involving pork bellies can be the underlier of a *new* derivative contract. For that matter, that new derivative contract (that has a previous derivative contract as its underlying asset) can then become the underlying asset for yet *another* derivative contract. And so on and so on. The problem with this endless slippage as a financial practice, however, is the evergrowing distance between derivatives and their concrete underlying assets.

Appadurai explains how the repeated commoditization of prior promises by new promises dilutes and disseminates the force of the promise across many market players. The result is that each trader bears only a tiny portion of the burden of the larger interlinked system of promises, that is, of the overall value of any particular derivatives market. Says Appadurai: "This opens the systemic possibility of failure, breakdown, and collapse even when the bulk of individual trades meet their local conditions of felicity" (8). Add to these already dicey fiscal practices such deceptive (if not fraudulent) undertakings as predatory mortgage lending or the creation of "collateralized debt obligation" tranches where those high-risk (subprime) mortgages can be grouped together with low-risk (prime) mortgages to be sold to unsuspecting investors and you have the makings of the 2008 collapse of the American housing market.[15] In this neoliberal version of finance capitalism, no intervening step of industrial commodity production is required. Just a lot of cash and a highly active financial imagination. Remarks Appadurai:

> the fact that money itself has no limit, being a manmade symbolic object, finds in the derivative form its highest technical expression. The derivative, which is primarily a way to take a risk on a prior risk, opens the prospect of making money whether the future price of an asset *goes up or down*.
> (12)

That last point is vital. It means that risk-taking in the derivatives market has no connection to actual commodity values in the real world of goods and services. Speculative finance by the wealthy, then, has become a money-making game indifferent to—but not disconnected from—the actual lives of everyday people around the world. Speculators care more about not leaving any money on the table than they do about the general economic welfare. In the complicated derivative instrument of the "credit default swap," for example, one speculator makes money based on the *broken* contract promise between another pair of speculators. Although it seems capitalistically counterintuitive for contracts to be founded on the *breaking* of other contracts, at the time of the 2008 crash about $55 trillion was in play in the credit default swap market—almost ten percent of the overall derivatives market (Appadurai 152–153). If this is not runaway speculation, it's difficult to image what is. Worst of all, when the tower finally topples and the crisis finally hits—that is, when there are no more buyers willing to purchase the next round of securitized bundles of derivative promises and so the markets freeze (see Appadurai 12–14)—it is not the rentier class, who have caused the fiasco, that pays the financial price. As we saw in the subprime mortgage crisis, it is the average taxpayer who foots the bill for the bank bailouts. The lives of actual mortgage holders are ruined, not those of the superrich or of the bankers and professional investors who play the speculative game. No wonder pragmatic billionaire and investor Warren Buffet called derivatives—*before* the 2008 meltdown—"weapons of financial mass destruction" (qtd. in Chang 239).

Sphere 3: Ideology

The basic tenets of neoliberal ideology already have been described above. In the name of "individual freedom," proponents of neoliberalism hold that the entrepreneur in us all must be realized. We all must set loose our inner-tycoons within an institutional framework upholding free markets, free trade, and private property rights. The engine of our well-being is the competitive market. However, as evidenced in the review of the business and financial climates fostered by this worldview, when it comes to liberty under neoliberalism, "capital has more freedom than people" (Iber 54). Moreover, money is sucked ineluctably to the wealthy. How does this bamboozling occur? The most pernicious aspect of neoliberal ideology needing to be demystified is that of individuality. If Foucault characterizes the danger to the citizen living under modern panoptic discipline as "Visibility is a trap" (*Discipline and Punish* 200), equally it can be said that, within the neoliberal regime of power, *individuality is a trap*. Neoliberal notions of individuality push beyond the standard Horatio Alger, American Dream myth of "pulling yourself up by your bootstraps." In the employment-insecure, no safety-nets, we're-all-in-this-alone economy of neoliberalism, everyone is exhorted to cultivate Brand You to be peddled on a precarious and merciless job market. While such rugged individualism holds an heroic charm that's easy for privileged white males to imagine about themselves, the untold reality of this fanatic singularity is that it makes You extremely tractable, not to mention vulnerable. More than being constructed as a wage-laborer within industrial capitalism (as theorized by Marx and, in more detail, by Foucault), the individual under neoliberal hegemony is subjected to and crafted into a subject by new techniques of power as well.

Gilles Deleuze theorizes that Foucault's "discipline" society has developed one step more into a "control" society. Whereas Foucault's carceral-based panoptic discipline molds, concentrates, bureaucratizes, fixes identity and relationships within the modern state, and thus *confines* the individual, Deleuze's concept of control modulates, disperses, shifts, monitors identity and relationships, and thus puts the individual to additional and particular *uses* within the modern state. Surveillance is the crucial mechanism in the operation of both social orders, so the function of the control society builds upon that of the discipline society. But Deleuze points out neoteric methods and outcomes of surveillance that have changed the face of political economy. He cites the innovations of a new "generation of machines, with information technology and computers" as a technological development "deeply rooted in a mutation of capitalism" (180). With regard to outcomes, he indicates how late 20th-century capitalism is no longer directed toward production, but "toward metaproduction"; that is, what capitalism "seeks to sell is services, and what it seeks to buy, activities. It's a capitalism no longer directed toward production but toward products, that is, toward sales or markets" (181). Factories have given way to businesses, Deleuze declares, to a corporate culture that saturates us all with and in the marketing ventures of capitalism. Observes Deleuze:

> We're told businesses have souls, which is surely the most terrifying news in the world. Marketing is now the instrument of social control and produces the arrogant breed who are our masters. Control is short-term and rapidly shifting, but at the same time continuous and unbounded, whereas

discipline was long-term, infinite, and discontinuous. A man is no longer a man confined but a man in debt.

(181)

Already discussed above is Dienst's notion of a "regime of indebtedness" that transfers wealth upward to a class of creditors engaged in free-wheeling finance capitalism. Working from Deleuze's theories, Dienst finds that, "In the current moment, indebtedness supplements and overtakes enclosure to become the crucial apparatus of control" (121). The neoliberal individual, far from finding herself living in a utopia of personal liberties spurred on by the ubiquity of market transactions, exists instead in a meat-grinder of privatization, deregulation, personal debt, slow growth, and cycles of financial crashes then bank bailouts (58–61). With most of its citizens struggling to keep their heads just above water—and increasingly now just below—the neoliberal state is free to go about its core purpose of accumulation by dispossession.

Also using Deleuze as his starting point, Appadurai takes this victimization of the individual one step further, showing how we have become the *products* of neoliberal marketing as well. This exploitation is accomplished by way of the informational fragmentation of the individual. Deleuze asserts that in the control society, "We're no longer dealing with a duality of mass and individual. Individuals become '*dividuals*,' and masses become samples, data, markets, or '*banks*' " (180). A dividual is something that is separate and distinct, something divisible and divided. Deleuze suggests that, in the control society, individual people repeatedly are being broken down and divided into their component statistical parts that are then put to use not only by the state but particularly in the fluctuating markets of business and finance. He states, "Disciplinary man produced energy in discrete amounts, while control man undulates, moving among a continuous range of different orbits" (180). Appadurai elaborates on Deleuze's idea of the *dividual* by showing how this partitioning of the individual is a crucial link between the practices of Big Data and the financial form of the derivative.[16] The digital age, he notes, introduces

> a sweeping process through which contemporary Western individuals have been rendered subjects of a vast array of data search, collation, pattern-seeking, and exploitation, some of which has been captured in the recent category of "Big Data." Big Data pervades the activities of the state, private corporate enterprises, and many varieties of security apparatus.

For example, consumer demographics are gathered by point-of-sale information; the telephonic surveillance of the NSA depends on point-of-use data; social media companies such as Facebook "generate troves of interactional information of value to both the state and to the corporate world." Our new and remarkable technologies of communication—the internet, laptops, tablets, smartphones, and so forth with their many applications—are likewise sophisticated instruments of panoptic observation producing massive inventories of data that can be analyzed in any number of ways. Argues Appadurai:

The most critical implication of these new forms of data gathering and analysis ... is the ways in which they atomize, partition, qualify, and quantify the individual so as to make highly particular features of the individual subject or actor more important than the person as a whole.

(109)

In other words, we are turned into consumer purchases, credit scores, health profiles, educational test scores, and the like in such a way that renders the ordinary life experiences of *individuals* the highly valuable statistics of *dividuals*. At this point steps in the deregulated mechanisms of neoliberal finance.

As might be expected, the main instrument taking advantage of our dividuation is the derivative. To provide an example, Appadurai outlines how the derivative-driven collapse of the mortgage market was founded on the process of dividuation. Characterizing the derivative as "a new form of mediation" that creates new materialities (meaning, as discussed above, an increasingly long and unstable chain of derivatives where the value of assets separates more and more from real commodities), he points to the simple materiality of an actual house being mediated, by its division, into ever more abstract things: the house becomes a mortgage; the mortgage becomes an asset; the asset becomes part of an asset-backed security, the asset-backed security is exchanged as a debt-obligation, and so on (108). The real-life act of a person buying a house, then, is divvied into the ether of a "financial imaginary" (126) into which ordinary people rarely, if ever, go and from which the everyday individual little, if ever, profits. Appadurai sees this same principle at work throughout the current financial system: "*What contemporary finance does is to monetize all the other forms of quantification that surround us today, by taking advantage of the dividual forms that such quantification continuously produces*" (105; italics original). He names this formula for combining Big Data with derivatives as "predatory dividuation" and contends that it is an ideal tool for the masking of inequality. The technique multiplies obscure profit-making financial instruments that escape audit, regulation, and social control. Concludes Appadurai: "In short, the dividualism that financialization both presumes and enhances is counter to the interests of the large majority of society" (101–102). Since the simultaneous rise of the digital age and of the derivative form since the 1970s, the genuine risks of ordinary individuals in an uncertain world have been turned into, more and more, the secondary risks of speculators and traders in a fiscal world invented for their use, controlled for their profit, and indecipherable to outsiders. In an instance of adding injury to insult, within this arrangement "the risk is asymmetrically distributed between professional risk-takers (traders) at the expense of already dividuated actors who largely bear the downside risks of the market" (117). Hence Appadurai's use of the word *predatory*. The invention of the derivative monetizes risk, allows a small set of actors to take risks on risks, and permits financial technicians to make, in effect, all aspects of everyday life susceptible to monetization. The everyday citizen, then, becomes the risk-*bearer* for the endless risk-taking and profit-making of the financial industry. And, here we are back to Deleuze's key feature of the control society: "a man in debt." Notes Appadurai:

> We are all laborers now, regardless of what we do, insofar as our primary reason for being is to enter into debt through being forced to monetize the risks of health, security, education, housing, and much else in our lives.
> (125–126)

In the neoliberal economy, unless one is extremely wealthy, it is all but impossible not to incur debt of some kind: house, car, credit card, business, education, health, and more. That the common person's debt has become the gain of the elite signals a new form of capitalism has emerged. Appadurai characterizes the situation thus:

> From this point of view, the major form of labor today is not labor for wages but rather labor for the production of debt. Some of us today are no doubt wage-laborers, in the classic sense. But many of us are in fact debt-laborers, whose main task is to produce debt that can then be further monetized for profit by financial entrepreneurs who control the means of production of profit through monetizing debts.
> (127–128)

In *Brave New World*, Huxley imagines a discipline society preserving indefinitely industrial capitalism by way of the perpetual consumption of planned-obsolescent goods produced by citizens confined, through bioengineering, into a permanent pyramidal class structure. Our neoliberal brave new world is different. Ours is a control society allowing finance capitalism to run civilization and biosphere to ground. The key destructive economic mechanisms in the operation of the Regime are *debt, dividuation, and derivatives.*

Recently, social psychologist and Harvard Business School professor of Business Administration, Shoshana Zuboff, has warned that a caustic new economic formation threatens our humanity in the same way unchecked industrialization threatens our planet. Zuboff calls this arrangement Surveillance Capitalism, a practice that "unilaterally claims human experience as free raw material for translation into behavioral data." Pioneered by Google and taken up with a vengeance by companies such as Facebook, Microsoft, and others, surveillance capitalism transforms the personal data collected from individual users of digital technology into what Zuboff terms *"prediction products."* These products are then traded in a new kind of marketplace: the *"behavioral futures markets."* Companies eager to understand and thereby predict the likes and dislikes of potential customers purchase such behavioral products. More than *predicting* consumer behavior, however, Zuboff shows in her study how the practice of surveillance capitalism has turned to *shaping* consumer behavior. It is far more efficient—and profitable—to *modify* behavior rather than just keep an eye on it. Notes Zuboff: "With this reorientation from knowledge to power, it is no longer enough to automate information flows *about us*;

the goal now is to *automate us*." This business practice, "*instrumentarianism*," is a new kind of power "that knows and shapes human behavior toward others' ends" (8). Thus, the danger of surveillance capitalism: it is one more technique, and perhaps the most controlling and pernicious yet, of accumulation by dispossession, of channeling capital upward. Regular people are not involved in any value exchange of products and services. Instead, we are lured into having our personal information wrung from us over the internet to be packaged and sold without benefit to ourselves. We are not the customers of surveillance capitalism; we are its raw material. Explains Zuboff: "Surveillance capitalism's actual customers are the enterprises that trade in its markets for future behavior" (10). As is the norm for capitalism, the means of production rests in the hands of the wealthy few while the rest of us seemingly have no choice but to participate in their self-enriching mechanisms. By now, the internet has become an essential instrument for social participation of all kinds. That instrument is saturated with commerce, and that commerce is dominated by surveillance capitalism. According to Zuboff, resisting our dividuation appears to be a hopeless task, and so we suffer from "a psychic numbing that inures us to the realities of being tracked, parsed, mined, and modified." This attitude of defeat in turn prompts us "to stick our heads in the sand, choosing ignorance out of frustration and helplessness" (11). Such vulnerability is a master stroke of neoliberal doctrine. Not only are we wage-slaves, not only are we debt-slaves, but under surveillance capitalism, we have become existence-slaves as well. Our very being as humans is now used against our health, happiness, and prosperity.

Polanyi speaks of both good freedoms and bad freedoms afforded to us by the market economy. Among the bad freedoms he lists:

> the freedom to exploit one's fellows, or the freedom to make inordinate gains without commensurable service to the community, the freedom to keep technological inventions from being used for public benefit, or the freedom to profit from public calamities secretly engineered for private advantage.

Among the good freedoms he names: "Freedom of conscience, freedom of speech, freedom of meeting, freedom of association, freedom to choose one's own job." Polanyi's idea, writing in 1944, is through governmental regulations and safeguards to promote these good freedoms while minimizing those bad freedoms, thereby achieving: "Freedom not as an appurtenance of privilege, tainted at the source, but as a prescriptive right extending far beyond the narrow confines of the political sphere into the intimate organization of society itself." At the time, standing in opposition to this form of society was the liberal utopianism of Hayek, Friedman, and the other budding neoliberal thinkers of the Mont Pelerin Society. Polanyi points out how, in their writings, these zealous laissez-faire economists attack *all* planning and regulation as being denials of freedom; in their view, only unrestricted enterprise and private ownership constitute a free society. For Polanyi, such a social order would bring about the fullness of freedom for those whose income, leisure and security need no enhancing, and a mere pittance of liberty for the people, who may in vain attempt to make use of their democratic rights to gain shelter from the power of the owners of property.

(256–258)

In the course of time, political and economic circumstances allowed Hayek's views to gain footholds in the 1960s and 1970s, leading to an outright neoliberal takeover around 1980.[17] Since that point, a new owner–manager, billionaire–CEO class has arisen to impose various kinds of authoritarian states around the world as well as a principally anti-democratic world order. Paradoxically, the false orthodoxy leading the way is predicated on calls for individual freedom and getting big government off our backs.

Neolib + Neocon = Hegemon

With regard to the links between neoconservative and neoliberal ideologies, Harvey sees them dovetailing in a distinct way to form a hegemonic discourse. Basically, whereas neoliberalism is evasive about its authoritarian proclivities, stressing instead a libertarian fantasy that we are all equal individual actors in a free and fair economic arena, neoconservatism is unabashed about its imposition of authority. Neocons in the U.S. favor corporate enterprise and the restoration of class power in ways entirely consistent with neoliberal mistrust of democracy and protection of market freedoms. However, asserts Harvey, neoconservatism

> veers away from the principles of pure neoliberalism and has reshaped neoliberal practices in two fundamental respects: first, in its concern for order as an answer to the chaos of individual interests, and second, in its concern for an overweening morality as the necessary social glue to keep the body politic secure in the face of external and internal dangers.
>
> (82)

The order neoconservatism imposes as an antidote to neoliberal chaotic individualism is that of militarization. Since 9/11 especially, neocons have depicted America as a nation besieged by terrorist threats from without and within. Such threats call for decisive military actions abroad and close surveillance against potential enemies at home. For neocons, only an increasingly militarized society and an unquestioning "Support the Troops" popular mentality can safeguard our exceptional American liberties against legions of fanatics who "hate our freedom." The morality neoconservatism imposes along with this militaristic order is that of "moral majority," evangelical Christianity. This mindset features cultural (if not ethnic) nationalism, "family values," an obsession with right-to-life issues, literal interpretations of the Bible, and the like in open hostility "to the new social movements such as feminism, gay rights, affirmative action, and environmentalism" (84). For Harvey, then, neoconservatism sustains the asymmetric market freedoms of neoliberalism but makes explicit the concomitant autocratic and hierarchical means of social control (see 81–86).

Harvey writes at the height of the Bush 2 administration, when third-wave neoconservatism and neoliberalism became joined at the hip. Since that administration—which showcased the arrogant and aggressive credo of American exceptionalism—this particular combination of neoconservative and neoliberal doctrines has become right-wing articles of faith.[18] Such a worldview produces not only national vanity—America is the richest and most powerful military nation the world has ever seen—but a sense of national paranoia as well—as the lone shining beacon of Good in the world, everyone envies and is out to get us. Harvey remarks on this odd combination of pride and fear fostering racism, the restriction of civil liberties, mass incarceration, and the curbing of press freedoms at home while abroad the U.S. engages in covert actions and preemptive wars to eliminate anything resembling a threat to its dominance and national interests (196). Self-absorption, conceit, bellicosity, ignorance, and fear of diversity—these are the traits of a bully. These traits have found their apotheosis in the presidency of Trump. Both pride and fear resonate ominously in the single slogan "Make America Great Again." Along with neoliberal bald-faced greed and neoconservative bare-knuckled militarism, however, comes Trump's bizarre, eclectic, and apocalyptic mixture of alt-right bigotry, faux-populist posturing, chronic and brazen lying, deep and cultivated obliviousness, abject immorality, and reckless narcissistic amateurism when it comes to policy foreign or domestic. Defenders and critics alike of neoliberalism have long worried that as the neoliberal state inevitably corrodes all social fabric of the democratic state, the backlash will be the impoverished populace reimagining solidarities along all manner of other lines—religious, ethnic, cultural—centered around a "strongman" figure. Remarks Harvey: "Neoliberalism in its pure form has always threatened to conjure up its own nemesis in varieties of authoritarian populism and nationalism" (81). As a self-obsessed, New York City trust-fund dandy looking to join the growing ranks of criminal autocrats around the world (a boy's club headed up by Vladimir Putin), Trump is the all-American incarnation of such a strongman figure: the businessman despot. While the illegitimate, Russian-impelled election of Trump is calamity enough, worse is the way Republicans—as stewards of the neoliberal/neoconservative hegemony—attempt to ride herd on the populist Frankenstein monster they've created in order to fulfill conservative agenda items such as more tax cuts for the wealthy, increasing yet more military spending, and stacking the judiciary (especially the Supreme Court) with moralistic, procorporation judges. In other words, the Regime grinds on more precarious than ever.

To Sum Up

I asserted at the outset of this chapter that, as an economic theory and practice, neoliberalism produces dystopia while, as a political viewpoint and exercise, neoconservatism wages war against the chaos of that outcome. After a review of these two philosophies, I hope my assessment is evident. Neoliberal greed impoverishes the great majority of people, puts tremendous stresses on many more, enriches beyond measure the very few, all while plundering the natural environment. The result is a desperate and perilous world that looks to be teetering on the brink of cataclysm. Neoconservative vainglory then builds a wall around all that it deems to be Good and Right in a kind of holy crusade against the desolation provoked by neoliberalism. This partnership is both ludicrous and tragic. Yet here we are.

Why have I outlined in detail the nuts and bolts of this political–economic movement? Because, like all ideologies that come to dominate social life for a time, neoliberalism and neoconservatism are adept—maybe exceptional—at blending into the background. They present themselves not as ideologies but as something neutral and normal, not as factional belief systems but as some kind of law of nature or timeless and universal truth. Journalist and activist George Monbiot remarks how not only is neoliberalism in particular seldom challenged, it is seldom even named. No one seems to know exactly what to call this thing that currently dominates our lives. Neoliberalism? Market fundamentalism? Laissez-faire economics? Writes Monbiot,

> mention the dominant ideology in conversation—whatever you choose to call it—and most people will look at you blankly. Even if they have previously heard the term you use, they are unlikely to be able to define it. What greater power can there be than to operate namelessly?
>
> (3)

Because the Regime exerts its control with such anonymity, I've troubled to name and to locate it. Anything less would be irresponsible. Nothing would be easier than for an English professor to declare "neoliberalism and neoconservatism are terrible, horrible things," but not really explain adequately why I think that is. Such topics are, after all, not normally in the English professor wheelhouse. But we're pursuing cultural studies here, not aesthetics and formalism. More specifically, we're studying *satire*. In order to understand the import and the intensity of the Rant being investigated, readers must be more than superficially familiar with the insidious and nefarious workings of its target.

Notes

1 For brief accounts of the early history of neoconservatism, see Lobe 2; Vaïsse, "Why Neoconservatism" 1–2. For a detailed portrayal of the origins of the movement, see Vaïsse, *Neoconservatism* "Introduction" and Chapters 1–3.
2 For accounts of third-wave neoconservatism, see Vaïsse, "Why Neoconservatism" 3 as well as his *Neoconservatism* Chapter 7. For other book-length studies of neoconservatism, see as well Dorrien; Fukuyama; Heilbrunn. For an interesting (and hostile) Libertarian view of the neoconservative movement, see Thompson.

3 For these Five Pillars of Neoconservatism, see Vaïsse, "Why Neoconservatism" 3–7. For an even more detailed summary of the neocon approach to the world, see his *Neoconservatism* 232–239.
4 Gordon Gekko, venture-capitalist kingpin in the film *Wall Street* (1987), famously puts this notion another way, telling a room filled with shareholders that "Greed is good."
5 See Harvey 19–31, and generally Harvey's Chapter 1. For other accounts of the takeover by neoliberalism starting around 1980, see also Dienst, Chapter 1; Graeber, Chapter 12. For full-length studies of right-wing economic theory and practice starting in the 20th century, see Mirowski and Plehwe; Burgin; MacLean. For a readable and detailed 23 point refutation of neoliberal free-market economics, see Chang. For an excellent thumbnail sketch of what neoliberalism is and how it came to dominate the world currently, see Monbiot 217–221. For a bit more detailed outline of what is termed "The Neoliberal Habitat," see Zuboff 37–41.
6 For a recent, in-depth analysis of the subprime mortgage crisis, see Adam Tooze's study *Crashed: How a Decade of Financial Crises Changed the World*.
7 Examples of such neoliberal states include Augusto Pinochet's U.S.-backed coup and regime in Chile during the 1970s or, 30 years later, the government the Bush administration attempted to impose on Iraq.
8 See, as well, the 2013 global poverty study by Anup Shah. Nor is the U.S. innocent of this level of wealth inequity. In 2018, the United Nations Human Rights Council issued a special report on extreme poverty and human rights in the United States. The author of the report, Philip Alston, characterizes America as "a land of stark contrasts." In his Overview, he tells of the United States currently: "About 40 million live in poverty, 18.5 million in extreme poverty, and 5.3 million live in Third World conditions of absolute poverty. It has the highest youth poverty rate in the Organization for Economic Cooperation and Development (OECD), and the highest infant mortality rates among comparable OECD States. Its citizens live shorter and sicker lives compared to those living in all other rich democracies, eradicable tropical diseases are increasingly prevalent, and it has the world's highest incarceration rate, one of the lowest levels of voter registrations among OECD countries and the highest obesity levels in the developed world" (3–4). Among the many problems discussed in the report, Alston cites the plight of the embattled and shrinking middle class in America as well as the damaging consequences to democracy of extreme wealth inequality (19).
9 For example, a paper from The Urban-Brookings Tax Policy Center summarizes the TCJA thus: "TCJA will stimulate the economy in the near term. Most models indicate that the long-term impact on GDP will be small. ... The new law will reduce federal revenues by significant amounts, even after allowing for the modest impact on economic growth. It will make the distribution of after-tax income more unequal, raise federal debt, and impose burdens on future generations" (Gale ii).
10 For a discussion of these particular problems and contradictions with neoliberal business practices, see Harvey 64–70; for a close analysis of the neoliberal state in action, see Harvey's Chapter 3. For a debunking of the foundational neoliberal myth that markets can and must be "free," and that they must remain untouched by the state in order to work their economic magic, see Chang's Thing 1, Thing 16, and Thing 19.
11 For examples of erstwhile public institutions becoming money-making concerns for corporate America, see Jennifer Mittelstadt's investigation of the all-volunteer

Army, *The Rise of the Military Welfare State*; see also Jackie Wang's study of our increasingly privatized prison systems, *Carceral Capitalism*.

12 For a closer discussion of these mechanisms for "accumulation by dispossession," see Harvey 159–165; more generally, see his Chapter 6, "Neoliberalism on Trial."

13 In late May 2020, Trump White House economics adviser, Kevin Hassett, asserted in an interview that, after many weeks of workplace shutdown as a result of the coronavirus, "Our human capital stock is ready to get back to work." Not only is his term "human capital stock" debasing to individual laborers, but Hassett's claim of workers eager to risk infection was not supported by polling at the time. See Rupar.

14 For a highly readable general description of the problems associated with current neoliberal financial markets, to include derivatives, see Chang's Thing 22. For a detailed and technical account of the history, workings, and dangers of derivatives, see LiPuma and Lee (in particular, Chapter 2); Appadurai (in particular, Chapter 1). For the following explanation of the derivative form, I draw upon these two expert sources.

15 See Appadurai 10; see also LiPuma and Lee 33–36. For an excellent and entertaining demonstration of these complex ideas, see what has become known as the "Jenga Clip" from the film *The Big Short*: www.youtube.com/watch?v=3hG4X5iTK8M.

16 See in particular Appadurai's Chapter 7, "The Wealth of Dividuals."

17 See, for example, Deborah Cowen's study showing that the termination of military conscription in the United States was in fact an early neoliberal project pushed at Nixon through the 1960s by Milton Friedman and other "Chicago School" economists. They argued, in their quest to conceptualize everything in market terms, that the draft was a form of tax on the individual, and therefore it should be dismantled as an act of liberating citizens from big government. Nixon's elimination of the draft in 1973, then, was something of an initial victory for the neoliberals and a significant first step in their defining neoliberal notions of freedom and models of citizenship. See also Beth Bailey's book-length study, *America's Army*, where she argues, among other things, that the current all-volunteer force is an outgrowth of neoliberal ideology.

18 As Vaïsse points out about Republicans, "neoconservatism … seems to have won the battle for the soul of the party. And if not neoconservatism per se (the base of the GOP is less internationalist than the neocons), at least a hawkish version of foreign policy is prevailing among Republicans" ("Why Neoconservatism" 8–9). Can-do, self-righteous, quick-and-easy head-busting is enormously popular with the Republican base—every bit as popular as the mantras of "free markets" and "liberty." Like neoliberalism, though, neoconservatism is flawed and limited as a course of action. Military engagement often turns out not as planned. Nation-building is even more hectic and uncertain. Both demand gargantuan budgets. Due to these and other factors, Vaïsse finds that "neoconservative ideas will be hard-pressed to prove they can make a difference" (10). Neoconservatism, though, like neoliberalism, boasts many influential writers and thinkers, working in numerous well-funded foundations and publications, seeking to steer both popular opinion and elite policy in favor of its worldview. For a summary of both the shortcomings and the resilience of neoconservative doctrines, see Vaïsse, "Why Neoconservatism" 7–10 as well as *Neoconservatism* 260–270.

3 Ranting Against the Regime

The purpose of this chapter is to offer several brief examples of fictional works ranting against the machinations of the hegemon. These concise illustrations show how elements of satire, sci-fi, and monstrosity combine to condemn the operations of late 20th- and early 21st-century modern power. They demonstrate as well how specific facets of neoliberal and neoconservative ideology are exposed by Rants. The chapter concludes with a concise listing of the many working parts of the Rant. This overview is offered as a useful guideline for the final three chapters of the book, where works of speculative satire are examined closely.

Satire/Sci-fi/Monstrosity at Work

To demonstrate the tri-genre Rant against modern power, I review two earlier 20th-century works and two works of the 1980s. The earlier works are Aldous Huxley's *Brave New World* (1932) and George Orwell's *1984* (1949). While these novels, obviously, do not take on our current-day neoliberal/neoconservative hegemony, they do voice opposition to what is portrayed in them as a threatening false orthodoxy of their own day. Needless to say, Huxley's and Orwell's novels are also hugely influential works of modern dystopian fiction. All dystopian fiction subsequent to them stand in their shadow in some way, whether in direct stimulus or by inevitable comparison. More important, *Brave New World* and *1984* set the stage for the Rant being posited: visible in them is a deft combination of satire, sci-fi, and monstrosity that serves as prototype for the flurry of dystopian fictions produced in our own era. In my breakdown of these works, I pair Huxley's novel with Terry Gilliam's film *Brazil* (1985), as both works are easily acknowledgeable as satire. Orwell's novel is paired with Margaret Atwood's novel *The Handmaid's Tale* (1985), as both are works less immediately recognizable as satire. The point of my brief analysis is simply to establish the operation of Menippean cognitive estrangement and cognition effect—as theorized in Chapter 1—in each outrageous tale.

The exuberant use of exaggeration makes Huxley's *Brave New World* and Gilliam's *Brazil* readily evident as satire. Both works push their depictions of an oppressive modern state to nearly absurd extremes. In his novel, Huxley famously has the worship of Henry Ford replacing Christianity as a controlling

DOI: 10.4324/9781003110491-4

doctrine of faith (80–86); he also gleefully extends Ford's industrial innovation of the factory conveyor belt to the mass production of citizens via Bokanovsky's Process (6–7). In his film, Gilliam gives us a campy-noir, almost vaudevillian totalitarian state. Many of the characters are performed as eccentric types; sets are often garish and costuming over-the-top; technology is a bizarre combination of the newfangled and the old-fashioned; the plot is set in motion by a ludicrous bureaucratic mix-up of the names "Buttle" and "Tuttle"; there's even an edge of Keystone Cops to the government's jack-booted thugs. None of this hyperbole, however, occurs incidental to the argument of either piece—namely, that modern discipline easily can run amok. The pastoral power of the modern state, where to govern "is to structure the possible field of action of others" (Foucault, "Subject" 138), is depicted in both of these alternative societies as having gone horribly—yet all too familiarly—wrong. Regulation, domination, and exploitation characterize the futuristic World State of *Brave New World* as well as the British government that is announced to exist, at the beginning of *Brazil*, "Somewhere in the 20th Century." Thus, the actual inequalities of social reproduction and class oppression in the modern world have been heightened to painfully vivacious levels in these speculative satires.

Satiric exaggeration doubles as sci-fi *novum* in each work. In *Brave New World*, chemistry is used not only to retard embryos so as to fix a pyramidal hierarchy of workers from Alphas down to Epsilons, but in the "Social Predestination Room" (10) Neo-Pavlovian conditioning techniques are applied to children as well in order to indoctrinate them to their preset places in consumer society (19–29). Explains triumphantly the Director of the Central London Hatchery and Conditioning Centre, "The mind that judges and desires and decides—made up of these suggestions. But all these suggestions are *our* suggestions! ... Suggestions from the State" (29). Readers will find such egregious social engineering shocking and horrifying—unimaginable. As the story wears on, however, the disorientation of exaggeration begins brutally to wear off. We come to realize that we are not in never–never land; Huxley is not just spinning a yarn with the World State. Rather, he is depicting our own subject-formation within modern discipline—albeit grossly distorted in a funhouse mirror. This alternative reality is not much different from our own reality. Such early chemical and psychological programming is not so different from the birth lottery of prosperity/poverty practiced by capitalism. Early health and nutrition, educational–occupational opportunities, as well as overall cultural mindset are tied acutely to the social class into which someone chances to be born. Modern social disciplining is every bit as adept as Bokanovsky's Process at fixing a stable and pyramidal hierarchy of workers. Moreover, in the everyday life of the World State, we see nearly our middle-class own: a life of pleasant meaningless work combined with the mindless pleasures of shopping, popular entertainments, readily available sex, and, when the going gets tough, the powerful mood-enhancing drug *soma*. We, too, live in a Fordian construct.

Brazil delivers the same uncomfortable cognition effect to viewers. Despite the spoof of it all, we soon see that we are engaged in identical civic cockups as those depicted in Gilliam's film. "Somewhere in the 20th Century," we come to understand, is right here and now. In particular, the movie focuses on modern power as the struggle of ruthless elites to maintain their sway over a cowed and clueless middle class as well as the disenfranchised masses. Working in the mid-1980s, Gilliam makes prescient use of several tactics and circumstances that have come to mark this struggle, decades later, in our current neoliberal/neoconservative state. One is the idea of a government using the threat of terrorism as, in actuality, a ruse by which to keep its citizens in fear and thereby more tractable. The terror alert is always on *extreme* in Gilliam's British state. Nowadays, worldwide, governments of all stripes hold up the boogeyman of Terrorist to induce blind loyalty and silence political dissent. Another idea emphasized by Gilliam is the navel-gazing detachment of the superwealthy ruling class. When a bomb explodes in one of their chic restaurants, the rich immediately are screened off by the wait staff from having to witness the untoward calamity of the dead and injured. The narcissism of America's 1% today is no less callous, where even the gesture of *noblesse oblige* has fallen by the economic wayside. A third distressing notion offered by Gilliam is the maddening inanity of bureaucracy, office work, and wage-labor. In this organizational hellscape, the great majority of modern citizens, middle and working class alike, spend their lives treading economic water. The carrot held in front of them is the fairytale that their own hard work reliably and eventually will get them ahead. A fourth idea represented in the film is that of the state as a vast, complex, and almost living entity unto itself. Like Frankenstein's modern Creature, the modern state has been created by humans, but it's not really under full human control. Here is where we come onto the phenomenon of the monster. The malignant beast in *Brazil* is not an actual terrifying creature, such as Godzilla, but Foucault's technologies of power. Symbolizing this elaborate, everpresent, nearly sentient state monster are the miles and miles of ridiculous ductwork running everywhere in the film or the seemingly breathing mechanized entrails behind apartment walls. This Leviathan motivates and monitors everything—even the power elite who ostensibly run It. In both Gilliam's film and Huxley's novel, the state as monster is the rudest awakening of all for readers. Droll satiric exaggeration and perplexing sci-fi estrangement give way to the painful social recognition that we have created a modern monster—that is, a dangerous capitalist orthodoxy—in whose shadow we now live in fear.

One of the main devices by which Huxley and Gilliam ply this monster is the manipulation of narrative persona. Through character viewpoints not only are sympathetic connections with readers crafted, but first-hand encounters with monstrosity are fictively enacted. As a focal character in *Brazil*, we're given Sam Lowry (Jonathan Pryce). It's through the eyes of hapless, bumbling, midlevel-bureaucrat, good-hearted Sam that we encounter the horrors of the despotic state. He—likely like us—is caught up only half-knowingly in the machinations of modern discipline. As more and more wrongdoings of the present regime are made known to Sam, though, we, too, begin to contemplate the injustices and inequities of the state structures regulating our own lives. We empathize with Sam as he works a dead-end job by day and dreams of sprouting wings to take flight in defiance of the humdrum by night. We cheer on Sam as he starts to pursue his resistance to state power, tentatively in his real life but heroically in his dream life. The state as monster becomes manifest in the giant samurai warrior Sam battles in his dreams. These recurring, developing sequences in the movie provoke a painful note of farcical valor in Sam's character that is at once hopeful and difficult to watch. Sam becomes bolder and bolder as a knight in shining armor in this dreamscape. As tempting as it might be, we can never quite bring ourselves, though, to believe that Sam will, in the end, take up arms against the real monster of state. Cruelly, Gilliam leads us down that Menippean garden path. The last several minutes of *Brazil* masquerade both as hero saga—Sam at last finding his courage to join the rebellion led by Harry Tuttle (Robert De Niro)—and love story—Sam at last winning his dream girl, Jill Layton (Kim Greist), and escaping with her to the idyllic countryside. The snare of satire grabs us, however, when we discover instead that these are the desperate fantasies of Sam, whose mind has broken under torture. The Deputy Minister of the Ministry of Information, Mr. Helpmann (Peter Vaughan), is applying enhanced interrogation techniques to Sam in an effort to get to the bottom of a suspected terrorist plot. The grim irony of the movie is that no such plot exists. It has all been the Buttle-Tuttle confusion from the start. There's no good reason to destroy Sam in this way. He knows absolutely nothing of note. He poses no actual threat to the government. Sam Lowry is but a run-of-the-mill citizen at the mercy of modern subject-formation. In terms of Cohen's Monster Theory, however, what takes place in Gilliam's movie is the inversion of any number of modern binaries: social order/radical chaos; good Us/bad Them; human culture/monster wilds; just state/criminal rebellion; freedom/tyranny; and so on. In other words, the monsterizing agency of dominant social norms turns out to be more monstrous than that which it eschews and excludes. Just as Hrothgar and Beowulf are far more the monster than Grendel, the state apparatus maintained by officials like Helpmann is the beast terrorizing citizens the likes of Sam. Sam is eliminated because the state decides, unfairly and prejudicially, to monsterize him. Time and again in the Rants explored in this book, we will see this basic binary of good humans/bad monsters problematized, reversed, or erased.

In *Brave New World*, Huxley similarly uses the lens of character to bring the reader to see this same inversion of monstrosity. While there is no one focal character or narrator in Huxley's novel, we're given insight into and thus the opportunity to sympathize with a handful of key persons, each one representing a different take on the World State. Bernard Marx and Helmholtz Watson are two Alphas suffering from "a mental excess" that has produced in them "the knowledge that they were individuals" (67). Each man "had realized quite suddenly that sport, women, communal activities were only, so far as he was concerned, second bests. Really, and at the bottom, he was interested in something else. But in what? In what?" (67). As the story plays out, we watch what each man does with this alarming insight into his society. Turning into an emblematic liberal, Bernard comes to "genuinely believe that there were things to criticize" about the World State, yet "at the same time, he genuinely liked being a success and having all the girls he wanted" (157).

In spite of the flawed system, Bernard is content to stay in the belly of the beast. Helmholtz, by contrast, becomes radicalized against state control. In a futile attempt to free Deltas from their conditioned slavery, he participates in a soma riot (212–214). For his crime, he's given a choice either to remain in the mindless comfort of the World State to carry out his duties as an Alpha or to be exiled to a remote island. Helmholtz chooses hardship and intellectual freedom: "I believe one would write better if the climate were bad. If there were a lot of wind and storms, for example" (229). He'll be shipped off to the Falkland Islands. In the eyes of the World State, Helmholtz has become a monster to be cast out.

Even more compelling as signifying characters are John the Savage and Mustapha Mond. One is a stranger coming to the World State; the other is one of ten World Controllers of this highly disciplined society. Their actions and interactions confront readers with intellectual and emotional extremes to weigh and to compare. It's not difficult to commiserate with John, once he realizes that the "brave new world" he has so wanted to experience turns out to be, instead, a monstrous industrial nation peopled by industrially created monsters. Taken on a tour of an electrical equipment factory, John sees first-hand the physically and mentally stunted Deltas, Gammas, and Epsilons who have been scientifically fabricated to become quite literally components in the assembly line. His reaction to this heinous biotechnology: "the Savage had suddenly broken away from his companions and was violently retching, behind a clump of laurels" (160). As readers, we imaginatively retch alongside him. In terms of Cohen's theories, John the Savage fits the role of monster to the World State. As an uncouth spawn of the Savage Reservation, he is a creature from beyond the borders representing everything deemed aberrant by the state: biological offspring, no chemical or psychological conditioning, member of a family unit, believer in primitive religion, reader of old literature. At the same time, with a mother from the World State (the soma-addicted Linda), John equally originates from *within* the culture that carefully engineered out all of those offending qualities. In this way, his presence in London poses something of a threat to the stability of state "normal." He is a walking manifestation of official abjection. John takes the monstrous action, for example, of attempting to prevent Deltas from ingesting soma, thereby exposing the pitiless disciplining of the state. Helmholtz joins him in this small act of insurrection. John's pleas to the Deltas, although wasted, are nonetheless exactly right:

> Throw it all away, that horrible poison. ... I come to bring you freedom. ... But do you like being slaves? ... Do you like being babies? Yes, babies. Mewling and puking. ... Don't you want to be free and men? Don't you even understand what manhood and freedom are?
>
> (211–213)

Of course, the Deltas do not and cannot. Like everyone who lives in the World State, they have been painstakingly conditioned to behave and to think in ways prescribed by the World Controllers.

Mustapha Mond represents the real monster of Huxley's fiction. As a monster, however, Mustapha could not be more charming, reasonable, and even kind. In many ways, he is Huxley's most maddeningly effective invention of speculative satire. Far from being a madman or a venal despot, Mustapha has arrived at a logical decision regarding human society given the troublesome record of human history and the problematic circumstances of human existence. He has opted for stable, trivial, artificial happiness over volatile, profound, tangible knowledge. As he explains the situation to Helmholtz and John:

> The world's stable now. People are happy; they get what they want, and they never want what they can't get. ... they're so conditioned that they practically can't help behaving as they ought to behave. And if anything should go wrong, there's *soma*.
>
> (220)

Of course, the point at which the World State has ended history is that of a capitalistic pyramid where the few *haves* rule over the many *have-nots*: "'The optimum population,' said Mustapha Mond, 'is modeled on the iceberg—eight-ninths below the water line, one-ninth above'" (223). Theirs is the quintessence of the modern state, using science to mass-produce a pleasure-induced quiescence in its population, yet keeping a tight rein on the social reality it has engineered. Mustapha readily admits:

> I'm interested in truth, I like science. But truth's a menace, science is a public danger. As dangerous as it's been beneficent. It has given us the stablest equilibrium in history. ... But we can't allow science to undo its own good work. That's why we so carefully limit the scope of its researches—that's why I almost got sent to an island.
>
> (227)

Brave New World, then, is unabashed in its exposé of the provisionality of the present. *All* social order—to include our own—is a makeshift social order. When John and Mustapha debate the existence of God, the Savage advocates for the traditional view of that deity as a transcendental signifier: "But isn't it *natural* to feel there's a God?" Mustapha counters that God, instead, is a signifier subject to freeplay—that it is *cultural* to feel there's a God:

> You might as well ask if it's natural to do up one's trousers with zippers. ... One believes things because one has been conditioned to believe them. Finding bad reasons for what one believes for other bad reasons—that's philosophy. People believe in God because they've been conditioned to believe in God.
>
> (234–235)

Huxley's state monster—an agent of social construction—also acts, paradoxically, as an agent of *de*construction. Mustapha calmly kicks some of the most dearly held western spiritualist and essentialist beliefs in the teeth: "The gods are just. No doubt. But their code of law is dictated, in the last resort, by the people who organize society; Providence takes its cue from men" (235–236). Most state oppressors genuinely believe in—or at least persistently maintain that they do—whatever ideology buttresses the social order they impose on their citizenry. To hear Mustapha so calmly and bald-facedly admit to the artificial makeup of the World State is unsettling in the extreme. The grip of the World State is even stronger than that of the repressive government depicted in *Brazil*. At the close of *Brave New World*, there is no promise of heroic overthrow. Potential rebellious Alphas such as Helmholtz and Bernard conform to the system. The pathetic nature of John's suicide prevents our salvaging even a moral victory from the tale. The World State looks ready to grind on for more centuries to come.

Menippean bleak warnings are delivered by Orwell's *1984* and Atwood's *The Handmaid's Tale* as well. As works of speculative satire, their methods of delivery are also bleak. Unlike *Brazil* and *Brave New World*, there is no flippancy or absurd levity to Orwell's and Atwood's stories. Instead, readers are ground into grim submission by them—as are the characters within these works. At this point, we come to an important quality of satire to keep in mind: *satire does not have to be funny*. At least, satire need not be funny in the pleasant, generally understood comedic way. Readers can be forgiven for equating the satiric with the comic. After all, wit, irony, parody, sarcasm, lampoon, travesty, burlesque are the frequent techniques of satire. Yet, polemic remains the key ingredient. Satire attacks current human behaviors that, in the eyes of the satirist, fall into the general categories of self-seeking criminality (knavery), ruinous ignorance (folly), or a combination of the two. As a genre, then, satire can be as akin to philosophy and to tragedy as it is to comedy. In fact, many of the works seen as the most powerful specimens of satire offer grim assessments of their here and now, if not of the overall human condition. Juvenal's famous *Satire X*, usually given the title "The Vanity of Human Wishes" and often translated or imitated through the centuries, sets the standard for such satiric–tragic visions. In that satire (as well as in many of his others), Juvenal delivers a torrent of withering observations, arguments, and exempla. This perpetual stream of vituperation, delivered with indefatigable passion, earned the Roman satirist the critical descriptor of *saeva indignatio* (savage indignation). This excess also prompted Dryden to comment in his "Discourse Concerning Satire" that Juvenal is always "on the gallop." That is, the humor involved in such satire is founded on frenetic wit and the amplification of outrage—in a word, on *exaggeration*. In Juvenal's satiric world, *every* vice or folly, no matter how trivial, is treated as moral affront and heinous transgression, even such things as overeating or women taking exercise. The effect of this hyperbole makes Dryden confess that "Juvenal … gives me as much pleasure as I can bear; … his spleen is raised, and he raises mine" (2: 130). By this, I take Dryden to mean that his experience when reading Juvenal does not result in pleasurable pleasure, as might be the result of encountering mirthful satiric humor, such as that of Horace. Instead, the levity available in Juvenal is only a gallows humor—unpleasurable pleasure—educing, at most, grim and ironic laughter because the situation being treated is depicted as utterly dark and hopeless. A French expression originating in the early modern era conveys well this idea: *rire jaune*. Translating literally as "yellow laughter," the idiom means a forced, mirthless, unhealthy, or hollow laughter that badly conceals, in fact, agitation and discontent. This uncomfortable, almost involuntary and painful form of humor marks many notable works of early modern satire, such as the Earl of Rochester's *A Satyr Against Reason and Mankind* (1679), Swift's *Gulliver's Travels* (1726), and Pope's *The Dunciad in Four Books* (1744). The device of dismal Juvenalian exaggeration triggering yellow laughter in readers and viewers—thereby raising their spleen (bad temper and spite) rather than their mirth—is a common trait of Rants. The narrative *vir iratus* of Juvenalian satire frequently is used as a means to target those misadministering the state. As severe alarms against the unthinkable, Rants against modern hegemony often are characterized by a savage indignation altogether devoid of comedic enjoyment.[1] Orwell's *1984* is a perfect instance of such satiric excess. So fierce is the depiction of that dystopian world, readers hardly surrender to the slightest reluctant, sobering, tragic chuckle.

At the heart of Menippean and sci-fi cognitive estrangement and cognition effect in *1984*—that is, of readers being provoked into rethinking their current reality—is Big Brother as the monster of state. Where Huxley's *Brave New World* foresees biological and psychological tampering with humans as the primary agent of governmental manipulation, Orwell's novel predicts panoptic surveillance and the distortion of public discourse as the path forward for totalitarianism. So far, Orwell's sociotechnological forecasts are in far greater evidence than Huxley's more tongue-in-cheek vision of futuristic oppression. The World State has a fantastic quality to it, something like an amusement park gone horribly wrong. Oceania, on the other hand, with its inescapable grime, palpable lies, and planned deprivation, is all too familiar. Modern readers experience something similar to it every day. With regard to voicing opposition to a dangerous false orthodoxy, Orwell was mistaken in his fear of Stalinist Communism being the grave threat to humanity. Huxley's Fordism—that is, capitalism—has turned out to be the more accurate prediction for calamity.[2] Nonetheless, Orwell is remarkably prescient in his portrayal of the means of ruthless modern power. Just as all tales of scientifically created monsters breaking free of control inevitably seem to bear a resemblance to *Frankenstein*, all stories involving a heavy-handed state unavoidably seem influenced by Orwell's Big Brother. *1984* has set the standard for monocratic nation-states, real and fictional alike. Orwell's monster state exists only to terrorize the individuals living within it, dominating them in mind and body. Unlike Huxley, however, Orwell is less fanciful with his satiric embellishments, making their effect that much more chillingly realistic. The Ministry of Peace wages perpetual war, The Ministry of Truth tells nothing but lies, The Ministry of Love promotes hatred and fear, The Ministry of Plenty rations out starvation, and so forth. Such nomenclature would be funny were it not for the recognizable governmental doubletalk at work and the human misery caused by these institutions. If it takes readers a while to realize that Huxley's World State is a wild elaboration of their state, no such cognition gap exists with Orwell's Oceania. Readers understand almost immediately that they are in the modern here and now—one where the potential brutality of modern discipline goes altogether unchecked.

As we saw in *Brave New World* and *Brazil,* Orwell likewise relies heavily on the creation of a sympathetic narrative persona to bring across his points of view. Winston Smith, an inconsequential member of the Outer Party, is the prototype of so many luckless victims of the modern state (to include, obviously, Sam Lowry). Winston's ordeal of false rebellious hope leading to savage reinfliction of state discipline functions as a painful teaching device for readers. Through him, we learn how The Party, *Ingsoc* (English Socialism), runs its pitiless state. We also glimpse the current geopolitical order. Three such autocratic mega-states, Oceania, Eurasia, and Eastasia, wage endless war not so much to gain advantage over each other, but as a means to maintain internal control over their populations. As mentioned above, Orwell's polemic target is the political and social orthodoxy of Stalinism. Its representative in the novel, the mysterious O'Brien, works in the Ministry of Truth and is a member of the Inner Party. Like Mustapha Mond, O'Brien is the monster of *1984*, enforcing an intolerable "normal" from his pinnacle of pyramidal power. Like Mond, O'Brien monsterizes those who do not conform to the dominant social order of his monster state. Unlike Mond, however, who founds his control of the citizenry on superficial social happiness, O'Brien operates a bestial brand of statism grounded in *realpolitik*. While torturing Winston, O'Brien explains to him:

> The Party seeks power entirely for its own sake. We are not interested in the good of others; we are interested solely in power. Not wealth or luxury or long life or happiness; only power, pure power. ... We know that no one ever seizes power with the intention of relinquishing it. Power is not a means; it is an end. One does not establish a dictatorship in order to safeguard a revolution; one makes the revolution in order to establish the dictatorship. ... Now do you begin to understand me?
>
> (217)

O'Brien's very definition of hegemonic power is the ability to mete out suffering and fear: "Power is in inflicting pain and humiliation. Power is in tearing human minds to pieces and putting them together again in new shapes of your own choosing" (220). O'Brien envisions a civilization not founded on vague claims of love and justice, but on the blunt fact of hatred: "Progress in our world will be progress toward more pain" (220). At this point in Orwell's Menippean tale, we should be enjoying/suffering a good stark Juvenalian snigger.

Along with "an endless pressing, pressing, pressing upon the nerve of power" (221), The Party maintains and amplifies its hold on people with the emphatic and Machiavellian use of Saussurean semiology and Derridean *différance*. That is, the Inner Party constructs, deconstructs, and reconstructs reality constantly to suit its political purposes. This practice is likely Orwell's most unnerving observation about modern power: "truth" is ever the invention of those in charge. As he remarks at the end of his 1946 essay, "Politics and the English Language":

> Political language—and with variations this is true of all political parties, from Conservatives to Anarchists—is designed to make lies sound truthful and murder respectable, and to give an appearance of solidity to pure wind.
> (139)

As an editor who revises historical evidence in the Records Department of the Ministry of Truth, Winston recognizes fully the informational sham at work in Oceania. The Party's is no run-of-the-mill propagandistic campaign, however. Their goal is cognitive and, eventually, linguistic domination. Via *doublethink*, "the power of holding two contradictory beliefs in one's mind simultaneously, and accepting both of them" (176), citizens are habituated to eschew critical thinking. Via the introduction of *Newspeak*, the purpose of which "was not only to provide a medium of expression for the world-view and mental habits proper to the devotees of Ingsoc, but to make all other modes of thought impossible" (246), the dominant is in the process of being enforced as the Universal. Says O'Brien to Winston: "You are imagining that there is something called human nature which will be outraged by what we do and will turn against us. But we create human nature. Men are infinitely malleable" (222). These dark, Orwellian threats to intellectual autonomy reveal to us, as does *Brave New World*, "that the meaning of the world as we find it is always already interpreted for us in a matter of historical accident, not natural necessity" (Brian Smith 352). We exist only within cultural construct, and any given social "reality" is the invention of hegemony.

In current-day terms, the phenomenon Orwell points out to readers is that of bullshit. In his 2005 treatise "On Bullshit," philosopher Harry Frankfurt examines this deceptive communicative practice. According to Frankfurt, what the bullshitter hides is the fact that the truth-values of her statements are of no real concern to her; her intention is neither to report the truth nor to conceal it. Writes Frankfurt: "He does not care whether the things he says describe reality correctly. He just picks them out, or makes them up, to suit his purpose" (55). The modern world is awash in such bullshit. From advertising to social media to news outlets to political parties, bullshit flies thick and fast in the 21st century—and seems always to be on the increase. One of the primary functions of modern satire is to expose bullshit, in particular political and corporate bullshit. In his 2015 farewell episode of *The Daily Show*, Jon Stewart delivers his own treatise on the subject, pointing out that, "Bullshit is everywhere." His main concern is with "the more pernicious bullshit; the premediated, institutional bullshit designed to obscure and distract. Designed by whom? The bullshitocracy." According to Stewart, this truly harmful form of bullshit, perpetrated by those in power, comes in three varieties: making bad things sound like good things (e.g., the Patriot Act); hiding the bad things under mountains of complexity (e.g., the Super PAC); cloaking an unwillingness to act under the guise of unending inquiry (e.g., climate change). Stewart ends his lecture, however, on a note of hope:

> But the good news is this: bullshitters have gotten pretty lazy, and their work is easily detected, and looking for it is kind of a pleasant way to pass the time, like an I Spy of bullshit. So I say to you tonight, friends, the best defense against bullshit is vigilance. So, if you smell something, say something.

Modern satire urges us to have up perpetually our critical-thinking/smelling guard. Orwell's speculative satire produces precisely this indispensable outcome of forcing readers to rethink their current reality. The bullshit disseminated by those governing Oceania may be amplified by Orwell to an extravagantly malevolent degree, but it is entirely recognizable to us as modern political bullshit. One of the important effects of reading *1984*, then, is for us to ponder our own cultural moment. Just what manner of bullshit is our modern state shoveling onto us? At the time of this writing, the reply to that question comes in a single word: Trump.

Atwood's *The Handmaid's Tale* is likewise an engrossing meditation on modern bullshit. In place of Stalinism or Fordism, this time Christian fundamentalism is the target of polemic. With the Republic of Gilead, Atwood creates a totalitarian theocracy and military dictatorship every bit as ferocious as Orwell's Oceania. Public executions and, in particular, the repression of women define this evangelical state. What is subjected most to satiric exaggeration and attack in Atwood's novel is western patriarchy. In something of an inversion of Marleen Barr's concept of feminist fabulation, *The Handmaid's Tale* creates, paradoxically, an anti-feminist nightmare in order to combat traditional sexism and misogyny.[3] Rather than depicting powerful women characters doing the presently impossible and living free from reproductive slavery, Atwood gives us exactly the reverse: woman as thing. Suvin's principle of cognitive estrangement, then, occurs not by way of displacing the contemporary familiar, but of amplifying it to the nth degree. The story depicts such a grotesque degree of male domination over women—yet one not outside the realm of possibility for certain American religious–political groups—that patriarchy is exposed for the ideological illusion and egoistic fraud it is. According to Atwood, one of the things that speculative fiction can do that socially realistic narratives cannot is experiment with polity in this overt way. Speculative fiction, she writes:

> … can explore proposed changes in social organisation, by showing what they might actually be like for those living within them. Thus, the utopia and the dystopia, which have proved over and over again that we have a better idea about how to make hell on earth than we do about how to make heaven. The history of the 20th century, where a couple of societies took a crack at utopia on a large scale and ended up with the inferno, would bear this out.
>
> ("Aliens")

Published at the outset of the neoconservative evangelical movement in the United States, *The Handmaid's Tale* takes 1980s readers for a test drive in the unbridled sexism of American right-wing Christian zealotry. Along the way, Atwood makes very sure that readers stop, get out, and kick the Menippean tires.

The narrative touchstone for us to learn about the horrors of Gilead is the Handmaid herself, Offred. Literally the name means "of Fred," signaling that she belongs to the Commander, a high-ranking government official. Because of drastically low birthrates in Gilead, due mainly to sterility from pollution, the Commander periodically and ritualistically rapes Offred in hopes of procreation. Everything is justified in this hierarchical, ultraconservative regime by literal readings of the Old Testament. As her tale unfolds, Offred comes to know the Commander personally. Much of their talk involves the tactics of power. Before Gilead, the Commander was part of a radical Christian group called the "Sons of Jacob." They conspired to assassinate the U.S. President and massacre the Congress in order to institute their theocracy. Along with bloody purges of all nonbelievers, a priority of Gilead was the reestablishment of old-timey patriarchy. Founders of the Republic believed that modern manhood had become weak and lost its way. Their rule of God has now set that right. Women are not allowed to read or handle money and property. They are monitored and compelled into social categories based on their fertility and perceived morality. Women are considered inferior to men and have no rights or freedoms in Gilead. Remarks the Commander of former American society: "Those years were just an anomaly, historically speaking. ... Just a fluke. All we've done is return things to Nature's norm" (285). In *1984*, O'Brien knows unequivocally that The Party manipulates "truth." In *Brave New World*, Mond, as a World Controller, is completely aware of the contrived operation of that super state. In contrast, Atwood gives us an autocrat who is under the delusion that he rules according to an irrefutable Truth. The Commander's sexist and murderous convictions derive from an unthinking faith. Atwood thus depicts a monstrous statecraft differently motivated than those set forth by Orwell or by Huxley, and one similar, perhaps, to Gilliam's blinkered and paranoid British government in *Brazil*. Nonetheless, modern regimes of power consistently betray an underlying common trait: the consensus of the elite posing as objectivity. It seems a moot point to decide whether the astute or the dull-witted powerbroker is the more devastating.

Like most protagonists terrorized by a dystopian state, Offred finds herself a waif amid forces. Atwood goes out of her way to make sure that we, as readers, are as well. Similar to Swift's Gulliver, Offred is an ill-informed and often unreliable narrator. At the end of her story, she doesn't know whether she's being rescued by anti-Gilead insurgents or carted off by Gilead secret police to be tortured. What is more, the wry closing of the novel—an academic conference centuries hence on "Gileadean Studies"—calls into question the veracity of Offred's entire story. We are left unsure if Offred even existed or not.[4] An effect of creating such anxiety and uncertainty in the reader is to make us feel the awful powerlessness of being ostracized, monsterized, enslaved, and erased by the vagaries of social convention. Offred's being helpless and in the dark is potentially our winding up helpless and in the dark, depending on if there's a radical change of ideology at the top of the state apparatus. For many centuries in western society, such shifts are a real threat, especially to all who are not white, male, heterosexual, able-bodied, and wealthy. In fact, the Commander embodies the unthinking privilege of hegemonic men. At some level, vague even to himself, he understands the constructedness of the Gilead state, acknowledging to Offred at one point that, "Better never means better for everyone. ... It always means worse, for some" (274). As we've seen, though, instead of pursuing this insight, the Commander retreats to his comfortable, self-serving Christian orthodoxy, maintaining that the Commanders govern not just according to God's eternal laws but to the essential qualities of human nature. Offred catches him out in this glaring contradiction, though, when the Commander enjoins her to dress up and accompany him for an evening at "the Club"—that is, the whorehouse for Gilead officialdom. When Offred questions the hypocrisy of such an establishment, the Commander excuses it by saying, "But everyone's human, after all." When she asks what that means, he explains: "It means you can't cheat Nature. ... Nature demands variety, for men. It stands to reason, it's part of the procreational strategy. It's Nature's plan. ... Women know that instinctively." When Offred implies ironically that the whole purpose of the Gilead state, then, appears to be to enable these few powerful men to "merely have different women," the Commander replies, without irony, "It solves a lot of problems" (308). And boom goes Atwood's satiric dynamite. The Republic of Gilead is founded far more on male sex drive than on devotion to Christ. Although the Commanders have convinced themselves that they follow God's Word, their vaunted Christian republic is nothing more than a frat house manned by sexual predators. At that moment, Offred sees the Commander for the petty and ignorant man that he is. For the oppressed of the modern state, however, discovering the character traits of their overlords hardly matters. Like Winston Smith and Sam Lowery, Offred stands defenseless when faced with the prospect of torture and execution.

> I want to keep on living, in any form. I resign my body freely, to the uses of others. They can do what they like with me. I am abject.
> I feel, for the first time, their true power.
>
> (368)

This confession by Atwood's terrified narrator, living as a fictional citizen of Gilead, puts readers in mind of actual women and girls around the world facing, every day, extant sexual and social exploitation at the hands of men. Even if Gilead is an exaggerated evangelical–patriarchal state beast, we recognize instantly the everyday origins of its sexist monstrosity and zealot's orthodoxy.

Ideology Exposed

Along with these four examples of speculative satire against an abusive modern state, I offer illustrations as well of specific characteristics of the neoliberal/neoconservative hegemony—as spelled out in Chapter 2—coming under attack in such polemics. As pointed out at the end of Chapter 2, recognizing the functioning of power can be a problematic undertaking. Due to normalization, the dominant easily can masquerade as the universal; ideologies go out of their way to portray themselves not as human constructs, but as laws of nature or as timeless truths. As a result, dogmas blend into the woodwork and credos become part of the social landscape. Hence the importance of distortion and exaggeration in the Rant. For a reader to be jarred into the reexamination of current social circumstances, a significant degree of cognitive estrangement must take place. Even then, certain entrenched features of the hegemonic discourse can remain in the background. For example, *The Handmaid's Tale* is quite successful, in its creation of a dystopia, at exposing the cruelties of religiosity and patriarchy. Those messages are hard to miss. But will readers likewise discern how Offred, by having her credit cards and bank accounts summarily cancelled, is a victim of accumulation by dispossession? Less certain. Or, in post-Marxist terms, will readers appreciate the excruciating detail with which Atwood depicts the hegemonic adversary of a modern state as well the hopelessness of individuals being ground in the gears of liberal–conservative discourse? Such depth of cultural response and analysis is unlikely. In other words, Rants can lead readers to ideology, but they can't always make readers think. Nonetheless, when it comes to decrying the economics of neoliberalism, Rants commonly depict wealth inequity, corporations as unchecked private agents, debt peonage, workplace abuse, and individualism as a trap. When it comes to exposing issues of neoconservatism, Rants often highlight the oppressive practices of militarism, religiosity, and primacy. Following are brief cases in point.

For a full-blown invective against neoconservatism, James McTeigue's *V for Vendetta* (2006) is unsurpassed. The Norsefire régime that rules a totalitarian, near-future England incarnates the principles of militarism, religiosity, and primacy. What is more, in their depiction of Norsefire, McTeigue as director and the Wachowski siblings as screenwriters/producers give audiences a damning portrait of the Bush 2 administration—an administration wholly given over to neocon doctrine. In a post-9/11 world, both governments—the fictional Norsefire and the actual Bush Whitehouse—propagate fear and hate as a means to power and control. Although the methods of Norsefire, of course, are heightened in the film, their qualities and actions are quite recognizable as right-wing Republican policy. The parallels are many and apparent.[5] Norsefire is a paranoid martial state founded hypocritically on Christian fundamentalism. The régime is convinced of its divine preeminence as a special nation in the world, and thus believes itself justified in using any means required to attain political ends. These measures include propaganda, surveillance, curfew, secret police, ethnonationalism, the rounding-up of dissenters/gays/Muslims, concentration camps, torture, medical experimentation, constant Terror alert, as well as staging fake "terrorist" attacks for political and economic gain. Such techniques are all amplifications of the basic neocon playbook—although some in the movie seem less exaggerations than others. In the America leading up to the 2008 presidential election, such a spectacular filmic rejection of dystopian neoconservatism equated, arguably, to a message of vote Democratic. In short, McTeigue's film is a thoroughgoing speculative satire excoriating the neocon orthodoxy of the day.

Far less plainly, neoliberalism in the form of finance capitalism comes in for condemnation as well in *V for Vendetta*. In the scene at the memorial to "The Victims of the St. Mary's Virus," V (Hugo Weaving) spells out for Inspector Finch (Stephen Rea) and his partner Dominic Stone (Rupert Graves) the criminal path by which Norsefire rose to power. Its leader, Adam Sutler (John Hurt), has been a member of the Conservative Party. In that role, he began a special government project, in the name of national security, at the Larkhill Detention Centre, a program alleged to be a search for biological weapons. In fact, its purpose was to supply Norsefire with a way to seize power. Via brutal experimentation on detainees (to include V himself), Larkhill scientists discovered a potent virus, presenting Sutler with that avenue to power. Explains V to Finch: "Imagine a virus, the most terrifying virus you can, and then imagine that you, and you alone, have the cure. If the ultimate goal is power, how best to use such a weapon?" Norsefire decided to use that weapon on England itself. In three counterfeit "terrorist" attacks, they released the virus at a school (St. Mary's), at a tube station, and contaminated a water treatment plant. The deadly pathogen claimed over 80,000 victims, setting off a countrywide panic. In the national elections following close on to these attacks, Sutler won by a landslide, offering the public the usual hardline, xenophobic, law-and-order stance of right-wing demagogues. Asserts V of Norsefire's scheming, "the true genius of the plan was the fear. Fear became the ultimate tool of this government." In Trump's America, this statement is painfully familiar. Where neoliberal economics enters the picture, on top of neoconservative politics, is with the idea of a business monopoly manufacturing a crisis in order to generate profit. As soon as the election was won by Norsefire, a cure to the virus was suddenly and wondrously "discovered." Recounts V:

> Then not long after the election, lo and behold, a miracle. Some believe it was the work of God himself. But it was a pharmaceutical company controlled by certain party members that made them all obscenely rich.

The stock prices of that pharmaceutical company, Viadoxic, went through the financial market roof as a result of its owning the patent to the cure. With the virus, then, not only did Norsefire steal political advantage, but it swindled its way to financial superiority as well. The two go hand-in-hand if a modern faction is to attain, as V puts it, "complete and total hegemonic domination." When it comes to power these days, where neoconservatism is in operation, neoliberalism is close by—and vice versa.

An excellent example of this neolib–neocon conjunction comes in James Cameron's 2009 mega-hit, *Avatar*. In that movie, we see distant-future corporate imperialism in action. That is, in the year 2154, a failing Earth has established a mining colony on the planet Pandora in order to commandeer natural resources—whether the native inhabitants like it or not. The resource being mined, pointedly named "unobtanium," is seen less as something vital for human survival back on Earth and more as a rare commodity vital for corporate profits and happy shareholders. Explains corporate manager Parker Selfridge (Giovanni Ribisi) to scientist Grace Augustine (Sigourney Weaver) while holding up a small lump of the treasure:

> This is why we're here. Unobtanium. Because this little gray rock sells for twenty million a kilo. That's the only reason. It's what pays for the whole party. It's what pays for your science. Comprendo?

Thus, this is not a story of humans gallantly exploring strange new worlds, seeking out new life and new civilizations, of boldly going where no human has gone before. Rather, this is a story of neoliberalism in outer space. We're out scratching around for the best interstellar bottom line, and we're bringing our corporate structure with us. An essential part of such colonization, of course, is military muscle. For this function, the company, Resources Development Administration (RDA), has hired as security chief a former Marine tough-guy, Colonel Miles Quaritch (Stephen Lang). He's altogether insane in his zeal for commercial mission. Together, Selfridge and Quaritch personify a fiscal–military alliance that demonstrates the dangers of corporations as unchecked private agents. RDA is a lawless actor on the final frontier. It's made clear in the film that this same corporate–militarist behavior has brought Earth to the brink of ruin. Cameron sprinkles the dialog with references to wealth inequity and the bellicose use of armed forces back home. Our hero, Jake Sully (Sam Worthington), is a disabled Marine combat veteran wounded in foreign action. His injuries have landed him down-and-out and in a wheelchair. When his scientist twin brother is murdered in a robbery (as Jake says bitterly in voiceover, killed "for the paper in his wallet"), RDA convinces Jake to take his brother's place as an avatar-driver on Pandora. As one of the company men tells Jake: "And the pay is good. *Very* good." Jake obviously needs the money. We also learn from him in a voiceover: "They can fix a spinal, if you've got the money. But not on vet benefits. Not in this economy." In other words, Jake is a discarded worker/soldier. A century and a half from now, like today, the elite class is more than willing to put military personnel in harm's way, but unwilling to pay the high cost of caring for them adequately once they're harmed. The overriding concern of the wealthy is not social justice or the general welfare, but corporate profits. As Selfridge spells out the situation on Pandora for Jake: "Look, killing the indigenous looks bad. But there's one thing that shareholders hate more than bad press, and that's a bad quarterly statement." Although Cameron sets his sci-fi a good ways into our future, his socioeconomic moment and commentary remains fixed in our early 21st-century present.

Likewise, the futuristic portrayal of militarism in *Avatar* is unflattering and grounded in the current-day. Neocon military adventurism looks to be alive and well in the 22nd century. As a Marine, Quaritch did "three tours of Nigeria," and Jake just has emerged from the "mean bush" of Venezuela.

Internationalism and unilateral military engagement still seem the policy of the day. Even more specific references to a neoconservative mindset come with several distinct allusions to the Bush Administration's prosecution of its oil war in Iraq. For one, the military forces on Pandora are private, not public; that is, these are corporate mercenaries. Muses Jake in voiceover: "Back on Earth, these guys were Army dogs. Marines. Fightin' for freedom. But out here they're just hired guns. Takin' the money. Workin' for the Company." Shades of private "security companies" such as Blackwater (which has since renamed itself), earning millions of taxpayer dollars through government contracts, but operating in Iraq and Afghanistan without public oversight or accountability. Another indicator that Pandora, at least in part, stands in for Iraq is the manner in which Quaritch wars against the indigenous Na'vi. His approach is the Bush doctrine of Pax Americana and "peace through strength," meaning preemptive military strikes and the use of overwhelming force. In a pep-talk to his corporate troops, Quaritch growls: "Our only security lies in pre-emptive attack. We will fight terror with terror." His crusade is even referred to as "some kind of Shock-and-Awe campaign"—the very name of the tactics touted by Bush as the 2003 invasion of Iraq began. Jake summarizes best how the principles of primacy and unilateralism serve the colonial invader: "This is how it's done! When people are sittin' on shit that you want, you make them your enemy! Then you're justified in taking it." When all is said and done, RDA is a future neoliberal-neoconservative version of multinational corporate giant Halliburton, now with the middle man of government conveniently cut out.

For a Rant wholly dedicated to a socioeconomic critique of neoliberalism, Neill Blomkamp's *Elysium* (2013) fits the bill perfectly. Although not a particularly satisfying or successful movie for its plotline, it nonetheless atomizes poignantly, through the exaggeration of dystopia, the cruelties of present-day economics.[6] The film checks every box of neoliberal praxis, and from its outset viewers understand they're in for a story of rich-versus-poor. The opening shot flies over vast slums and ruined city skylines; a superimposed script tells us: "In the late 21st century Earth was diseased, polluted and vastly overpopulated." The shot changes to Earth from the vantage point of high orbit, and we're informed: "Earth's wealthiest inhabitants fled the planet to preserve their way of life." The camera then pans to a massive, wheel-shaped space station. Nestled within its ring are long tracts of posh neighborhoods, every mansion featuring a large swimming pool and finely manicured lawns. The image could not be more telling: here is the ultimate gated suburb, a supremely secure setting where the privileged few can enjoy their opulence far, far away from the unwashed masses.[7] Blomkamp is fully intentional in his social commentary. Just prior to the release of *Elysium*, the director/screenwriter told *Entertainment Weekly* that his movie is not about the future at all, but is a statement about the contemporary human condition (Sean Smith). Similarly, in an interview with *I Am Rogue*, he says, "Everybody wants to ask me lately about my predictions for the future. No, no, no. This isn't science fiction. This is today. This is now" ("The Future is Now"). Blomkamp clearly employs sci-fi cognitive estrangement in order to trigger a fiscal cognition effect on viewers, his general message being that the 1% are vultures. Moreover, he's quite aware that his story is founded on polemic and ridicule. In 2015, after *Elysium* had met with only lukewarm critical success, Blomkamp mused in an interview, "I still think the satirical idea of a ring, filled with rich people, hovering above the impoverished Earth, is an awesome idea. I love it so much, I almost want to go back and do it correctly" ("New 'Alien' "). Like *Avatar*, then, *Elysium* is a Rant targeting the hegemon, but with particular emphasis on exposing the neoliberal side of the power equation.

Our touchstone character is Max Da Costa (Matt Damon), a Los Angeles slum-dweller in the year 2154 (curiously, the same year *Avatar* is set) trying to get his life on track after being arrested for car theft. Through Max, viewers experience the many downsides of neoliberal society. All of them are immediately familiar: chronic and crushing poverty, crumbling infrastructure, lack of adequate public services (such as transportation and health care), widespread unemployment and insecure employment, low wages, inescapable debt, criminal gangs, byzantine bureaucracy along with brutal policing (both now performed by a robot force), and so on. Max has taken a job as an assembly line worker for Armadyne Corp, dead-end and utterly exploitative employment in itself. Add to that the workplace abuse of hazardous conditions, zero safety protocol, and managerial threats. When Max suffers an industrial accident, getting bombarded with a lethal dose of radiation, we witness the utter callousness of Armadyne corporation and its CEO, John Carlyle (William Fichtner). Solely concerned with keeping the production line moving and losing no profit, Carlyle issues orders for Max to be immediately removed from the factory. The only corporate attention Max receives after his injury is being informed by a robot medic, in a grimy infirmary, that he will die in five days. The robot then makes Max sign for some palliative medication and thanks him for his service. Shades of Jake Sully.

To add insult to Max's fatal injury, Armadyne Corp manufactures Elysian weaponry, to include the robots that police the Earth. On his way to work that morning, Max had been accosted by two robot cops at a bus stop. In an aggressive check of his parole status, they ended up knocking Max to the ground, breaking his wrist, and ordering him to report to his parole officer without delay. That officer, we discover, is also an automaton. Without listening to Max's side of the bus stop incident, the administrative robot straightaway extends Max's parole by a further eight months. It is oppressive enough for a worker to be alienated from her own labor in the classic Marxist sense, say, by working on an assembly line manufacturing high-end automobiles that the worker could never hope to afford on her factory salary. It is worse yet to be a worker, such as Max, alienated from, in effect, his own life by the products he assembles at Armadyne Corp. That is to say, Max builds the very robots that brutalize and summarily punish him. Moreover, his plight comes as the result of dividuation within a highly developed control society. As an individual, Max can be so closely tracked and monitored that his criminal record can never be forgotten. Thus, as seen in his interaction with the parole officer robot, neither will Max ever be forgiven, no matter the mitigation of extenuating circumstances or his good behavior. The automated system forever knows and deals with Max according to that one specific aspect of him, making a particular feature more important than the person as a whole. That, of course, is the entire point of dividuation, because Max then can be used for profit-making by Armadyne.

Carlyle's corporation obviously rakes in billions, if not trillions, producing these authoritarian machines. Like private prisons currently, where there is no incentive to lower recidivism rates because these incarceration companies need a steady stream of prisoners to fill their cells, what would it profit Armadyne to decriminalize Max? Quickly slapping more parole time on him makes good business sense. For that matter, the more poverty-driven crime there is, the fatter the corporate bottom line is going to be and the happier Armadyne shareholders (who all live safely on Elysium, no doubt) are going to be. The more offenders and parolees there are, the greater the need for robot cops and robot parole officers to arrest and punish them. Here, then, the panoptic disciplining mechanism (literally now) of the police blends seamlessly with the controlling implementation of surveillance capitalism. Similar to debt peonage, Max is caught up in a massive crime peonage scheme. In this way, Max's individuality is a trap. Max will never be able to pay off his "debt to society"—meaning really escaping his being a cog in the neoliberal profit-making machinery of crime and punishment. Even if he makes it out of parole status, the violence and poverty of his surroundings always will encumber his life, likely driving him into another criminal violation. Armadyne Corp makes too tidy a sum managing what amounts to a slum-prison planet for the wealthy elites to want to change anything.

The behavior of the residents of Elysium is predictably appalling. Many of them look to be simply rich manikins living the high-life. The Elysian officials running this orbiting country club seem split between hypocritical liberals and ruthless conservatives. President Patel (Faran Tahir) wrings his hands over the "moral" issues involved when it comes to protecting the space station against gatecrashers from Earth. Opposing him is Defense Secretary Delacourt (Jodie Foster), who is unabashed about blowing unauthorized spaceships to smithereens when they get too close to Elysium. Obviously, neither executive is at all concerned about the egregious planetary wealth gap that is the root cause of the situation. Provocatively, the special focus of Blomkamp's *haves* versus *have-nots* tale is the issue of healthcare. Elysians enjoy the technology of the "Med-Bay," a medical device that cures instantly any disease. Meanwhile, on the planet below, billions of people go without anything resembling adequate medical attention. In fact, most of the Earth-bound who attempt illegal immigration up to Elysium on tattered spaceships risk the perilous crossing in order to access a Med-Bay, which are programed, of course, only to serve the official citizens of the space station. To make a long and clunky storyline short, Max makes his way to Elysium initially looking only to cure his own fatal condition. Along the way, he does battle with the monster of a lunatic mercenary, Kruger (Sharlto Copley), hired by Delacourt to protect plutocracy. In the process, Max transitions into the Savior figure, in the end sacrificing his own life so that a fleet of medical shuttles can descend to Earth bringing the benefit of the Med-Bay to all. Ham-fisted narrative, to be sure, but noteworthy post-Marxist points are made nonetheless. For one thing, only the oppressed can free themselves; oppressors do not give a damn about authentic social reform. For another, the only humanity and solidarity on display in the film comes from the underclass. Only among slum-dwellers do we see friendship loyalty, romantic love interest, parental devotion, teamwork, heroic sacrifice, and other hopeful communitarian qualities. In this way, *Elysium* vividly and memorably defines the neoliberal-neoconservative adversary in the central conceit of Earth's well-to-do joyriding in space on their giant Ferris wheel. Equally, Blomkamp's movie depicts agonistic pluralism and the inception of a radical and plural democracy challenging and altering the neoliberal status quo. However sentimentalized the film may be, audiences are shown a better kind of society for which to fight, one where the benefits of liberal democracy, in the form of advanced medical care, are redistributed to the many identities of the multicultural masses.

And So …

In his study *The Bonds of Debt*, Richard Dienst concludes with a discussion of how, "A new politics of indebtedness is emerging everywhere—in government ministries and parliaments, workplaces and households, streets and forests" (172). People around the globe are reacting to this neoliberal normal in a variety of ways: with resignation and capitulation, with deferral and negotiation, with evasion and refusal. Dienst wonders, though, how long people will put up with a situation that can only get worse. He speculates:

> And when it turns out that none of the austerity plans on offer do anything more than reinforce the basic imbalances of the prevailing growth regime, electorates may set their governments a new political task: to break the resistance of the creditors, clip the wings of capital flight, recast the terms by which accumulated wealth can be appropriated by the general economy that produced it, and thereby, at last, help the rentier class toward its long-delayed euthanasia.
>
> (175)

Yet how might popular resistance to neoliberal policy be realized? What are practical steps that might be taken? At the end of *A Brief History of Neoliberalism*, David Harvey similarly contemplates alternatives to the neoliberal ascendancy. He remarks:

> The story-telling from the White House and the spin-meistering from Downing Street have to be rebutted then stopped if we are to find any kind of exit from our current impasse. There is a reality out there and it is catching up with us fast.
>
> (198)

Harvey points out how there are many energetic resistance movements to accumulation by dispossession, but they tend to be localized, group-specific, and lacking an adequate macro-viewpoint of the crisis. At this point, after a generation or so of dominance, neoliberal and neoconservative propaganda is also well naturalized into both national and global social fabrics. In the United States and around the world, conservative ideology, legal systems, and militaristic police power are firmly consolidated. Harvey points out as well, as do Laclau and Mouffe, how progressives have yielded to the neoliberal canard that "class" is no longer a valid economic category or political topic, and so "class warfare" is no longer a matter for serious concern (200–202). These are just some of the obstacles facing any kind of egalitarian revisioning of capitalistic practice. Harvey outlines, however, a series of lessons we must learn if there is to be any chance of fighting back against neoliberal domination. As we have seen above, and as we will see in the subsequent chapters of this book, most of Harvey's lessons are the specific teaching points of the post-Marxist Rant. These lessons are as follows.

One, label class struggle as class struggle; instead of foolishly buying the palpable lie that class no longer exists as a social grouping, fight back against the obvious upper-class takeover foisted on us by neoliberalism.

Two, expose neoliberalism for the utopian nonsense it is; instead of believing the ludicrous myth that anyone who works hard can get rich, voice democratic demands for economic justice and security, fair trade, and full political participation.

Three, promote alternative individual rights to the neoliberal individual privileges of profit rate and private property; instead of possessive individualism, advocate for fair life chances, social solidarity and support, difference, a healthy environment, and control over production by direct producers.

Four, reclaim the moral high ground; instead of acceding to sanctimonious claims about the holiness of The Market or to the self-serving religiosity of evangelical Christianity, show the neoliberal–neoconservative orthodoxy for the greedy, hypocritical, and brutal social contrivance it is.

Five, attack the right wing for its *lack* of democracy; instead of buying into the happy noise of "individual liberty," expose the machinations and dirty tricks of neoliberal authoritarianism (Harvey 202–206).[8] In various ways and to various degrees and in various combinations, speculative satire can help readers and spectators understand all of these vital lessons that led to the critical reexamination of our current social order.

In the last chapter of *Debt: The First 5,000 Years*, David Graeber writes:

> it could well be said that the last thirty years have seen the construction of a vast bureaucratic apparatus for the creation and maintenance of hopelessness, a giant machine designed, first and foremost, to destroy any sense of possible alternative futures.

The purpose of that machine is to make certain "that those who challenge existing power arrangements can never, under any circumstances, be perceived to win." The powers that be deploy a vast and expensive array of armies, police, prisons, intelligence agencies, private security firms, surveillance techniques, as well as propaganda engines of every variety to "create a pervasive climate of fear, jingoistic conformity, and simple despair that renders any thought of changing the world seem an idle fantasy" (382). As a result, we are "left in the strange situation of not being able to even imagine any other way that things might be arranged. About the only thing we can imagine is catastrophe" (383). Perhaps Graeber's assessment helps to explain the craze for dystopian fiction in recent decades. Apocalypse is very much *in* around the turn of the 21st century. Audiences love to be entertained by watching the world crumble in sundry ways: alien invasion, cataclysmic natural disaster, A.I. takeover, zombie swarms, colossal city-stomping monsters, pandemic hysteria, and the like. Yet speculative satire is different from these tales of sheer catastrophe. Rants work to countermand the hegemonic articulations of hopelessness manufactured by the corporate–military Regime. Rants furrow our brows, upset our expectations, make us uncomfortable with our normal, and then put us on the mental pathway—the social imperative—of imaging another way. Speculative satire does not indulge in escapism; it advocates for our escape from bullshitocracy.

Now that the groundwork has been laid for understanding the functioning of speculative satire, from this point forward I undertake close readings of various kinds of Rants. Chapter 4 examines two Rants, one a film and the other a trilogy of novels, that depict the hell it can be to endure life under a neoliberal/neoconservative rule. Chapter 5 reviews several Rants that focus on specific pernicious features of the Regime. Chapter 6 takes into consideration the extraordinary technological inventions of A.I. as they figure in the telling of speculative satires. The aim of these readings is not to provide an exhaustive catalog of every fictive piece that might qualify as a Rant. Nor will the depth and detail of all these readings be the same; some will be more elaborate than others. Instead, my goal is to explore the many devices by which speculative satire provokes us to amend how we see the world. Toward that end, I offer a summary and helpful guide to the form's most salient features.

The Rant Playbook

Satire

- a bleak Menippean forewarning against a false orthodoxy
- a passionate argument exploring important cultural issues of the day
- someone/something blamed; someone/something praised
- distortion/exaggeration used as a rhetorical tool
- narrator/persona used as a rhetorical tool
- invasion of other genres and forms used as a rhetorical tool
- yellow laughter impelled by amplified gloom and savage indignation

Science-fiction

- a *novum*/strange newness featured
- cognitive estrangement triggering a cognition effect—that is, the strange newness elicits a critical reexamination of the current social order
- utopia/dystopia used as a rhetorical tool
- a showcasing of social issues, notably Marxist, feminist/gender, race/postcolonial concerns

Monstrosity

- weird creatures and strange things disturb categories of "normal" and disrupt well-worn ways of framing "reality"
- borders of social constraints both policed and crossed, exposing cultural norms as arbitrary
- social Others scapegoated as monstrous, exposing bigotry and the workings of raw power
- the human/monster binary often flipped, exposing the customary as the monstrous

Foucault and Deleuze

- evidence of hegemonic devices of modern discipline and subject formation applied by a powerful minority to regulate the actions of a disempowered majority
- evidence of hegemonic devices of control monitoring and modulating identity and relationships in order to put the individual to particular uses within the modern state
- the "Truth" propagated by a dominant minority challenged, discredited, and ultimately detached from the power of that minority, exposing the oppression of a dominant discourse
- depictions of people resisting subjectivity by the modern state, such as against forms of domination, against forms of exploitation, against forms of submission to authority
- modern hegemony revealed as *not* permanent, but always under pressure and renegotiation

The Regime at Work

- evidence, however overt or subtle, of neoconservative polity at work, notably militarism, religiosity, and primacy
- evidence, however overt or subtle, of neoliberal economics at work, notably wealth inequity, corporations as unchecked private agents, debt peonage, workplace abuse, and possessive individualism
- evidence, however overt or subtle, of dividuation and surveillance capitalism at work, notably in ways furthering neoliberal accumulation by dispossession

Post-Marxism

- the current neoliberal hegemonic adversary clearly defined
- indication of a better kind of society for which to fight
- various identity positions—of gender, race, class, ethnicity, sexual orientation, bodiedness, and so forth—depicted in struggle against hegemonic subjectivity and articulations
- depictions of people striving to extend the benefits of liberal capitalistic democracy to *everybody* via the redistribution of wealth and the equality of all identities
- evidence of the freeplay of political power, of agonistic pluralism via constant hegemonic construction/deconstruction/reconfiguration

Harvey's Lessons for Fighting Back:

- class struggle labeled as class struggle
- neoliberalism exposed as utopian nonsense
- possessive individualism exposed as greed and selfishness; alternative individual rights such as socioeconomic justice, solidarity, and environmentalism promoted
- moral high ground reclaimed
- the right wing attacked for its authoritarianism and *lack* of democracy

Certainly, not all of the works examined in Chapters 4, 5, and 6 will tick every box of The Rant Playbook. Some texts accentuate particular qualities of the Rant over others. Few texts actively touch on *all* of the many traits of the Rant listed above, but instead focus more narrowly on a handful of key attributes. However, regardless of the combination of characteristics any individual Rant marshals in its attack against the Regime, the overall aim of the work is the same: to stimulate in the reader first perplexity, then critical thinking, then reexamination of the here and now. Speculative satire cares nothing for Timeless Beauty, but everything for timely awareness.

Notes

1 The black humor of Kurt Vonnegut is a good example, in our own era, of this kind of sobering mirth. For other critics theorizing similar strains of bleak, despairing satire, see Steven Weisenburger's idea of "degenerative satire" as well as Howard Weinbrot's notion of "apocalyptic satire." For Weisenburger, degenerative satire "functions to subvert hierarchies of value and to reflect suspiciously on all ways of making meaning, including its own" (3). Norms operate in this kind of satiric text, but they are conditional, not universal norms, that is, "values without truth-values" (6). For Weinbrot, apocalyptic satire is that offering no answers and no hope; it is a "losers' satire in a nation of rubble" ("Apocalyptic" 105). Such satire "forces us to look at serious weaknesses in our culture, in ourselves, and in other dark places that need exposure" (109).

2 In many regards, however, Stalinism and free-market capitalism are not so different as technologies of modern power. Both systems share, for example, the decidedly disastrous practice of trickle-down economics. See Chang, Thing 13.
3 See Kate Manne's study of current-day patriarchy, *Down Girl*, where she distinguishes between sexism as an ideology and misogyny as its disciplining practice.
4 Atwood's long-awaited sequel to *The Handmaid's Tale*, titled *The Testaments* (2019), likewise uses the device of revealing, at the end of the novel, that the accounts we've just read of life in Gilead are in fact historical documents being discussed at the Thirteenth Symposium on Gileadean Studies in the year 2197.
5 In a chapter titled "Love and Violence in *V for Vendetta*," I've written a full analysis of this film that explores these issues and corresponds well with my conception of the Rant; see Combe and Boyle.
6 In a 2015 interview, Blomkamp states that he didn't get the story quite right: "I just think the script wasn't … I just didn't make a good enough film is ultimately what it is. I feel like I executed all of the stuff that could be executed, like costume and set design and special effects very well. But, ultimately, it was all resting on a somewhat not totally formed skeletal system, so the script just wasn't there; the story wasn't fully there." See "New 'Alien.'"
7 For a sobering look at the prospects for world growth and population, see Mike Davis' 2006 study, *Planet of Slums*. Reports Davis: "In 1950 there were 86 cities in the world with a population of more than one million; today there are 400, and by 2015 there will be at least 550. Cities, indeed, have absorbed nearly two-thirds of the global population explosion since 1950, and are currently growing by a million babies and migrants each week." Blomkamp's conception, then, of wealth-flight from out-of-control hypermegalopolises is thoroughly plausible. Predicts Davis: "The global countryside, meanwhile, has reached its maximum population and will begin to shrink after 2020. As a result, cities account for virtually all future world population growth, which is expected to peak at about 10 billion in 2050" (1–2).
8 In his "Conclusion: How to rebuild the world economy," Chang enumerates as well eight principles for restructuring capitalism away from the destructive practices of the neoliberal model.

4 Living Under a Lousy Orthodoxy

This chapter explores two thoroughgoing depictions of life lived under the control of the Regime. A particular culprit in this formula for oppression, as discussed in Chapter 2, is the modern corporation. In its single-minded goal of maximizing profit for shareholders, the neoliberal corporation has become an amoral and socially destructive institution.[1] Without effective democratic checks on corporate power, little stands in the way of abusive if not lethal corporate irresponsibility toward people (whether as workers, consumers, the raw material for Big Data, or collateral damage) and the environment (enough now to endanger the planetary climate). Most of the Rants considered in this book, in fact, involve corporate wrongdoing (to word it mildly). In some works, corporations star as the villain. In others, corporations to various degrees lurk in the background, having set the neoliberal table, so to speak, for the calamities at hand. As usual, working alongside the profit-taking dystopia of corporations is the militaristic and self-righteous mindset of neoconservatism, violently safeguarding the exploitative status quo. The two Rants examined below, in their extreme and unforgiving visions of the near-future, work to alert us to this catastrophic pairing.

Snowpiercer (2013)

This curious film by Joon-ho Bong, based on the 1982 graphic novel *Le Transperceneige* by Jacques Lob and Jean-Marc Rochette, drew well at the box office and fared extremely well with critics.[2] Similar to *V for Vendetta*, *Snowpiercer* qualifies as a first-rate example of a movie Rant. As a work that ticks most of the boxes of The Rant Playbook, Bong's film is best studied by walking through that list of traits. By way of a bleak Menippean forewarning against a false orthodoxy, Bong gives us our planet frozen dead due to not just the folly of climate change, but also our stupid pursuit of "a revolutionary solution to mankind's warming of the planet" by releasing a substance, "CW-7," into the atmosphere that's designed to bring "average global temperatures down to manageable levels." That experiment goes terribly wrong, killing just about everyone, yet global warming is *not* the primary warning being issued by the film. The primary warning of the film is against capitalism. The telling and painful irony of *Snowpiercer* is that the last remnant of humanity

DOI: 10.4324/9781003110491-5

surviving on earth has organized itself into the very socioeconomic base and superstructure responsible for killing off humanity. The fanciful supertrain, named Snowpiercer, that circles the globe on a yearly loop socially reproduces exactly the class structure and ideology that brought about the global disaster in 2014. By 2031, when the apocalyptic tale is set, this Capitalism Express has been in perpetual motion for 17 years pathetically going nowhere and appallingly serving no other purpose than preserving and imposing the workings of the Regime on the last handful of humans. Indeed, Bong's central metaphor is that of capitalism as an end-of-history, stasis-making mechanism of pyramidal hierarchy and oppression embodied as this weird train. We need look no further, then, for the false orthodoxy under attack than our current-day neoliberal/neoconservative hegemony. Those creeds are on full and bare-knuckled display in the movie.

With regard to elements of satire operating in the film, coming in for polemic blame is not only the fundamental brutality of capitalism but also the miserable lack of human imagination when it comes to creating society. How selfish and blind do the upper-class passengers of Snowpiercer have to be to replicate the social order that produced this cataclysm in the first place? Obviously, very selfish and blind. Much like the space-station elites of *Elysium*, they are depicted as bourgeoisie living at the top of a pyramidal society (in this case, the forward cars of a supertrain) without empathy for or awareness of the awful conditions existing at the base of that social structure (here, life in the tail section). The severe distortion and exaggeration of *Snowpiercer* drive home, unapologetically, these important cultural issues of resource distribution and equity. Drawing us into and propelling us through this capitalist nightmare is a lower-class hero, Curtis (Chris Evans). He is the satiric persona touchstone of the adventure. We follow his travails as he battles his way forward from the tail section of Snowpiercer to its very engine. There Curtis intends to confront and kill the builder, owner, and man in charge of the train, Wilford (Ed Harris). Curtis is appealing as both the brains and the brawn of this rebellion. He is a quiet and even reluctant leader, but unshakable in his resolve to push forward through the train cars. Were *Snowpiercer* a run-of-the-Hollywood-mill sci-fi action film, Curtis would triumph in his quest. Like Jake Sully of *Avatar*, he would bring about a new day of justice and freedom for the oppressed, winning the love of a feisty heroine in the process. Bong gives us, however, nothing like that standard hero story. As a lead character, Curtis is akin to V from *V for Vendetta*: dark, brooding, troubled, and more than willing to meet violence with violence. Here is where the satiric invasion of another genre comes into play as a rhetorical tool in *Snowpiercer*. Bong creates the trappings of the traditional quest-romance narrative, but only as a way to disappoint our expectations of that form and, thereby, make sharper his Menippean polemic. Curtis looks every bit the part of the questing hero, with Gilliam (John Hurt) in the role of Wise Old Man and young Edgar (Jamie Bell) as the loyal sidekick. Opposing the quest is a formidable adversary in Minister Mason (outlandishly acted by Tilda Swinton) and, of course, the ultimate enemy of the piece—and dragon needing to be slayed—Wilford. As Northrop Frye explains the basics of this genre, the central form of romance is dialectical: "everything is focussed on a conflict between the hero and his enemy, and all the reader's values are bound up with the hero." That hero is analogous to a messiah or deliverer, and he is associated "with spring, dawn, order, fertility, vigor, and youth." The enemy, on the other hand, is associated "with winter, darkness, confusion, sterility, moribund life, and old age" (187–188). The antagonism between Curtis and Wilford fits this bill perfectly. For most of the film, Curtis' harrowing journey to the front of the train looks to be a textbook story of young Good versus old Evil. Yet Bong complicates and scuttles this well-worn plotline when Curtis, after many trials and tribulations, at last reaches the engine. At this point in the movie, we discover his anything but heroic past as a murderer and a cannibal during the early days aboard the train.

In an edgy conversation with train security expert Namgoong Minsoo (Kang-ho Song), Curtis recounts the initial chaos and horror of the tail section: "Wilford's soldiers came and they took everything. It was a thousand people in an iron box ... no food, no water." Curtis then confesses gloomily: "After a month, we ate the weak. You know what I hate about myself? I know what people taste like. I know that babies taste best." In fact, Curtis had killed Edgar's mother and was about to devour baby Edgar when Gilliam stepped in, implausibly cutting off his own arm and offering it as food to the ravenous gang in exchange for letting the baby live. That act sparked an acute (and barely believable) sense of solidarity among the tail-sectioners. People began voluntarily to cut off limbs to offer as food. Says Curtis: "It was like a miracle. I wanted to ... I tried. A month later, Wilford's soldiers brought those protein blocks. We've been eating that shit ever since." These revelations explain much in the way of Curtis' reluctance to be the leader of the rebellion. We learn as well that his motivation for this ostensible quest is personal, not communal. Like V, Curtis is set on revenge-killing, on vendetta. He admits, "Eighteen years I hated Wilford. Eighteen years I've waited for this moment. And now I'm here. Open the gate. Please." Curtis, then, is disappointingly *not* our messianic quest-hero, as we had been led to believe. Similar to the faux-ending sequence in *Brazil*, where Sam Lowry for a moment seems to attain the heroism of his dream-self, audience hopes of a gratifying tall tale are raised, then dashed.

Film critic Inkoo Kang comments how Bong's "film only becomes interesting when Curtis suddenly ceases to be the noble, level-headed leader he was initially presented as and reveals his true ruthless self." Rather than finding these dark admissions noteworthy and game-changing, however, Kang worries that "Evans is so wooden ... that those revelations provoke more disgust than compassion, and investing in him as the hero ultimately becomes a chore." In other words, she seems disappointed that the movie is not living up to its quest-romance promise—even when the hero becomes more interesting when breaking with that formula. Kang concludes about the film: "'Snowpiercer' warms the heart, but doesn't penetrate it." Likely that's because this movie, as a Rant, endeavors to warm and to penetrate the brain. Nothing turns out how we anticipate the resolution of Curtis' quest. Curtis does not kill Wilford, nor does he take control of the train to initiate a new dawn of equality for all passengers. Gilliam turns out to be not the Wise Old Man of quest, but the Company Man of capitalism, working in league with Wilford to manufacture necessary, periodic "rebellions" in order to thin the population of the tail section. Most significantly, at the end of the film we discover that Namgoong and his teenage daughter, Yona (Ko Asung), have been pursuing a different plan all along: escape from the train. When Namgoong detonates an explosion to an outer door, however, an avalanche is triggered that derails and destroys the train, killing everyone aboard. The only survivors are Yona and a young boy, Timmy (Marcanthonee Reis), who offboard into a barren, snowy, alpine landscape to spot immediately a Polar Bear. That's a sobering and problematic moment for viewers. On the bright side, some life has survived the human-made deepfreeze. On the not-so-bright side, it seems rather dubious now that humans will. But, alas, Menippean cautionary tales are not designed to uplift.

Moving on to the elements of sci-fi in *Snowpiercer*, the *novum* of a frozen world and a supertrain carrying the last humans hurtling through it is exceedingly new and strange. It doesn't take long, however, for our cognitive estrangement to turn into a gruesome cognition effect: we're simply seeing our current social order stripped down to its basic inequalities and barbarities. After an opening montage of the 2014 climate disaster in the making, we're fast-forwarded 17 years to what looks to be a grubby cattle car on a moving train. Armed soldiers barge in to conduct a routine head count, not of livestock but of the overcrowded, intimidated, grimy people inside. From these interactions, we quickly gain a sense of the *haves* versus *have-nots* social order of this odd train-world, and that there is rebellion afoot. When an officious, well-dressed woman enters the car to tape-measure the height and arm reach of two small children and, for unexplained reasons, take them from their parents, a scuffle breaks out. During the skirmish, Andrew (Ewen Bremner), father to one of the children, throws his shoe in futile resistance to the abduction, striking the woman in the head. His crime brings swift and violent repercussions. In what seems an often-practiced punishment, Andrew's arm is thrust outside the train, into the subzero temperatures, to be frozen off. During his ordeal, which his car-mates are forced to witness, Minister Mason makes her first appearance. As Wilford's administrator of order on Snowpiercer, she delivers an admonishing speech to the hoi polloi. At this early point in the movie, we are left with no doubt that the dystopia we see onscreen will be a rhetorical tool to foreground Marxist issues. Scolds Mason while brandishing the offending footwear:

> Passengers! This is not a shoe. This is disorder. This is size-10 chaos. This—you see this? This is death. In this locomotive we call home, there is one thing that's between our warm hearts and the bitter cold. Clothing? Jeans? No: *order*. Order is the barrier that holds back the cold and death. We must all of us, on this train of life, remain in our allotted stations. We must each of us occupy our preordained particulate positions. ... In the beginning, order was prescribed by your ticket. First bus, economy, and freeloaders like you. Eternal order is prescribed by the Sacred Engine. All things flow from the Sacred Engine. All things in their place. All passengers

in their sections. ... When the foot seeks the place of the head, a sacred line is crossed. Know your place! Keep your place! Be a shoe!

While the plight of the tail-sectioners is performed with grim realism, Bong renders the elite passengers riding at the front of the train ridiculous caricatures of the well-to-do. In an over-the-top upper-class landscape similar to *Brazil*, they thoughtlessly enjoy all manner of luxury—fresh food, private space, classical music, bars, discos, hair salons, saunas, swimming pools, aquariums, and so on. Mason in particular is played by Tilda Swinton with Monty Python-like excess. The blatant comic sarcasm aimed at the wealthy of course accentuates the sense of socialist outrage generated by the film. Curtis is thoroughly disgusted as he makes his way forward, like a working-class Grim Reaper, through the galling opulence of the front sections of the train. Along with signposting the extremes of the capitalistic class system, this stark contrast by Bong also brings into play monstrous aspects of the Rant.

Several facets of monstrosity can be seen at work in *Snowpiercer*. An obvious one is how the lower-class passengers have been scapegoated as monstrous social Others, revealing the bigotry and raw workings of modern power. During the comic-horrific scene in the school car, a cute, blond schoolgirl blurts out, "I heard all tail-sectioners were lazy dogs and they all drink their own shit." This is while several tail-sectioners stand nearby as "guests" in the classroom. The nasty little know-it-all likely heard such a thing from her front-section parents as part of the privileged culture in which she grows up. These schoolchildren are being acculturated into such vicious and self-serving upper-class beliefs. Equally plain is how Curtis looms a Frankenstein Monster in the film. As a Rebel Workingman, Curtis has been created by Wilford. Like Victor's Creature vexing his maker, Curtis is enraged by Wilford's brutal neglect and set on revenge. *Snowpiercer* just makes evident the bourgeois-versus-proletariat undertones of *Frankenstein*. Unmistakably, by way of the extended metaphor of the train as the world, Curtis is upsetting the applecart of capitalistic pyramidal hierarchy. He's crossed the border marking the back of the train from the front of the train, wreaking havoc on "normal" social order. Likewise readily available when reading the movie is flipping the human/monster binary. If Curtis appears as the monster to the passengers at the front of Snowpiercer, Mason certainly is the monster to the passengers trapped at its back. Not only is Mason ludicrously eccentric in her implementation of power, she's bloodthirsty as well. Before the gruesome ax-fighting scene in the tunnel, Mason delivers a second reprimand to the mutinying tail-sectioners, calling them ungrateful hooligans and scum. She concludes her scold with a chilling bit of information: "Precisely 74% of you shall die." Her official mission is to decrease the numbers of the underclass herd. Confident in her superior forces, Mason icily tells Curtis, "My friend, you suffer from the misplaced optimism of the doomed." She then prepares to witness the carnage, saying to herself, "This is going to be good." During the melee, we catch glimpses of Mason enjoying the bloodshed with ghoulish delight. More than just reversing the human/monster binary, however, Bong's film by its end erases that dyad. The momentous clash of Hero versus Enemy that we anticipate as the finale of *Snowpiercer* plays out quite differently. Unlike all action movies, and in particular all superhero movies, audiences are not treated to an extended, cathartic fight scene between Good and Evil. Instead, we're presented with an extended dinner conversation about social organization—a conversation that becomes a seduction into capitalism.

Held at gunpoint, Curtis unwillingly sits down to a steak dinner prepared by Wilford. At first Curtis is determined to resist, verbally sparring with his host.

Wilford: Do you think my station is without its own drawbacks? It's noisy. And it's lonely.
Curtis: Right. Steaks. Plenty of room. This whore to bring you anything you want.
Wilford: Curtis, everyone has their preordained position. And everyone is in their place, except you.
Curtis: That's what people in the best place say to people in the worst place. There's not a soul on this train that wouldn't trade places with you.
Wilford: Would you trade places with me?
Curtis: Fuck you.

Patiently, however, Wilford explains the facts of their situation to Curtis, which seem incontrovertible. They are all prisoners inside this train. The train is a closed ecosystem that must always be kept in balance: air, water, food supply. Most of all, the population must always be kept stable. Such population control, explains Wilford, is the trickiest problem of all:

> For optimum balance, however, there have been times when more radical solutions were required. When the population needed to be reduced—rather drastically. We don't have time for true natural selection. We would all be hideously overcrowded and starved waiting for that. The next best solution is to have individual units kill off other individual units. From time to time, we've had to stir the pot, so to speak. The Revolt of the Seven. The McGregor Riots. The Great Curtis Revolution. A blockbuster production with a devilishly unpredictable plot.

Wilford then reveals to Curtis a devastating piece of news: that Gilliam and Wilford worked together, staging these "revolutions" when needed. Says Wilford, "Oh, don't tell me you didn't know. Gilliam and I—our plan. ... The front and the tail are supposed to work together. He was more than a partner, really. He was my friend." Although incredulous, Curtis comes to see that everything he's done has been part of Wilford's plan to reduce the population of the tail-section by 74%. Wilford sums up:

> And as Gilliam well understood, we need to maintain the proper balance of anxiety and fear, chaos and horror in order to keep life going. If we don't

have that, we need to invent it. In that sense, the Great Curtis Revolution you invented was truly a masterpiece.

In reaction to these social engineering eye-openers, Curtis is crestfallen and shocked to inaction. At this point, Wilford makes his rhetorical move.

Leading his guest to the nose of Snowpiercer and gently walking the tail-sectioner into the spinning core of the engine, Wilford entices: "Cozy, yes? Peaceful. You are now in her heart. I've devoted my entire life to this. The Eternal Engine. It is eternity itself." In a movie filled with clamor and violence, the stillness of this moment is profound. Wilford leaves Curtis to enjoy it: "Have you ever been alone on this train? When was the last time you were alone? You can't remember, can you? So please do. Take your time." As Curtis stands alone inside the slowly rotating engine, the symbolism seems sexual: man-penis snugly inside a twirling engine-vagina. Overwhelmed by it all, Curtis falls to his knees. Wilford pops back up to pitch his offer:

> I am old. I want you to take my Station. It's what you always wanted. It's what Gilliam wanted too. You must tend the Engine. Keep her humming. Look, Curtis. Beyond the gate. Section after section precisely where they've always been and where they'll always be. All adding up to what? The train. And now the perfectly correct number of human beings. All in their proper places, all adding up to what? Humanity. The train is the world. We the humanity. And now you have the sacred responsibility to lead all of humanity. Without you, Curtis, humanity will cease to exist. You've seen what people do without leadership. They devour one another.

That last remark by Wilford is literal: Curtis *has* seen leaderless people devour one another. More than seen it, Curtis has *done* it. Wilford and Gilliam seem to have been grooming Curtis for the job of engineer from the moment he onboarded Snowpiercer as a 17-year-old. Far from being a rebel, then, Curtis has been an unknowing cog in Wilford's social mechanism all along. He will replace Wilford as the authoritarian saving the violent, ridiculous, and pathetic passengers—that is, humanity—from themselves: "This is what Gilliam saved you for. Curtis. This is your destiny." When Yona rushes into the engine room, our erstwhile hero looks down on her harshly, almost imperiously. Curtis appears to have given into Wilford's temptation, seduced by the Eternal Engine. Fortunately, Yona pries up a floorboard to reveal Timmy, one of the abducted tail-section children, rhythmically at work below amid the grinding mechanisms of the locomotive. The sight jolts Curtis back to his workingman self. Enraged that Wilford uses lower-class children for replacement parts, Curtis pummels Wilford then sacrifices his own arm reaching through the turning gears to rescue Timmy. Just before Namgoong's explosive device wrecks the train, there is a symbolic embrace where Namgoong and Curtis shield between them Yona and Timmy. Even Wilford is touched by this tender family huddle, remarking to himself the instant before detonation, "Nice."

The Marxist lesson of this dénouement is clear: the seductive Engine of Capitalism itself is the monster in *Snowpiercer*. Wilford is no evil genius or willful destroyer of the Good. He's a deluded industrial capitalist obsessed with trains. As we learn from the video shown to the schoolchildren, Wilford built "a luxury locomotive cruise-line connecting railways of the entire world into one" and set his self-sustaining "miracle train" on it to run a yearly circuit. The project was more or less a folly, not a hedge against the CW-7 going wrong and certainly never a plan to enslave humanity. Wilford, then, is merely a devotee of the status quo doing the only thing he knows how to do: maintain the status quo. For him, it is either capitalism or chaos. Moreover, Wilford clearly believes that capitalism is not just the only form of social organization available to humanity, but that it is the socioeconomic crown of creation. Wilford sees capitalism as an endpoint, the end-of-history social structure that will perpetuate itself endlessly. Obviously, he is mistaken. The locomotive clearly is breaking down. Wilford himself admits, "She's getting sensitive recently." Parts are wearing out, making it necessary to turn children into mechanical things. These are hardly the traits of "the Eternal Engine." Hence all the talk by Wilford and Mason about everyone having "their own preordained position" on the train is nonsense. Passengers are positioned by organizational choice, not by fate. It is at the directive of the wealthy and powerful on the train that the capitalistic class system is replicated.[3] The entire movie, in fact, is a story of their fanatical efforts—by repression, by deception, by violence—to keep the Capitalism Express on the track. Wilford's capitalism/chaos binary is a lie. *Snowpiercer* demonstrates how, as an apparatus of power, capitalism not only fails to keep the violence of chaos at bay, as Wilford would have Curtis believe, but capitalism is itself the *source* of chaotic violence. Without class violence, capitalism as a system cannot operate. Thus, the film brims with fierce lower-caste suppression of all kinds. Wilford's train is not an efficiently functioning society rumbling ideally down the rails; it is a chattering, speeding, multicar charnel house.

As viewers, we are meant to share Curtis' stark and deepened awakening into the contrivance of social organization. Bong's far-fetched morality tale is designed to jolt us out of any facile, partial, and self-serving understanding of our own economic system. The manner of capitalism enacted on Snowpiercer is *not* the only kind of "train" that humanity could be riding. What is more, Bong's bizarre supertrain is an objective correlative for the global socio-economic status quo in 2013. The neoliberal elite, partnered with neoconservative force, have humanity careening down a track of global destruction and self-annihilation. The especially bleak forewarning of this speculative satire is that even if we can blast our way off of this insane choo-choo train, environmentally it might already be too late.[4]

I have considered closely the satire/sci-fi/monster mainstay elements of *Snowpiercer* to arrive at a reading of the movie as a Rant. Taking a look at its ancillary aspects, as spelled out in The Rant Playbook, repay examination as well. With regard to the theories of Foucault, they're applicable everywhere in Bong's film. As we've just seen, the movie is one long demonstration of the hegemonic devices of modern discipline, punishment, and subject formation carried out by a powerful minority to control the actions of a disempowered majority. The arm-freezing of Andrew and the prison-car confinement of Namgoong and Yona demonstrate the carceral workings of the train. The many gun-toting soldiers and blade-swinging thugs (a kind of train-lumpenproletariat) violently keeping order leaves no doubt that Snowpiercer is an extreme police state as well. Power creates Truth on the train, and obviously Wilford's hegemony is always under challenge. Hard at work, then, is Althusser's notion of a modern Repressive State Apparatus where force or its threat uphold the status quo. Equally operational on the train is Althusser's concept of an Ideological State Apparatus (ISA), that is, nonphysically violent ways to maintain control over a population by way of inveigling people into an imaginary relationship with their real conditions. Modern ideology specializes in telling us that we are free subjects, when in fact the system to which we accede is run by elites who do not have our best interests in mind (see Althusser 162–183). Among the most notorious modern ISAs is schooling, a circumstance taken full satiric advantage of by Bong. His school car scene is maybe the most screwball and disconcerting in the movie—which is saying a lot. The sequence evokes the yellow laughter of Juvenalian excess by combining a 1950s warm-and-fuzzy innocence with a 2010s bitter experience, all performed on a knife-edge of tension and with the hyperbole of farce. The upper-class schoolchildren are well-scrubbed and obediently enthusiastic as the sugar-sweet, young, pretty, and pregnant Teacher (Alison Pill) shoves ludicrous propaganda down their little throats. The appalled tail-sectioners witness these lessons in disbelief. Following the curiously dated informational video about Wilford, the Teacher poses a leading question to the class about CW-7 freezing the world: "So what did the prophetic Mr. Wilford invent to protect the chosen from that calamity?" The children shout back in well-drilled unison: "The Engine!" Teacher, pupils, and Minister Mason all then chant, with accompanying gestures, in praise of the miracle machine: "Rumble rumble, rattle rattle, it will never die!" The Teacher next leads the class (Mason again joining in) in a song of praise for Wilford's wonderful Engine.

Teacher: What happens if the Engine stops?
Children: We all freeze and die.
Teacher: But will it stop, oh, will it stop?
Children: No! No!
Teacher: Can you tell us why?
All in chorus: The Engine is eternal. Yes! The Engine is forever. Yes! Rumble rumble, rattle rattle!
Teacher: Who is the reason why?
All in chorus: Wilford! Yah! Wilford! Wilford! Hip hurray!

After this anthem, Mason turns simpering to Curtis to remark, "I love that one. Such a tonic." Concerted interpellation is taking place among the forward passengers. Bong ends his lampoon of modern education with a reminder of the ferocity underlying such brainwashing. The man wheeling through a cart of "New Year Eggs from Mr. Wilford" delivers a concealed gun to the Teacher. She opens fire on the tail-sectioners, killing Andrew and being killed herself by a knife hurled into her throat. Needless to say, such stark violence jars harshly with the wholesome, child-friendly setting of the schoolroom. As Foucault theorizes, however, modern subjectivity must be imposed at any cost. Submission to Wilford's domination, exploitation, and authority comes about through a variety of techniques of power.

Along with separating Truth from Power and thereby exposing the oppression of a dominant modern discourse, *Snowpiercer* depicts as well, in spades, the Regime at work. Notable dynamics of neoliberal economics in the film are extreme wealth inequity (forward cars/tail cars), acute accumulation by dispossession (tail-sectioners have nothing so that the forward-sectioners can have everything), unchecked corporate power (Wilford Industries as a corporate state under the authority of a single CEO), and unremitting workplace abuse (the sadistic finishing touch being child labor). Neoconservative polity is no less in evidence. The preemptive aggression of well-funded militarism secures the primacy of Wilford and the capitalism he imposes on the train-world. Wilford has become the focus of religiosity as well. In *Brave New World*, the citizens of the World State practice Fordism as their form of worship. Similarly, in *Snowpiercer*, Wilfordism looks to be the official religion of the train. Mason in particular incessantly insists on Wilford-as-God, always characterizing him as "divine" and "merciful" while calling his locomotive the "Sacred Engine." However, the "Eternal order" of every passenger's "preordained position" on Snowpiercer that Mason insists upon is a twisting of Christian dogma into neoliberal tenet. As in *Brave New World*, Wilford's deification is strictly a capitalistic phenomenon with merely Christian trappings. The ruling elite in both Rants care nothing for the spiritual comfort of people but everything for keeping citizens in their correct economic place. The modern power technique Foucault theorizes as "pastoral power" describes exactly this strategy. As an earthly (as opposed to heavenly) shepherd of subjects (as opposed to souls), the modern state seeks to know—and thereby shape—the inside of people's minds. Whereas the traditional pastorate fashions hearts and minds for salvation, the pastoral state molds the attitudes and thinking of individuals into a functional sameness that suits the social system ("Subject" 131–133). Mason's title as "Minister" seems an apt conflation of these church and state purposes: she spouts quasi-religious Wilfordian creed as one of many techniques to maintain civic order aboard Wilford's train.

Signs of post-Marxist theory abound in *Snowpiercer* as well. The current neoliberal hegemonic adversary is unambiguously defined in Wilford as plutocrat managing his despotic Train of Fools. The train *is* the Regime. What has brought humanity to ruin is our current neoliberal/neoconservative hegemony. In contrast, the tail-sectioners, who are treated with far more pathos than bathos by Bong, signify a better kind of society for which to fight, one looking to redistribute resources to all identity positions on the train. Snowpiercer itself, then, can be read as a stunning incarnation of Laclau and Mouffe's concept of a hegemonic articulation, that is, an attempt to fix social discursivity at a nodal point. In this case, the nodal point takes the incredible form of an end-of-history capitalist supertrain perpetually looping a closed track. Wilford's entire enterprise, in fact, betrays a post-Marxist crisis of democratic liberalism where the bourgeois have severed capitalism from democracy, keeping the benefits of liberal capitalistic democracy to themselves while denying equity and justice to the rest of society. By the same token, although Wilford imposes hegemonic subjectivity on the passengers of his train, Bong does not indulge in portraying Curtis as an old-school Marxist Worker Hero destined to save the train-world from the naked evils of capitalism. The agonistic pluralism at work in his film is far more nuanced. As Harvey points out, "There is no proletarian field of utopian Marxian fantasy to which we can retire" (202). At the end of the movie, Curtis dissolves as a workingman hero fighting the boss to become akin to a tragic hero discovering knowledge too late. Terribly, as noted above, Curtis discovers that his underclass rebellion is *part* of the social order he's struggling to tear down. Truly radical and plural democracy in *Snowpiercer* occurs in Namgoong's extremist plan to offboard the train. The freeplay of political power depicted in this film thus includes a total social reboot: rather than continue to live within the lunacy of the modern state, Namgoong is willing to risk the ultimate back-to-nature scheme. Interestingly, Bong is sanguine about the chances of the two young "train babies" surviving outside of Snowpiercer. In an interview, he says:

> These kids have never known what it was like to step on the earth. So it's almost like Neil Armstrong touching down on the Moon when they leave the train for the first time. They have no memory of what it's like to be on the Earth. For them to procreate, it's going to take a little time. So, for me, it's a very hopeful ending ... those two kids will spread the human race.
> (Abrams)

If that's the case (quite a big *if*), this non-white, non-European, new Eve and Adam pairing won't be socially reproducing the neoliberal state anytime soon.

Finally for this analysis of *Snowpiercer* as a Rant, does it display Harvey's lessons for fighting back against the neoliberal monocracy? Unequivocally, yes. The movie ticks all items on that list. Is class struggle labeled as class struggle? Check. Is neoliberalism exposed as utopian nonsense? Check. Is possessive individualism exposed as greed and selfishness? Check. Are alternative individual rights, such as socioeconomic justice, solidarity, and environmentalism, promoted? Check. Is the moral high ground reclaimed? Check. Is the right wing attacked for its authoritarianism and *lack* of democracy? Double check. Bong's film does not mask its politicality for the sake of bigger box office returns. Like *V for Vendetta* and *District 9*, *Snowpiercer* pushes boundaries of imagination in order to show audiences the chicanery of plutocracy engineering the conditions of social crisis so that it can pretend to be justified in pitilessly containing social unrest.

The MaddAddam Trilogy (2003–2013)

Margaret Atwood has written much and been much written about. My scope here is limited: to discuss as Rants her three recent works of speculative fiction, namely, *Oryx and Crake* (2003), *The Year of the Flood* (2009), and *MaddAddam* (2013). Each novel was a national bestseller in the U.S. and sold well internationally. Collectively known now as *The MaddAddam Trilogy*, their story is currently in development as a TV mini-series (Otterson). Although by no means strictly a writer of speculative fiction, Atwood is well established and respected in the field of science fiction.[5] These three novels deal with a range of threats to 21st-century humanity: corporate reach into every aspect of our lives, the widening wealth gap, swelling global population, environmental degradation, and technology rushing ahead of our ability to use it wisely. Notes Atwood, "I don't write about Planet X, I write about where we are now." Among her biggest concerns in the trilogy is biotechnology run amok. "We've just opened the biggest toy box in the world," remarks Atwood, "which is the genetic code" (Lee). Critic J. Brooks Bouson characterizes these works as "admonitory satires" and finds that Atwood engages in "environmental consciousness-raising" by way of her darkly satiric tale of human annihilation (341). Similarly, Coral Ann Howells calls Atwood's dystopian vision a "ferocious satire on late modern American capitalist society" (164). As, in effect, a Rant a decade-long in the making, Atwood's trilogy more than satisfies the many qualities of the form I've delineated. Rather than run through the entire Playbook, however, of particular interest in my analysis of Atwood's Menippean vision will be the destructive neoliberal and neoconservative doctrines at work in the novels, the ecological movement of radical and plural democracy opposing that hegemonic discourse, and the characters of Snowman and Crake as monsters.

Neolib–Neocon on the Rampage

Atwood begins her trilogy with an epigraph from Swift's *Gulliver's Travels*:

> I could perhaps like others have astonished you with strange improbable tales; but I rather chose to relate plain matter of fact in the simplest manner and style; because my principal design was to inform you, and not to amuse you.

Readers familiar with Lemuel Gulliver for the unreliable narrator that he is will be on the alert, as a result of this epigraph, for Atwood's fictional world to plunge them into the perplexing maze of satire. Although we *will* be astonished with strange improbable tales, plain matter of fact will also be related to us; although we *will* be amused as we read, we will likewise be informed. The plots of *Oryx and Crake* and *The Year of the Flood* cover the same time period and catastrophic events—a plague that basically wipes out humanity—but told from the perspective of different characters. *MaddAddam* then picks up the story to contemplate the aftermath of such a cataclysm as well as the beginning, perhaps, of an entirely new kind of humanity. The Menippean forewarning of the trilogy is unmistakable: human greed and foolhardiness, epitomized by corporations combining neoliberal economics with revenue-making scientific innovations, doom us all by creating a slow-moving environmental disaster we attempt to deny, ignore, and even profit from. The sci-fi *novum* of unsettling familiarity emerging out of initial strangeness comes by way of the many flashbacks Atwood tells. She places readers in a disorienting, postapocalypse present but continually recounts past events leading to the planetary ruin. In this way, the strange newness of the devastated world makes more and more painful sense as we read. We realize how the many seeds of our collapse exist here and now. Among the satiric distortions and exaggerations confronting us are weird animal splice-ups, such as "pigoons," "rakunks," and "wolvogs," as well as an entirely new kind of human, The Crakers, all stemming out of ill-advised experiments with genetic engineering—a technology proceeding apace and sometimes haphazardly today. Atwood's overall approach to satire is novelistic in that she works primarily through careful and detailed character development. While obviously a larger-scale disaster is taking place, our focus is on real people undergoing specific hardships. The science fiction happens in the background, more or less. Prominent in the trilogy are class issues of *haves* and *have-nots*, racial and postcolonial matters (particularly in *Oryx and Crake*) with regard to the developed world exploiting the underdeveloped world, as well as many concerns of feminist fabulation. Atwood puts before us the social evils of patriarchal violence toward women, prostitution, and child pornography while also suggesting that a new female-empowered social order is surfacing (especially in *MaddAddam*). Monstrosity is likewise on hand in Atwood's "alien free" form of sci-fi. The corporations loom as globe-devouring beasts. The genetic creatures they create are also dangerous and unnerving hybrids. A criminal justice system turned corporate—and, so, entertainment-based—produces male brutes known as "Painballers" who prowl the derelict landscape. With the *MaddAddam Trilogy*, then, Atwood makes use of all the elements of speculative satire as she diligently and pointedly severs modern Truth from the raw Power propping it up.

More specifically, Atwood's cautionary tale is centered around a blistering post-Marxist critique of the neoliberal state. The hegemonic adversary clearly identified and constantly ridiculed in the trilogy are the powerful corporations that have thrown off all public controls and come, in effect, to govern the world. The socioeconomic conditions during the decades leading up to the horrendous plague are easily recognizable as those developing out of our current social reality. In North America, society has split in two: an educated and affluent elite who reside safely in corporate suburban "Compounds" and everyone else who lives willy-nilly in urban "pleeblands." We first start to learn about this bifurcated civic order through the character of Snowman, whose preapocalypse name was Jimmy and who grew up as the world transitioned out of our own.

> Jimmy had never been to the city. He'd only seen it on TV—endless billboards and neon signs and stretches of buildings, tall and short; endless dingy-looking streets, countless vehicles of all kinds, some of them with clouds of smoke coming out the back; thousands of people, hurrying, cheering, rioting.
>
> (Oryx and Crake 27)

People from the Compounds go into these cities rarely and never without protection. The pleeblands are seen as lawless places. We discover as well that these changes are relatively recent, perhaps just a generation removed from us: "Outside the OrganInc walls and gates and searchlights, things were unpredictable. Inside, they were the way it used to be when Jimmy's father was a kid, before things got so serious, or that's what Jimmy's father said." That is, "You could walk around without fear … Go for a bike ride, sit at a sidewalk café, buy an ice-cream cone." Jimmy himself, in fact, had experienced some of these "old ways" as a small child (27). Atwood, then, situates us in a near-distant future that makes perfect—and awful—sense.

Corporations require employees to live in Compounds not out of concern for their safety but out of anxiety over protecting intellectual property and maintaining a competitive edge. The business climate is an unregulated Hobbesian state of nature where all have right to all.

> When there was so much at stake, there was no telling what the other side might resort to. The other side, or the other sides: it wasn't just one other side you had to watch out for. Other companies, other countries, various factions and plotters. There was too much hardware around, said Jimmy's father. Too much hardware, too much software, too many hostile bioforms, too many weapons of every kind. And too much envy and fanaticism and bad faith.
>
> (Oryx and Crake 27–28)

Compounds, in fact, are latter-day castles designed "for keeping you and your buddies nice and safe inside, and for keeping everybody else outside." When Jimmy asks his father, "So are we the kings and dukes?" his father's laughing answer is, "Oh, absolutely" (28). To apply post-Marxist terms to this situation, Atwood imagines a world fixed at a neoliberal nodal point rife with liberal–conservative discourse. Those few living inside the Compounds are a fusion of modern and feudal hegemonic subjectivity and articulations: a capitalistic–aristocratic elite who enjoy the benefits of market-generated wealth, while at the same time denying those benefits to the rest of the population by way of enforcing a nondemocratic régime. In short, democratic liberalism has given way to possessive individualism. As a result of this neoliberal configuration, the vast majority of people living outside the Compound-castle walls are reduced to scrambling and clawing for the economic scraps. Such blunt wealth inequity and physical segregation of rich from poor is but a slight exaggeration of our present-day world. We are well on our way to this outright hostile arrangement of Compound versus pleeblands. Throughout the trilogy, Atwood also makes blatantly familiar to us the tactics and symptoms of neoliberal accumulation by dispossession.

Sprinkled through the novels are instances of capitalistic exploitation and increasingly futile attempts to resist corporate power. In *Oryx and Crake*, we hear about coffee bean wars raging worldwide. A genetically altered "Happicuppa coffee bush" has been designed that easily "could be grown on huge plantations and harvested with machines." While great for corporate profits, the innovation "threw the small growers out of business and reduced both them and their labourers to starvation-level poverty." In response, a global resistance movement to Happicuppa coffee springs up: "Riots broke out, crops were burned, Happicuppa cafés were looted, Happicuppa personnel were car-bombed or kidnapped or shot by snipers or beaten to death by mobs; and, on the other side, peasants were massacred by the army" (*Oryx and Crake* 179). It seems that, in the near future assembled by Atwood, the neoliberal state has reached a tipping point: either citizens will resist and reform the big corporations, bringing them to heel, or corporations will take over completely. We hear from various characters of the many corporate wrongdoings afoot and both individual and public efforts to fight back. Jimmy's mother, for example, argues that she and Jimmy's father should leave their research positions at NooSkins, a subsidiary of a giant pharmaceutical corporation called HelthWyzer. To her mind, the genetic splicing work they do is "yet another way to rip off a bunch of desperate people." She contends, "Don't you remember the way we used to talk, everything we wanted to do? Making life better for people—not just people with money. You used to be so … you had ideals, then" (56–57). Jimmy's mother decides to abandon the family, steal sensitive corporate information, and escape the HelthWyzer Compound to join a resistance movement. Corporate security services immediately start tracking her down. A similar family rift happens to Jimmy's friend, Glenn—who will become Crake. His parents are also HelthWyzer scientists, and in the course of his work, Glenn's father discovers an awful truth: in order to boost profits, HelthWyzer is in the practice of creating diseases *and* their cures. As Glenn describes the scheme to Jimmy:

> The best diseases, from a business point of view, … would be those that cause lingering illnesses. Ideally—that is, for maximum profit—the patient should either get well or die just before all of his or her money runs out. It's a fine calculation.
>
> (211)

When Glenn's father tries to turn whistleblower, Glenn's mother and a fellow employee, Pete, report him to the company. Corporate security then murders Glenn's father and makes it look like a suicide. Like Jimmy's mother, Glenn's father is someone who "believed in contributing to the improvement of the human lot" (183) through science, but finds that goal being grossly perverted by neoliberal corporatism.

Where *Oryx and Crake* is a novel told from the vantage point of characters living inside the Compounds, *The Year of the Flood* shifts perspectives to characters living in the pleeblands. As is to be expected, in this setting corporate abuse of workers and customers is even more callous. The preplague backstory of Toby, for instance, includes the economic horror story of her middle-class parents going under once a developer targets their house and ten acres to buy for the encroaching urban sprawl heading their way. Her father refuses to sell, which results in corporate interests arranging to have him fired from his job in sales and her mother—who operates a HelthWyzer franchise—to come down with a strange illness. Toby's mother, it turns out, becomes a victim of the HelthWyzer illness/cure plot uncovered by Glenn's father. In an ostensive act of largess, HelthWyzer arranges special care for Toby's mother with company doctors. However,

> They charged for it ... and even with the discount for members of the HelthWyzer Franchise Family it was a lot of money; and because the condition had no name, her parents' modest health insurance plan refused to cover the costs. Nobody could get public wellness coverage unless they had no money of their own whatsoever.
>
> (Year of the Flood 25–26)

This kind of health insurance nightmare is all too prevalent today. Predictably, Toby's father takes out a second mortgage, pours all of his time and money into his wife's care, eventually is forced to sell their house to the developer (for a much reduced price), and then gets fired for absenteeism from his new job—all to no avail. Toby's mother dies, after which her father commits suicide. Debt peonage, job insecurity, lack of adequate public health care or safety net, defenselessness against deep corporate pockets—these are all benchmarks of the neoliberal state.

Through Amanda, we hear of another grim example of middle-class family disaster, this one sparked by "the droughts in Texas." We're told how her parents lost their Happicuppa coffee franchise, could find no other jobs, could not sell their house because no one would buy it, and "ended up in a refugee camp with old trailers and a lot of Tex-Mexicans." At that point, more climate devastation struck:

> Then their trailer was demolished in one of the hurricanes and her father was killed by a piece of flying metal. A lot of people drowned, but she and her mother held on to a tree and got rescued by some men in a rowboat. They were thieves, said Amanda, looking for stuff they could lift, but they said they'd take Amanda and her mother to dry land and a shelter if they'd do a trade.
>
> (Year of the Flood 84)

The "trade," of course, was for sex. The shelter they wound up in was "a football stadium with tents in it" where survival also required trades for sex. There was no medical care available, and Amanda's mother died from bad drinking water. "'A lot of people shat to death,' said Amanda. 'You should have smelled that place'" (84). Amanda decided to walk north "along with thousands of other people." She faced not only personal dangers on the way but corporate obstacles as well, the most daunting being the Wall. Explains Amanda: "The Wall they're building to keep the Tex refugees out, because just the fence wasn't enough. There's men with sprayguns—it's a CorpSeCorps wall" (85). "CorpSeCorps" is the brand name of Corporation Security Corps, a security firm that begins as a contractor providing safety measures for various corporate Compounds but grows, in time, into the private armed services of the corporations. Climate disasters, economic downturns, unemployment, housing crisis, inadequate disaster relief, lawlessness, refugee crisis, company thugs, extreme forms of immigration control—Atwood hits every note of our current downward spiral at the hands of the Regime.

In the third novel of the trilogy, *MaddAddam*, we come to understand the bigger picture of how the corporate takeover occurred. For one thing, faux ecologically friendly scams such as "Bearlift" placated a gullible public into thinking sound countermeasures were being taken in the face of climate change. Zeb, an anti-corporation insurgent, explains the con to Toby:

> It lived off the good intentions of city types with disposable emotions who liked to think they were saving something—some rag from their primordial authentic ancestral past, a tiny shred of their collective soul dressed up in a cute bear suit.
>
> (MaddAddam 59)

Basically, restaurant leftovers were airlifted and dropped to starving polar bears. Zeb knows that such nonsense projects served a corporate function; they "sounded a note of hope, distracted folks from the real action, which was bulldozing the planet flat and grabbing anything of value." Zeb concludes of such corporate public-relations tricks: "That was back when they were still massaging their trust-me images. ... Once they got a hammerlock on power, they didn't have to bother so much" (69). That hammerlock came in stages. First, companies made money hand over fist. Big Pharma in particular was instrumental in swelling corporate coffers, not only by inventing and planting in the population curable diseases but also through endless vanity products. Second, with their vast wealth, corporations began to influence institutions of public trust, such as a free press or departments of government oversight. Trying to expose corporate crimes became futile—and, as in the case of Glenn's father, fatal. Notes Adam, Zeb's half-brother and the leader of the radical resistance movement called God's Gardeners,

> if we were to try going public with this information we wouldn't be believed. We'd only sound paranoid, and after that we would have unfortunate accidents. The press is Corps-controlled ... and any independent regulation is independent in name only.
>
> (255)

Finally, corporations positioned themselves for a hostile takeover of the state. Through the neoliberal tactic of shrinking public services by starving government tax revenues, companies were able to extend their reach into public policy and law-making itself. In particular, CorpSeCorps moved in "when the local police forces collapsed for lack of funding" (25). Says Zeb: "With the CorpSeCorps takeover of so-called law-and-order functions, the Corps had the power to bulldoze and squash and erase anything they liked" (329). At that point, corporate preeminence became absolute.

> Old-style demonstration politics were dead. … any kind of public action involving crowds and sign-waving and then storefront smashing would be shot off at the knees.
>
> (242)

In the end, Atwood shows us a world where corporations have become, if not the outright government, the shadow government wielding the real power. Under the thumb of such neoliberal dominance, the individual rights of citizens cease to exit.

Alongside neoliberalism, working in tandem, the destructive practices of neo-conservatism are portrayed in *The MaddAddam Trilogy* as well. CorpSeCorps is the militaristic instrument of primacy enforcing neoliberal free economic reign by the corporations. The security company is the muscle behind neoliberal Truth, gradually subsuming the state functions of police, army, intelligence services, border patrol, and everything else. CorpSeCorps ends up, in fact, being the only organization allowed to have weapons, and thus capable of totalitarian rule. Even while exercising this military superiority, however, the pretense remains one of neoliberal business-as-usual—that is, the Free Market is selecting winners and losers in a fair and open economy. Thus the security firm stays, for the time being, a somewhat shadowy entity flexing its muscle behind the scenes and mainly in the pleeblands. Zeb explains to Toby the reasoning behind this corporate charade regarding CorpSeCorps: "Corporations still wanted to be perceived as honest and trustworthy, friendly as daisies, guileless as bunnies. They couldn't afford to be viewed by the average consumer as lying, heartless, tyrannical butchers" (*Year of the Flood* 266). Nonetheless, the public state has become a private state, run not by democratic rule of law but by an oligarchy fueled by disproportionate market wealth and political influence as well as the advanced technology that big money can buy. In this way, the satiric exaggeration and sci-fi *novum* imagined for us by Atwood is more forecast than invention. She grounds her fiction in our current social reality then prognosticates by how much more, several decades hence, the Regime will be dictating our lives.

Along with this grim warning against zealous militarism, Atwood offers as well some wry satire on neoconservative religiosity. In *MaddAddam*, we're introduced to "The Church of PetrOleum," which we're told is "affiliated with the somewhat more mainstream Petrobaptists" (111). In this send-up of Prosperity Theology, Atwood participates in a centuries-old tradition of anti-cleric and anti-religious hypocrisy satire. The target of her mockery is "The Rev," who is the father of Adam and Zeb and a shyster preacher with a Texas megachurch. Of The Rev's creation of a cult following we are told:

> That was the way to go in those days if you wanted to coin the megabucks and you had a facility for ranting and bullying, plus golden-tongued whip-'em-up preaching, and you lacked some other grey-area but highly marketable skill, such as derivatives trading.
>
> (111)

The equivalence of sham pastor with derivatives stockbroker is an instructive detail by Atwood, linking together, as it does, the religious fanaticism of neo-conservatism with the profit zeal of neoliberalism. The Rev cooks up a preposterous theology "to help him rake in the cash" based on Matthew 16:18, "Thou art Peter, and upon this rock I will build my church" (112). As Zeb tells Toby:

> It didn't take a rocket-science genius, the Rev would say, to figure out that *Peter* is the Latin word for rock, and therefore the real, true meaning of "Peter" refers to petroleum, or oil that comes from rock. "So this verse, dear friends, is not only about Saint Peter: it is a prophesy, a vision of the Age of Oil, and the proof, dear friends, is right before your eyes, because look! What is more valued by us today than oil?"
>
> (112)

Such specious interpretation has a profound effect on his willing-to-believe, self-seeking flock. What better way to counteract the science of fossil fuels driving cataclysmic climate change than with blind faith in a book written centuries before such technology was even imaginable? The Rev further embroiders his Prosperity-cum-Oil Gospel with mumbo-jumbo about how *oleum* is the Latin word for oil and how "oil is holy throughout the Bible!" Kings, prophets, and priests are anointed with oil as a sign of special election by God, points out The Rev. "What more proof do we need of the holiness of our very own oil, put in the earth by God for the special use of the faithful to multiply His works?" It is our sacred duty, therefore, to retrieve the Holy Oleum from the ground: "Lift up your voices in song, and let the Oleum gush forth in ever stronger and all-blessed streams!" (112). When the bottom line can be united with sanctimony, no matter how absurd, America wins.

Radical and Plural Ecology

Opposing the neoliberal/neoconservative ascendancy in *The MaddAddam Trilogy* is an underground movement calling itself God's Gardeners. This "green religion" teaches "the convergence of Nature and Scripture, the love of all creatures, the dangers of technology, the wickedness of the Corps, the avoidance of violence, and the tending of vegetables and bees on pleeblands slum rooftops" (*MaddAddam* xv). In satiric terms, this movement represents the positive behaviors being recommended and praised in Atwood's polemic. While Atwood mounts a passionate argument against the Regime, equally, she sets out an avid case in favor of the philosophies of God's Gardeners. *The Year of the Flood* is filled with their hymns, homilies, and celebrations of their Saint's Days. These are an interesting mixture of religious beliefs and scientific understandings. For example, during the "Feast of Adam and All Primates," the character Adam, who is the founder of the Gardeners and holds the position of "Adam One," sermonizes:

> we affirm our Primate ancestry—an affirmation that has brought down wrath upon us from those who arrogantly persist in evolutionary denial. But we affirm, also, the Divine agency that has caused us to be created in the way that we were, and this has enraged those scientific fools who say in their hearts, "There is no God."
>
> (Year of the Flood 51)

In their blending of faith and reason, the Gardeners hold that humans are both spirit and matter—"Word" and "dust"—and thus subject to God's creation "through the long and complex process of Natural and Sexual Selection." Our Fall, then, according to Gardeners doctrine, is forgetting our animality. Declares Adam One:

> Our appetites, our desires, our more uncontrollable emotions—all are Primate! Our Fall from the original Garden was a Fall from the innocent acting-out of such patterns and impulses to a conscious and shamed awareness of them; and from thence comes our sadness, our anxiety, our doubt, our rage against God.

The commandment we disobeyed, then, was "to live the Animal life in all simplicity"; instead, we craved and obtained "the knowledge of good and evil" and so "now we are reaping the whirlwind" (52). Adam One concludes:

> In our efforts to rise above ourselves we have indeed fallen far, and are falling farther still; for, like the Creation, the Fall, too, is ongoing. Ours is a fall into greed: why do we think that everything on Earth belongs to us, while in reality we belong to Everything? We have betrayed the trust of the Animals, and defiled our sacred task of stewardship.
>
> (52–53)

Atwood recommends to us not so much a return to nature as a much more informed adherence to the workings of nature—and in particular, to our part within those natural workings. She doesn't seem to want us to be living in caves, but neither does she want a handful of us living in posh suburbs, while the rest struggle to survive on a ruined planet. Somewhere in between might be a good thing.

At the end of *The Year of the Flood*, Adam One speaks to his followers for what might be the last time. A horrible pandemic has swept the earth, all but erasing human life. He reminds the Gardeners, though, that, "It is not this Earth that is to be demolished: it is the Human Species." This plague is one "that infects no Species but our own, and that will leave all other Creatures untouched" (*Year of the Flood* 424). Adam One's message, and Atwood's, is that although we seem to think we own the earth, in fact the earth is quite indifferent to us. If we want to destroy ourselves with what the Gardeners call the "Waterless Flood," that is, some manner of human-made disaster that will put a halt to "all buying and selling" and throw us back into God's Garden of the natural world (126), so be it. Nature will carry on without noticing we are gone. Our stupidity will be the end of us, and in the trilogy that stupidity takes the form of the neolib–neocon status quo. The Regime is the Waterless Flood. When offering a prayer for the souls of all those who have died from the plague, Adam One includes pointedly:

> those who have persecuted us; those who have murdered God's Creatures, and extinguished His Species; those who have tortured in the name of Law; who have worshipped nothing but riches; and who, to gain wealth and worldly power, have inflicted pain and death.
>
> (425)

Atwood is explicit in assigning culpability for the end of civilization; she is likewise direct when offering approbation for those who pursue, instead, a reasoned and humane path.[6] As critics have noted, Atwood takes a stance of deep ecology and radical environmentalism in the trilogy. She is intent on environmental instruction as she warns against the extreme dangers of the convergence of neoliberal capitalism and biotechnology resulting in the algorithmic commodification of life itself.[7] Thus, although painting a dismal picture of our near-future, Atwood provides us with a glimmer of a better way to behave.

In post-Marxist terms, God's Gardeners represent as well the struggle of radical and plural democracy against the possessive individualism of the dominant liberal–conservative discourse. The group signals a better form of society, one that's communitarian, less technophile, environmentally aware, diverse in its membership, and, thus, worth pursuing. It also enacts agonistic pluralism as it fights to establish a new hegemonic order to replace the malicious control of the corporations. In *Oryx and Crake*, we learn that there are various "terrorist" organizations mounting resistance to corporate power. One group in particular, MaddAddam, runs an intriguing website and employs the tactic of releasing gene-spliced, nuisance bioforms into the environment to disrupt corporate profits and sabotage infrastructure—for example, a pesticide-resistant weevil addicted to eating the Happicuppa coffee bean or a tar-eating microbe that turns asphalt highways into sand (216). In *The Year of the Flood*, we discover that Zeb is not only a high-ranking member of God's Gardeners, but the secret originator of this more radical and direct-action opposition group.

MaddAddam turns out to be a collection of "Top scientists—gene-splicers who'd bailed out of the Corps and gone underground because they hated what the Corps were doing." Zeb's goal is to cripple the economic and industrial mechanisms of civilization so that "the planet could repair itself. Before it was too late and everything went extinct." He's not looking to kill people; Zeb "just wanted them to stop wasting everything and fucking up. ... He wanted to make them think" (*Year of the Flood* 333). Inevitably, a primary mission for CorpSeCorps is to crush such resistance movements. Because of its radical methods and provocative strikes, MaddAddam is a particular target of the corporate security forces. Adam One also conducts a willful defiance against the corporations. By spreading the God's Gardeners movement and by procuring infiltrators within the Compounds themselves, Adam One engages in a more cautious form of confrontation. In time, the movement's proenvironment and anti-commercial stance poses a real threat to the neoliberal state. When a crackdown comes against activist groups, CorpSeCorps links God's Gardeners to the bioattacks of MaddAddam and raids all Gardeners enclaves, driving the movement into hiding. Explains Adam One to his followers:

> Why did the Corps strike? Alas, we were becoming too powerful for their liking. Many rooftops were blossoming as the rose; many hearts and minds were bent towards an Earth restored to balance. But in success lay the seeds of ruin, for those in power could no longer dismiss us as ineffectual faddists: they feared us, as prophets of the age to come. In short, we threatened their profit margins.
>
> (275)

God's Gardeners is no merely violent insurgency. In defying the corporations, it works to redistribute—if not redefine—wealth and to recognize all people—not just the corporate elite—as worthy of a secure and sustainable habitat. Nor does Atwood invent this group as any kind of "centre-left" or "third way" party, as warned against by Laclau and Mouffe. Adam One, Zeb, and the Gardeners are under no illusion that with the coming of the information society and the process of globalization antagonisms between rich and poor have disappeared. Their revolutionary vision constitutes a drastic social alternative to the corporate state.

Monstrous Lost Boys

In *The MaddAddam Trilogy*, good cases could be made for any number of weird creatures monstrously disrupting current conceptions of normal, for any number of borders crossed in ways that expose all cultural norms as arbitrary, or for social Others scapegoated in ways that, under analysis, expose in fact the bigotry and machinations of modern power. To conclude my analysis of Atwood's speculative satire, however, I focus on an intriguing flip of the human/monster binary, one that exposes the dominant discourse as monstrous in any number of ways. The inversion involves the characters Snowman

(Jimmy) and Crake (Glenn). In *Oryx and Crake*, Snowman serves as the focal character, if not protagonist, of the narrative. We follow his struggle for postplague survival as he also tends to the odd, new humanoids concocted by Crake—what Snowman calls "the Children of Crake" or "the Crakers." Along the way, we hear through him the backstory of himself (as Jimmy) and Crake (as Glenn) as adolescent friends growing up in the Compounds, as friends keeping in touch through university, then eventually as co-workers at the powerful RejoovenEsense corporation where Crake conducts his secret, apocalyptic experimentations. Snowman is our first touchstone into Atwood's fictional world, and it is through his mediation that we learn most of its basic features. For his part, Crake plays the integral role in the first novel—and, albeit less visibly, throughout the trilogy—as the scientist who bioengineers both the plague that destroys humanity and the new version of humans to take our place. These actions place Crake at the center of Atwood's trilogy as its prime mover. Discerning his thinking, motivations, and significance is thus an indispensable interpretive task. Both of these characters, then, are crucial to the tale being told. As young white males who we watch grow into manhood, at first glance they look to be the stuff of not only the Bildungsroman, but the hero figure of innumerable novels in the British-American tradition. What else are novels for, after all, but the celebration of young white males? In her satiric invasion of the novel genre, however, Atwood plays a trick. Far from being the heroes of a coming-of-age story, Snowman and Crake are inverted into a pair of privileged, dumb-and-dumber monsters of satire. Specifically, they emerge in the trilogy not as sympathetic figures suffering the slings and arrows of outrageous apocalypse, but as neoliberal lost boys risibly enmeshed in what critic Nina Baym memorably describes as melodramas of beset manhood.

In her analysis of the formation of the American novel canon by patriarchal critics, Baym discusses the quintessential myth and promise of America: that the rugged individual (meaning a man), armed only with his bootstraps, can make his own way in an unspoiled wilderness without the help or, more important, the hindrance of society. Writes Baym:

> This promise is the deeply romantic one that in this new land, untrammeled by history and social accident, a person will be able to achieve complete self-definition. Behind this promise is the assurance that individuals come before society, that they exist in some meaningful sense prior to, and apart from, societies in which they happen to find themselves. The myth also holds that, as something artificial and secondary to human nature, society exerts an unmitigatedly destructive pressure on individuality.
>
> (131–132)

Given America's origins as vast tracts of what Europeans saw as virgin territory for the taking, it makes sense

> that the essential quality of America comes to reside in its unsettled wilderness and the opportunities that such a wilderness offers to the individual

as the medium on which he may inscribe, unhindered, his own destiny and his own nature.

(132)

Such mythology drives not only James Fenimore Cooper's "Leatherstocking" novels and every cowboy movie starring John Wayne, but the rags-to-riches tales of Horatio Alger as well as our own current neoliberal ideology of possessive individualism. The intrepid individual is all—whether riding the range or shining shoes or wheeling-and-dealing on Wall Street—and society is only a snare for that heroic, self-determining soul. In her depictions of Snowman and Crake, Atwood seems to be having fun at the expense of this core American fable. Growing up, Jimmy and Glenn both are wannabe nonconformists looking to buck—heroically, in their minds—the upper-middle-class, corporate-controlled society around them. They chafe at the tightly monitored Compound life in which their professional-scientist parents raise them. As Jimmy laments about the paltry option of going to the mall after school:

There wasn't much else to do after school in the HelthWyzer Compound, or in any of the Compounds, not for kids their age, not in any sort of group way. It wasn't like the pleeblands. There, it was rumoured, the kids ran in packs, in hordes.

(Oryx and Crake 73)

Glenn's reaction to the privileged humdrum is to assume an offhand, detached persona so common in teenage boys, a "kind of cool slouchiness" giving off "the sense of energies being held back, held in reserve for something more important than present company" (72). They are a pair of mavericks without a high plains to drift, with no more Manifest Destiny to fulfill. Their unknown wilderness to explore is not the wide-open prairie, but the slums of the pleeblands. It's as if Atwood is announcing the death of the American frontier myth: it's over; we've stolen and ruined all the land; we've corporatized the planet; no more are young men able to light out for the Territory to avoid being civilized. The extent of Jimmy and Glenn's teen rebelliousness, predictably, is cruising the internet for violence and pornography, playing video games, and hacking into the online accounts of the adults around them.

The second key aspect of this American myth of individuality, according to Baym, is its being sexualized. That is, if the rugged individual is understood to be male, then both what he runs from—society—and what he runs toward—the wilderness—are understood to be female.[8] Baym explains how "the entrammelling society and the promising landscape" alike "are depicted in unmistakably feminine terms"; moreover, this sexual definition "has melodramatic, misogynist implications." Here is where the element of beset manhood enters the equation. Young men find themselves, so runs the myth, torn between these two powerful female influences. On the side of domestication in these stories, "the encroaching, constricting, destroying society is represented with particular urgency in the figure of one or more women" (133). For Jimmy and

Glenn, these threatening women are their mothers. Glenn's mother seems a woman wholly of social convention. As discussed above, she betrays Glenn's father when he's preparing, heroically, to expose HelthWyzer crimes, opting instead for the safety of the Compound life and eventual remarriage to her boss, a right-wing bore who Glenn is compelled to address as "Uncle Pete" (*Oryx and Crake* 89). Atwood thus gives the young Crake a tragi-droll air of Hamlet, complete with coldly watching his mother die a horrible death from an incident of bioform sabotage (176–177) and, in due course, enacting his revenge on Uncle Pete by melting him with a rogue virus (253). As for Jimmy, his mother menaces in a different way. Her form of constricting socialization is not one of conventionality, as with Glenn's mother, but the opposite: one of social consciousness and activism. Again as discussed above, Jimmy's mother escapes the Compounds to join the anti-corporation underground resistance, a fact that beleaguers, embarrasses, and conflicts Jimmy as he grows up. Jimmy never musters the courage, as she did, to rebel against the corporate life he so disdains. Instead, he floats aimlessly through his college education at a second-rate school, his professional career as a spin-doctor for corporate marketing, and any number of indifferent relationships with women. Like Glenn, Jimmy eschews the entangling society of his mother. Both young men cast women, whether mothers or lovers, in what Baym characterizes as "the melodramatic role of temptress, antagonist, obstacle—a character whose mission in life seems to be to ensnare him and deflect him from life's important purposes of self-discovery and self-assertion" (133). What these lost boys long for instead is alluring, uncharted, and virgin territory in which to fashion themselves. In *Oryx and Crake*, this new country is represented by Oryx.

Baym notes how the rejection of society for adventure by the young man entails another form of female influence: the call of the wild. She asserts: "the beckoning wilderness ... is given a deeply feminine quality. Landscape is deeply imbued with female qualities, as society is; but where society is menacing and destructive, landscape is compliant and supportive" (135). Jimmy and Glenn find exactly these qualities in the exotic figure of Oryx. Rather than being an "entrapper and impediment in the melodrama of beset manhood" (135), Oryx is an emotional and sexual enabler of these boys' self-aggrandizing fantasies. Through a retelling by Snowman, Atwood provides us with a full account of Oryx's harrowing experiences as a child from rural poverty in Southeast Asia sold into sexual exploitation (*Oryx and Crake* 115–144). Growing up as an object with "money value" (126), Oryx is unimaginable to Jimmy's sheltered upbringing, and he treats her with a mix of guilt-pity and jealous desire. Happenstance brings Oryx (a code name, we never discover her real one) to America and eventually into the employment of Crake. Under these circumstances, an edgy love triangle forms among them. For a time, Jimmy and Glenn alike are allowed by Atwood to venture into Oryx's promising landscape of sheer male self-gratification. Crake, who is coldly analytical and socially awkward, uses Oryx to advance his ego and his secret project. Jimmy, on the other hand, wallows blissfully yet anxiously in the delicious enigma of Oryx, always worried that she's lying to him but unable to resist wandering her lush terrain. Of course, both young men covet Oryx not as a real-life woman, but as a fantastic construction of their own making. Says Baym of these patriarchal yearnings: "The fantasies are infantile, concerned with power, mastery, and total gratification: the all-nurturing mother, the all-passive bride" (136).

Far from being a hero, then, Jimmy amounts to little more than a clever slacker and pathetic rebel without a cause. He is a forlorn inhabitant of what Michael Kimmel calls "Guyland," a social landscape wherein white adolescent males of reasonable means come of age, in the 21st century, in a reality vacuum of puerile pursuits—video games, internet pornography, fraternities, sports—paying little serious attention to their education, their careers looming beyond college, or the actual state of the world around them. As such, Jimmy is an incisive and damning satiric portrait by Atwood of a significant and recognizable aspect of current neoliberal hegemonic masculinity: the well-heeled loser who drifts along neglectfully buoyed by his gender, race, and economic status—all unearned benefits. Jimmy is monstrous for his self-indulgence, his self-pity, his disgraceful squandering of cultural advantages, and particularly for his navel-gazing indifference to the disintegrating society around him. As a member of the power elite, Jimmy has been afforded the wherewithal, potentially, to amend the broken social order. Such exertion and bravery, however, are inconceivable to him. Jimmy is a privileged lost boy of paralyzing indecision and inaction.

Blameworthy as Jimmy is, Glenn-cum-Crake is worse. He is a privileged lost boy not of cowardly apathy, but of asocial megalomania. Crake is Atwood's twisted apotheosis of the hero of American myth: the loner who achieves such complete self-definition, who rejects so utterly the artificial, secondary, and unmitigatedly destructive pressure of society on his precious core individuality, that he resolves to destroy society altogether. In the symbolic figure of Oryx, Crake turns, as Baym puts it, "to nature as sweetheart and nurture, anticipating the satisfaction of all desires through her and including among these the desires for mastery and power" (136). The mastery and power Crake seeks to exert, however, is not just over Oryx/the wilderness; he will overmaster the menacing society of his mother, as well. That is to say, if no virgin territory remains in the 21st century to accommodate the young man's escape, a perverse alternative is for him to eradicate that stultifying society into which he was born. We learn in bits and pieces throughout *The MaddAddam Trilogy* that this is precisely what Crake resolves to do. Atwood supplies the young Crake with many signs of a developing antisocial personality disorder as he grows into manhood. Slowly but surely, bringing down the whole system and harming people make more and more sense to Crake. Eventually, he becomes a top student, then a bioengineering whiz kid for the corporations. His ultimate goal, though, is not corporate success and riches, but to reboot humanity. Crake's undertaking calls for him to dupe and betray everyone around him.

Fooling greedy corporate executives is a simple matter for Crake. He leads them on with his scientific genius. A pair of his inventions promise to be incredible revenue-generators. First is the "BlyssPluss Pill," a wonder-drug that simultaneously boosts sexual performance while secretly sterilizing the user. The pill is a neoliberal bid to save the world—the world that neoliberalism has driven to the brink of destruction. Crake informs Jimmy:

> I've seen the latest confidential Corps demographic reports. As a species we're in deep trouble, worse than anyone's saying. They're afraid to release the stats because people might just give up, but take it from me, we're running out of space-time. Demand for resources has exceeded supply for decades in marginal geo-political areas, hence the famines and droughts; but very soon, demand is going to exceed supply *for everyone*. With the BlyssPluss Pill the human race will have a better chance of swimming.
>
> (Oryx and Crake 294–295)

In true neoliberal fashion, this last-ditch effort to shrink the global population will rake in tons of cash: "Needless to say, Crake continued, the thing would become a huge money-spinner. It would be the must-have pill, in every country, in every society in the world" (295). Crake's second invention is his "Paradice Project," that is, the Crakers. These are gene-spliced humanoids engineered to survive much better in nature than current humans and to have engineered out of them certain harmful features and behaviors. In the minds of Crake's corporate managers, the BlyssPluss Pill and the Paradice Project work in tandem: "The Pill would put a stop to haphazard reproduction, the Project would replace it with a superior method. They were two stages of a single plan" (304). In other words, RejoovenEsense plans to market a better brand of human, one custom tailored to meet the needs of the buyer: "Whole populations could be created that would have pre-selected characteristics. Beauty, of course; that would be in high demand. And docility: several world leaders had expressed interest in that" (304). One can hardly imagine a better example of the control society theorized by Deleuze: the hegemonic device of genetic engineering monitoring and modulating identity and relationships in order to put the individual to particular uses within the modern state. The Crakers are a neoliberal dream come true. For Crake, however, the mere genetic engineering of a superior race is small potatoes. He is not out to *play* God; Crake is out to *be* God. His goal is the sudden and wholesale substitution of his new and improved humans for the older model. The Paradice Project, then, is something of a gene-splicing version of Victor Frankenstein's ill-fated bid to defeat death. To achieve his grandiose ends, Crakes lets nothing and no one get in his way.

Crake misleads and manipulates both Jimmy and Oryx. Oryx sincerely believes in Crake's talents and goodness, telling Jimmy of their friend: "He wants to make the world a better place. ... He has found the problems, I think he is right. There are too many people and that makes the people bad" (*Oryx and Crake* 322). What Oryx doesn't realize—what no one knows—is that Crake has built into the BlyssPluss Pill a supervirus, one that spreads quickly and kills rapidly. Innocently, Oryx helps Crake distribute that lethal virus worldwide. Jimmy is less gullible, but his suspicions about Crake's actions and motives extend little beyond his own insecurities about their love triangle with

Oryx. Worries Jimmy: "Had he only been some sort of toy-boy for Oryx, a court jester for Crake?" (322). Because of his habitual self-involvement, Jimmy misses the signs of Crake's grander, more deadly narcissistic plan. Crake triggers the virus and planetary human extermination begins. As the pandemic unfolds, Jimmy experiences not a tragic but a satiric version of knowledge-too-late. Rather than moving us to pity and fear, Jimmy stirs our derision and exasperation. At the same time, in Crake, Atwood creates the 21st-century version of the rugged individualist—a young man who needs no one and nothing. Crake can only think in terms of himself. He has no affinity for a social collective of any kind. Unlike Adam One or Zeb, who fight against the neoliberal–neoconservative hegemony in an effort to change society, Crake is fatally imbued with its ideology of individualism. He is an utter creature of that cold-blooded creed, maybe even a monstrous representation of the Regime itself. By way of Atwood's satiric exaggeration, Crake amplifies neoliberal individuality to its extreme of sociopathy. His character does not overthrow the neoliberal state; he brings it to fruition. It is only logical and inevitable that a corporate culture hell-bent for profit, exploiting scientific innovations faster than consequences can be understood, will come crashing to a terrible end. As the preeminent scientist-rainmaker of that system, Crake incarnates the corporation as the civilization-destroying monster that it is.

If we care to wax symbolic in our reading of Atwood's Menippean warning, Crake is the neoliberal Beast, Oryx is the indispensable yet vulnerable Earth, and Jimmy is Us, the reader of speculative satire, stupidly looking on as one maltreats and kills the other. The question *The MaddAddam Trilogy* poses to readers, then, is simple: are we going to be as lost, as navel-gazing, as foolishly sluggish, as wretchedly awake-too-late as Snowman?

Notes

1 Zuboff points to a key event in the increasingly ruthless neoliberal mindset being the publication of an influential article in 1976 by economists Michael Jensen and William Meckling. Titled "Theory of the Firm: Managerial Behavior, Agency Costs and Ownership Structure" (*Journal of Financial Economics*, vol. 3, no. 4), this piece argues that corporate managers are like parasites feeding off the host of ownership. In order to stop this drain on profit and maximize market value of the firm, the pay and incentive structure for managers needed to be tied to "the market's signal of value, the share price" so as "to finally and decisively align managerial behavior with owners' interests" (Zuboff 38–39). Founded in Hayek's neoliberal theories, these ideas by Jensen and Meckling started what became known as the "shareholder value movement," which effectively shut down the prosocial practices of the 20th-century corporation. In this way, the "public corporation" and "its long-standing reciprocities with customers and employees" (40) became an economic dinosaur. Replacing it was the lean-and-mean, downsized firm along with the cult of the "entrepreneur." Zuboff characterizes this emergent neoliberal approach as "a single glorified template of audacity, competitive cunning, dominance, and wealth" (41).
2 Costing an estimated US$39,200,000, *Snowpiercer* brought in a cumulative worldwide gross of US$86,758,912 (*IMDb*). On *Rotten Tomatoes*, the film registers a

Critics Score of 94% on the "Tomatometer" with a Critics Consensus reading: "*Snowpiercer* offers an audaciously ambitious action spectacular for filmgoers numb to effects-driven blockbusters." Among the many positive comments on the movie, Claudia Puig of *USA Today* writes, "*Snowpiercer* is a rare hybrid that perfectly blends the dazzle of a futuristic action thriller with the intellectual substance of an art film." Peter Howell of the *Toronto Star* echoes, "You couldn't ask for a better metaphor for hell on Earth than what Bong Joon-ho has wrought with *Snowpiercer*: constant forward momentum while getting absolutely nowhere, suffering all the while." For less complimentary critics who see Bong's film as hitting us over the head too overtly with political messages, see Bowen; Zacharek.

3 As Bong says in an interview in *Vulture*: "I wanted to emphasize the idea of the train, the physical train, as an iron box, or metallic prison. That's really a symbol of the system that exists inside the train. There are so many characters, but they're all stuck inside. They say they want to move to the front, and they fight to get there. But they're still ultimately inside the train" (Abrams).

4 Most critical readings of *Snowpiercer* focus on the biopolitics of the human-triggered climate disaster driving the film and the horrible lengths to which humans might go to survive. See, for example, Andersen and Nielsen; Canavan; Gomel and Shemtov.

5 With regard to major awards and recognitions, Atwood was honored as a "creator" by the Science Fiction Hall of Fame in 2017, was named a finalist for the John W. Campbell Memorial Award in 2010 (for *The Year of the Flood*), and in 1987 was both nominated for the Nebula Awards and the winner of the Arthur C. Clarke Award (for *The Handmaid's Tale*).

6 In an interview following the publication of *The Year of the Flood*, Atwood states that "she believes in a love match between science and religion" as long as that religion "is not one of the standard ones" steeped in dogma and demonizing everyone else. Characterizing herself as a "strict agnostic" in that "she will not present as knowledge something that is unknown," Atwood asserts nonetheless of this science-religion combination: "I think that kind of reconciliation is coming and also has to come if we are to have any hope for the planet. Either one by itself is too (a) unreal, in the sense of misrepresenting the physical universe, or (b) bleak, in the sense of leaving a whole area of human experience unrepresented" (Lee).

7 Bouson regards Atwood's horrific and darkly satiric account of the gruesome final days of humanity as a wake-up call for readers. Amelia Defalco argues that Atwood dramatizes a catastrophic anthropocentrism in the trilogy, one where the arrogant forces of neoliberalism heedlessly turn organic cellular data into marketable, utilitarian objects. J. Paul Narkunas contends that Atwood writes speculative fiction in a way that challenges speculative capital as it seeks to monetize the elements of life. Although the fabrication of derivative speculation has become our current economic reality, applying that same make-believe to transgenics and biotechnology steps disastrously beyond the bounds of human knowledge.

8 Baym points out that the "subject of this myth is supposed to stand for human nature, and if men and women alike share a common human nature, then all can respond to its values, its promises, and its frustrations." However, within the patriarchy, "in order to represent some kind of believable flight into the wilderness, one must select a protagonist with a certain believable mobility, and mobility has until recently been a male prerogative in our society" (132–133). The loner-heroes of these tales of vicarious rough country adventure, then, as a matter of course are men—as are their authors.

5 Special Topic Rants

As a distinctive formula for political satire, Rants have the ability not only to challenge the dominant discourse but to zero-in on very particular social sore spots. Such works accentuate the miserable and the awful in our culture to the degree where audiences beg *make it stop*. But Rants don't stop. That's part of what makes them Rants. They push us to terrible extremes of emotions and ideas. Some Rants hone-in so finely on certain social ills, on specific practices of injustice or bigotry or merciless greed, on cataclysmic outcomes wrought by the Regime, that the single-mindedness of their Menippean forewarnings become difficult to bear. This chapter examines three such Rants.

Get Out (2017)

The special topic of Jordan Peele's debut film as a writer–director is white supremacist racism against African Americans. Don't be bamboozled by talk of a "postracial" America following the presidency of Barack Obama. Violent, hateful, and deep-rooted racism perseveres—and not, asserts this film, just among poor and uneducated whites. Wealthy white elites (e.g., Trump) are the particular target of Peele's satire. Observes critic Kelli Weston:

> *Get Out* blatantly engages with black suspicion of white people, or perhaps more accurately with black fear of white cannibalism, a fear that has, naturally, plagued the former ever since her introduction to America. Because for all its contemporary trappings, *Get Out* may well be the most penetrating cinematic depiction of slavery, from the nature of the institution to its far-reaching psychic consequences.
>
> (38)

Peele himself has commented of his film, "The real thing at hand here is slavery … it's some dark shit"; he has also categorized his movie as "a social thriller" (qtd. in Weston 38). How to classify Peele's film, due to its eclecticism and complexity, is in fact an interesting dilemma. One group of commentators points out how standard Hollywood pigeonholes simply don't accommodate Peele's social messages:

DOI: 10.4324/9781003110491-6
This chapter has been made available under a CC-BY-NC-ND license.

> *Get Out*, seen through the analytics of the flesh, succeeds insofar as it perfectly grasps how expressing the African American condition has always stretched the limits of bourgeois realism: we have always needed horror, sci-fi, fantasy, and other speculative genres to begin to get near the unspeakable truth of slavery and its afterlives.
>
> (After Globalism Writing Group 38)

Peele's more recent film, *Us* (2019), poses the same quandary, perhaps even more so than *Get Out*. Just how do we classify these curious and disturbing filmic texts? In my view, both are Rants. The elements of speculative satire especially are evident in the laser-focused attack of *Get Out*.

One outstanding device of satire in Peele's movie is that of genre invasion. In a film predicated on body-snatching, Peele convention-snatches from the standard plotline of the horror movie, and even more specifically from the mad-scientist horror movie, to apply toward scathing Menippean ends. We see two mad scientists at work in the film, namely, the white, educated, affluent, middle-aged, power couple of Missy and Dean Armitage. Missy (Catherine Keener) is an accomplished psychiatrist and expert hypnotherapist. Her job as an off-kilter genius is to trap unsuspecting young black women and men in "the sunken place," a state of "limited consciousness" where victims exist merely as powerless passengers in a small portion of their brain. There they are able to see and hear what's going on with their body, but not able to do anything about it. Dean (Bradley Whitford) is an eminent neurosurgeon. His unhinged task is then to transplant the brains of rich white people into those stolen black bodies. There, the white people live a new life while the original black owners are reduced to "an audience" without agency. This evil scheme is the intergenerational work, secret society, and financial enterprise of the Armitage family. In a clunky info-video titled "Behold the Coagula," family patriarch Roman Armitage (Richard Herd) explains to victims how they have been chosen "because of the physical advantages you enjoyed your entire lifetime. With your natural gifts and our determination we could both be part of something greater. Something perfect." He describes the "coagula procedure" (meaning the brain transfer operation) they're about to undergo as "a man-made miracle" that "our order has been developing ... for many, many years." This mind-suppressing and body-stealing technology is carefully described in the film, making it a sci-fi *novum*. However, this strange newness is not designed to trigger cognitive estrangement in audiences so much as activate excruciating reminders of entrenched American white supremacy.

The weird science in *Get Out*, then, is not a brave new world to contemplate but a sinister, novel way to enact the racial oppressions of the bad old one. Peele pushes the horror motif of the racialized mad scientist over the top. Missy malevolently controls the motor functions of our hero, Chris Washington (Daniel Kaluuya), with the mere tap of spoon to teacup. Dean delivers a stock hubristic, mad-scientist monologue while staring into the fireplace:

Fire. It's a reflection of our own mortality. We're born, we breathe, then we die. Even the sun will die someday. But we are divine. We are the gods trapped in cocoons.

White gods only, apparently. When it comes time for the brain transplant itself, the scene is one of full-on Klansman Dr. Frankenstein. Ominous choral music thunders. Two white candles burn ritualistically in the operating room. We're subjected to ghoulish images and sounds of cut-open skull. This send-up of the horror genre would be camp were it not for the fact that Peele deals with the deadly serious subject matter of racism. Underlying the farcical make-believe of the "coagula procedure" is the historical brutality of slavery and white supremacist ideology. These black victims are first interpellated by Missy into obedience; next Dean seizes their bodies to turn them into the absolute property of whites.[1] As a result, while moviegoers—white American moviegoers in particular—superficially enjoy the story-arc thrill-ride of the horror genre, alongside that fun they are forced to confront as well the profound reality of racial hatred and violence in America. Familiar delight ambushes viewers with unnerving instruction, causing audiences to squirm in their cushioned cineplex seats.

A second satiric device used expertly by Peele is that of distortion and exaggeration. As discussed above, the trappings of the horror film are heightened to nearly derisive levels in *Get Out*. Atmospheric music, tension-filled moments, anxiety-producing camera angles, and the like are embellished to the brink of being ham-fisted. But, of course, these are not amateurish mistakes; they are finely calculated prompts alerting us to the filmic manipulation at work in and, indeed, integral to the horror genre. Such movie-making brinksmanship by Peele is the same satiric technique as the mock-heroic, where the conventions of the epic are used facetiously as a way to condemn ingeniously and, thereby, more thoroughly the main target of the satire.[2] The satirist is not so much concerned with belittling the genre of the epic (or of the horror movie) as she is with using that genre as a vehicle for satiric polemic. The best way to exploit the genre as an instrument of satire is to call the reader's (or the viewer's) attention to the formulaic workings and ideologies of that form. By way of this maneuver, the audience both sees through the genre and, because of it, perceives the satiric target in an even more negative light.[3] Such is the case with Peele's distorted parody of horror movies in *Get Out*. He gooses the shtick of horror to a degree that focuses our minds all the more keenly on the genuine horror of racism. The most telling device in Peele's exploitation of the horror genre is his implementation of the ingredient cardinal to all horror films: the monster. In *Get Out*, that monster is not vampires or werewolves or space aliens or zombies or killer clowns or whatever other terror the imagination can conjure. The monster is the neoliberal white supremacist—depicted in many forms, in unbearable detail, and with devastating exaggeration.

The White Monster in *Get Out*. Where to begin? For one thing, it is intergenerational, as represented by the three generations of the Armitage family in the film.⁴ The grandparents display good old-fashioned, old-timey racism from the early- and mid-twentieth century. Not only do they use dated slang such as "doggone" and "funny business," but their beliefs about African Americans center around black physical superiority/mental inferiority as well as whites needing to caretake blacks, such as when the grandmother assures Chris: "The Armitages are so good to us. They treat us like family." The gruesome irony, however, is that Grandma and Grandpa Armitage have undergone the coagula procedure and been transplanted into young black bodies. Whenever the next victim is their house guest, such as Chris, they pose as the housemaid, Georgina (Betty Gabriel), and the groundskeeper, Walter (Marcus Henderson). This grisly arrangement makes the Armitage country estate a Gothic sci-fi slave plantation where the accustomed racist binary of white/black remains a constant principle of oppression but its practice has transformed terrifyingly into a weird new physical hybridity. (Behold the Coagula.) The middle generation of Armitages, Missy and Dean, along with being mad scientists, represent limousine-liberal racism. Theirs is a post-1960s seeming acceptance and toleration of racial difference. They say politically correct things (such as Dean declaring to Chris, "I would have voted for Obama for a third term if I could. Best president in my lifetime, hands down") and they display progressive social attitudes (such as warmly welcoming their daughter's black boyfriend), but beneath the broadminded veneer lurks bigotry as intense as that of the previous generation. This masked form of racism is signaled early in the movie by Dean's little tirade about the deer infestation in the area:

> I don't mean to get on my high horse but I'm tellin' ya, I do not like the deer. I'm sick of it. They're taking over. They're like rats. They're destroying the ecosystem. I see a dead deer on the side of the road I think to myself, that's a start.

As the story evolves, we come to understand that deer in *Get Out* are a symbol for black people. Thus, African Americans in Peele's film are scapegoated and othered—that is, monsterized—by white power in the usual ways. At the same time, as we've seen above, their bodies are perversely desired by whites, so much so that they have become fetishized commodities for purchase. Various aspects of monstrosity, then, comes at us thick and fast in *Get Out*. In the end, however, what we witness through the medium of horror is the White Monster monsterizing its black victims. This provoking objective correlative forces our reexamination of American social order, exposing the discipline exerted by white supremacy as arbitrary, brutal, self-serving, and nothing even remotely approaching "Truth."

The youngest generation of Armitage, brother and sister Jeremy (Caleb Landry Jones) and Rose (Allison Williams), embody two different Millennial manifestations of racism. Jeremy appears to be an outright white nationalist, simultaneously belligerent and craven. Like his grandfather, he regards black men as physically advantaged but intellectually deficient. As a member of the secret "order" mentioned by his grandfather in the "Behold the Coagula" video, Jeremy also sees black men as threats to be bested and adversaries to be destroyed. Drunk and rambling at the family dinner table, Jeremy starts to chest-pound at Chris while supposedly talking sports. He tells Chris that: "With your frame and your genetic make-up if you really pushed your body … I mean really trained, you know, no pussy-footin' around … you'd be a fucking beast." When he discovers that Chris took jiu-jitsu lessons as a kid, Jeremy treats the information as some kind of challenge to his white manhood. Focusing weaselly, frat-bro eyes on Chris, Jeremy white-mansplains to him: "The thing about jiu-jitsu is strength doesn't matter, right? It's all about this. [Points to his head.] It's a strategic game, like chess. It's all about being two … three … four moves ahead." His implication is, of course, that white men are smarter than black men. During the climactic sequence when Chris does battle with all the White Monsters of the Armitage household, he will outsmart Jeremy—that is, be two, three, four moves ahead of him—when the young white supremacist has him in a jiu-jitsu chokehold. In a film packed with telling racial details and inversions, it's one of many gratifying moments.

For her part, Rose enacts her younger-generation racism contrariwise to Jeremy. Instead of directing hatred toward black men, Rose pretends to love them. Chris is not the first black man she has procured then lured home to be prepared for consumption by whites. Her real passion, then, is appropriation. While seeming to love African Americans and their culture, Rose is really only interested in using them for her own gain. This attitude and behavior reflects the race-relations phenomenon identified by bell hooks in the 1990s as "eating the Other." Hooks theorizes how race and ethnicity in American culture have "become commodified as resources for pleasure" (23; see also Weston 39). In particular, black culture—music, fashion, sports, attitudes, language—has been embraced by the dominant white culture (especially youth culture) as trendy and cool (and lucrative), but mainly in ways where "the Other can be continually exploited, and that such exploitation will occur in a manner that reinscribes and maintains the *status quo*" (22). A large part of this ingesting of the exotic dark Other is sexual and involves breaking American taboos against miscegenation. Notes hooks: "the culture of specific groups, as well as the bodies of individuals, can be seen as constituting an alternative playground where members of dominating races, genders, sexual practices affirm their power-over in intimate relations with the Other" (23). This approach to racial difference sums up Rose's white supremacist ploy. She has no more regard for Chris than any other consumer item that gives her pleasure and brings her status. Meanwhile, according to hooks, the black Other is devoured and erased:

> Currently, the commodification of difference promotes paradigms of consumption wherein whatever difference the Other inhabits is eradicated, via exchange, by a consumer cannibalism that not only displaces the Other but denies the significance of that Other's history through a process of decontextualization.

(31)

Such an eradication is clearly what the Armitage family has in mind for Chris. Rose, like her limousine-liberal parents, personifies the type of white supremacist monster that is likely the most sinister to black people: the racist who pretends to accept and even to admire you. Similar to Martin Luther King, Jr. in his "Letter from Birmingham Jail," Peele warns black audiences that it is preferable to deal with outright bigots who openly express their racial hatred—because at least with them you always know where you stand—than it is to deal with furtive liberals who feign their impartiality and support—because when push comes to shove you'll abruptly discover, to your peril, that they only ever made a show of having your back.

Along with its being intergenerational, a second attribute of the White Monster in *Get Out* is its ubiquity, its inescapability, its terrifying reach and power as the dominant ideology. Peele drives home these points by way of satiric exaggeration. Whiteness is everywhere in the film. However, Peele denormalizes white upper-middle-class culture by constantly calling the viewer's attention to it with myriad farcical and cringeworthy details. To point out but a few: Dean and Chris discuss progressive politics while standing in a gazebo; all the rich, old, country-club-type white guests at the Armitage weekend event; Jeremy takes a swing at Chris with a lacrosse stick; the décor of the Armitage house is Pottery Barn chic; they have carrot cake for dessert; the basement rec room is straight out of Whitebread Hell—heavy wood paneling, dartboard, ping-pong and foosball tables, hardy pile carpeting, overstuffed leather chair, backgammon and other board games, a bocce ball set (one of which Chris uses to stave in Jeremy's skull), a trophy deer head hung on the wall above a vintage TV-stereo console. In other words, that which is revered in American society as the accoutrements of wealth and prestige is sardonically transformed by Peele into menacing particulars of the White Monster. We see with new eyes white discourse as not a chronicle of special achievement and justified entitlement but as a practice of violent oppression and abuse. Spike Lee, at the end of his acerbic racial satire *Bamboozled* (2000), delivers a devastating and enraging montage of racist stereotypes leveled against blacks by white popular culture, thereby exposing the distorted "truth" about blacks contrived by insidious white ideology. Throughout *Get Out*, Peele returns the favor: by caricaturing and monsterizing white supremacists, he reveals the hyped-up "truth" about whites propagated by the guile of white power. Nowhere is this satiric pulling-back-of-the-curtain more trenchant than in Peele's creation of the primary monster of his deadly serious, tongue-in-cheek horror flick: the Monstrous White Girl.

With the character of Rose, Peele renders topsy-turvy hundreds of years of white supremacist narrative about the perilous relationship between white women and black men. *Get Out* reverses all racist rhetoric upon which thousands of lynchings of black men in America were predicated: the murderous lust of black men for white women. Black men in this movie are the victims and the prey. Their predator is an attractive young white woman who is single-minded and ruthless in the hunt. Rose comes across as sociopathic, in fact, in her white supremacy. The moment her seduction performance of

Chris is at an end, she transforms from an affable, untailored, liberal-minded white girlfriend into an anal-retentive Bond villain. Her phone conversation with Chris's worried best friend, Rod (Lil Rel Howery), is particularly chilling. Dressed now in a stark white turtleneck with her hair pulled back into a prim and austere ponytail, Rose shows no emotion on her face while her voice fakes helplessness, confusion, and concern. Deadpan, she whimpers to Rod: "Wait … you haven't seen him? … Oh my God!" Rose is polished and cunning in covering her tracks for the kidnapping of Chris. Rod suspects her subterfuge and attempts to record the phone call in order to catch Rose in a lie. Rose is one step ahead of him, though, and redirects their conversation by brazenly accusing Rod of wanting her for himself: "Rod, just stop. … I know why you're calling. … I know you think about fucking me, Rod." Flustered by this groundless accusation, Rod panics and hangs up, cursing, "Shit! Ga! … She's a genius!" Rod was not about to become Rose's next quarry. Wearing an expression of cold triumph, Rose turns to look at her White Monster family, who has been watching her phone conversation with pride and approbation. Ironically, when Rod goes to the police to lay out his theory about the Armitage family abducting and enslaving black people, he is ridiculed by detectives—all people of color. In particular, Detective Latoya (Erika Alexander), scoffs: "Oh, white girls. They get you every time." In this horror scenario, however, racial cliché has become fact. This white girl *does* get the black man every time. Peele recasts the character of Rose from being the traditional object of black temptation and lust into being the lethal agent of white power. In the process, Rose is transformed as well from the horror film trope of "the final girl" into that of the undying monster.[5]

The most unnerving-cum-mordant depiction of Rose as the Monstrous White Girl occurs while Chris is in the process of fighting his way out of the Armitage home. During this sequence of extreme violence, we cut to Rose in her bedroom upstairs, sitting calmly cross-legged on her bed with earphones in listing to the song "Time of My Life" from the film *Dirty Dancing* (1987). Not only is that movie very white, but the song lyrics, in this situation, could not be more ironic: "Now I've had the time of my life / No, I never felt like this before / Yes I swear it's the truth / And I owe it all to you…" Again, Rose is dressed fastidiously in white and beige. On her laptop, she's searching for her next young black man victim. Rose appears to have a basketball player in mind this time. Behind her on the wall, over her headboard, are photographs of her past ten victims. Recalling the deer head in the rec room, these pictures are hung like trophies and signal that the bed and sexuality are the environs of her hunt. Topping the caustic and embellished traits that Peele gives to this wicked white girl, however, is Rose having at hand a small bowl of Fruit Loops along with a glass of milk. While searching the internet for the next body to snatch, she selects a single Fruit Loop, bites it in half with care, then chews meticulously. She washes that down with three strictly measured sips of milk through a straw. Thus, we have the monster at the heart of *Get Out*: a neurotic and soulless serial temptress whose obsessive purpose is the seduction and consumption of black men. Rose is a racialist Siren whose song lures

African-American men into believing that social equality is available to them. To their horror, these men find themselves instead abducted, packaged, and sold to white masters. Rose is an embodiment of the white supremacist orthodoxy upon which America is founded and under which people of color suffer to this day. She represents the *lie* of the American Dream: you can be anything you want to be—so long as you're white.

In the final showdown with Chris, Rose proves to be, as well, the monster-that-will-not-die (just yet). Even after being shot by the black man trapped in the sunken place inside of Walter, she's still reaching for her rifle. When Chris takes the gun from her, she plies her seduction tactic one last time, telling him, "Chris ... I'm so sorry ... I love you ... I love you." Justified in his rage, Chris begins to strangle her. At this remarkable moment in the film, Peele presents viewers with the antithesis of white supremacist dogma: not the black man beast attacking the innocent white woman, but the innocent black man desperately defending himself against the white woman beast. The damsel in distress is, in fact, the dragon; the dragon is, in effect, the damsel in distress. To make clear this state of affairs, Peele has a strangely triumphant smirk come to Rose's face as Chris strangles her. It's as though generating in Chris this violent reaction to her is the monstrous trick Rose wants to play on black men—that is, she looks to spur black men into being the racist stereotype whites have of them as lusting uncontrollably, and sometimes murderously, after delicate white womanhood. When Chris breaks off his stranglehold, Rose's expression turns to disappointment, as if she's failed to turn Chris into the universal Black Thug whites expect. A moment later, when Rose thinks a police car has pulled up, she deftly switches into white victim mode, calling out weakly, "Help ... help ... help me." At that moment, we think all is lost for Chris. The Monstrous White Girl has won. Surely, the racist cop from early in the film has arrived, and he will interpret this scene of carnage in typical white police officer fashion. In a plot-twist of genius, though, Rod steps out of his Airport TSA vehicle, fulfilling his role not only as Chris' loyal sidekick but becoming now Chris' knight in shining armor. Chris staggers to the car and climbs in. Rod sizes up the scene for a few moments, then delivers the best line of the film: "I mean, I told you not to go in that house." Notably, Chris and Rod ignore Rose altogether. The pair leave her to die in the middle of the road, while she watches her erstwhile victims drive away.

Finally, via the Menippean satiric persona of Chris, the moviegoer experiences the injustice, violence, and terror of racism. Chris is wholly sympathetic as a protagonist. We identify with and root for him as he negotiates first the oddity then the sophisticated barbarity of the Armitage estate. As noted above, Peele gender bends typical horror conventions by making Chris function as the "final boy" of the movie—unfortunate racial pun unavoidable in this case. Moreover, in Chris' heroic fight against the white monsters, audiences are exposed to a range of social issues characteristic of a Rant. In the silent auction for Chris, for example, we witness slavery revisited neoliberal style. To be sure, as in the American past, whites buy blacks as property. In this situation, more specifically, rich old white men look to buy and occupy Chris' young black body in a new and extreme form of accumulation by dispossession. What is more, wealth inequity nearly as much as race drives this outrageous crime. Although Chris looks to be solidly middle class, he possesses nothing like the money of these affluent couples who are the Armitages' weekend guests. Perhaps as a way to signal that race is not the only factor in this 21st-century act of enslavement, Peele includes one Japanese bidder for Chris. Chris' interactions with the man who eventually buys him, blind art dealer Jim Hudson (Stephen Root), likewise confirms that neoliberalism works alongside racism in this transaction. When these two chat prior to the auction, Hudson comments on the "ignorance" of the wealthy white party guests and says of them, "They mean well, but they have no idea what real people go through." He refers, of course, to the social detachment of extreme privilege enjoyed by the 1%. Hudson also relates that he is an admirer of Chris's photography: "You have a great eye. ... You've got something. The images you capture—so brutal, so melancholic. It's powerful stuff." Other than Rose, Hudson is the only white person in the film Chris connects with authentically. Expressing empathy for Hudson's blindness, Chris tells him, "Shit ain't fair, man." In what will turn out to be an ominous retort, Hudson answers, "Oh, you got that right. Shit ain't fair." Not only is Hudson anticipating Chris' pending betrayal by all the white people around him, but he refers as well, plausibly, to the wealth and power gap between rich and not-rich. That is to say, Chris is about to be ambushed by the double bind of racial *and* economic injustice in America. The nonracial motivation for Hudson's purchase of Chris is confirmed when the two speak again, this time just before the coagula procedure while Chris is a prisoner in the rec room. Over the old TV console, Hudson tells his acquisition: "I could give a shit what color you are. No, what I want is deeper. I want your eye, man. I want those things you see through." It's cold comfort to know that Hudson is not a racist, but instead a classist—blind money, so to speak. In true neoliberal fashion, this rich man regards his fellow human as a thing to be bought and used for parts, as an economic object in a marketplace as opposed to a whole person with a life to live. In this way, *Get Out* defines for us the hegemonic adversary needing to be battled: not just racism but neoliberal white supremacy. The film blows the whistle on the ersatz utopia promised by our current-day ruling ideology. Well-heeled white Americans are rebuked for their hypocritical disregard for democracy. In post-Marxist terms, the movie targets the hegemonic articulations of Democrats and Republicans alike for their imposition of a liberal–conservative discourse that restricts the advantages of democracy to the moneyed and predominantly white few.

All of this is a lot of politicality for a horror movie—but not for a Rant. Film critic Mary Elizabeth Williams writes of Peele's story:

> This isn't a facile fable about the very real evils of racism, one in which the villains are typical mouth-breathing rednecks. By focusing the storyline on a particular form of racism—the kind that's often disguised as peculiar envy—"Get Out' reveals something more insidious."

In her review, Williams goes on to discuss how "the film delves into the deep damage wrought from white insecurity, from its frustrated aspirational bigotry." Even more than deriding unselfconfident whites who wish they could run faster or have larger copulatory organs, *Get Out* explores a phenomenon fundamental to society: hegemonic ideology. Peele devises an extraordinary finale where white audiences are inveigled into cheering for what they have been ideologically conditioned to hate and fear most: a young black man doing violence to a rich white family. Were one to watch Chris' killing spree inside the Armitage house without the benefit of knowing the horror plotline leading up to it, one might imagine the sequence an unusually macabre home invasion and car theft. After all, in countless ways overt and subtle American whites are taught to believe that young black men inherently are threats to the status quo. Out of lust and poverty and a brute nature, so the doctrine goes, young black men are ever eager to rape and steal from and kill white people. Especially terrifying to whites is the idea of this violence occurring in their suburban enclaves, where they have intentionally retreated so as to be well removed from this troublesome mixed-race unrest. How amazing is it, then—if one stops to think about it—to have cineplexes full of suburban white people thrilled and relieved to see Chris impale Dean with a buck antler and stomp Jeremy to death? Through the magic of genre invasion, Peele momentarily suspends the dominant racist ideology disciplined into whites so that they see Chris not as a threatening black marauder, but as an innocent victim courageously fighting back against powerful and immoral forces. Thus, the more insidious thing revealed by *Get Out* is the awful power of ideology to shape our worldview as well as the extraordinary measures it takes to goad our rethinking of those implanted mindsets. Yet even as Peele exposes the lie of racist attitudes, he is heedful of them. Chris' killing of Missy is not graphically depicted. In what might be taken as an image of inverted rape, Missy stabs Chris through the hand with a letter opener as they struggle. Almost reluctantly, Chris then kills Missy—off-camera—with that same weapon. It makes sense for Peele to avoid, as much as possible, the deep cultural taboo against black men harming white women. As noted above, Chris purposely stops himself from killing Rose. To preserve his protagonist as the heroic final (black) boy of this social thriller, Peele engineers maximum audience sympathy for Chris during his harrowing escape from the clutches of the (white) monsters. Likely aiding white viewers to experience empathy for Chris is the fact that the Armitage family is filthy rich—not particular fan favorites of the economically challenged 99%. All racial groups in America are subjected to financial injustice.

By way of the character of Chris, then, Peele pushes many social commentary buttons. In Chris, we see someone struggling against ethnic domination, against exploitation by the rich, and against the imposition of an identity position that subjects him to pernicious authority. We likewise see an oppressed racial group, that of blacks generally and of young black men particularly, engaged in social antagonism with the hegemon. Chris' fight to survive the Armitage house of horrors is symbolically a fight for equal recognition as well as an act of agonistic pluralism. Peele's political message is clear: wealthy white people are unfit to run society; more voices from more identity positions need to be heard. Chris meets violence with violence in this combat against the Regime, destroying the oppressive apparatus of the Coagula group as well as thwarting the warped possessive individualism of its devotees. With regard to satiric praise in *Get Out*, commended most is brotherhood among young black men. Converse to portraying anything like formulaic black-on-black violence, that is, the stereotype of young black men—"thugs"—mindlessly killing one another in gangland turf-wars, this movie features young black men having each other's back. As we've seen, Rod goes to extraordinary lengths to recue Chris from the white monsters. Similarly, Rose's earlier victim, now shackled inside of Walter, tricks and shoots the Monstrous White Girl both to help Chris escape and to end his own nightmarish captivity. In the signature moment of the movie, when Andre (LaKeith Stanfield) is roused out of the sunken place by the flash on Chris' phone, he vehemently warns Chris: "Get out! … Get out of here! Get the fuck out of here!" Each of these acts is a demonstration of heroic concern for others that stands in stark contrast to the anti-social greed displayed by all white characters in the film. African-American brotherhood reclaims the moral high ground in Peele's movie. Moreover, this core message is directed at black viewers as a warning against the dominant false orthodoxy of whites. Critics have noted that framing the storyline of *Get Out* is a chorus singing "Sikiliza Kwa Wahenga," a Swahili phrase meaning "listen to (your) ancestors"; other lyrics of the song translate loosely as "something bad is coming. Run" (Pulliam-Moore; see also Weston 37). If the special topic and target of this Rant is avaricious white supremacy, the behavior recommended as, if not a corrective, at least a safeguard is black solidarity hand-in-hand with a renewed vigilance against everpotential white malice. Peele pulls no punches in his horror movie portrait of white privilege. White American racism is excoriated from start to finish as evil.

"Men Against Fire," *Black Mirror* (season 3, episode 5, 2016)

Arguably, any *Black Mirror* episode could be analyzed usefully as a Rant. The series is premised on imagining the problematic-to-adverse effects of developing technologies on human society in a near-future setting. Many episodes focus on a single topic of sociopolitical concern. For example, "Fifteen Million Merits" (season 1, episode 2) examines the fraud of reality talent contest TV shows as a way to distract the public from miserable jobs and lives. "Nosedive" (season 3, episode 1) envisions popularity on social media as the organizing principle for class structure. Every *Black Mirror* episode features an intriguing sci-fi *novum* presented in an exaggerated social situation as a way to jolt viewers into inspecting our current cultural and technological circumstances and where we might be heading. For this chapter, I look at one episode in particular, "Men Against Fire," as a special topic Rant scrutinizing the dangers of neoconservatism, and in particular the militarism central to that credo.

Along with militarism, neoconservative polity features religiosity and primacy. These two elements will be considered first. As set out in Chapter 2, neocons adhere to the doctrine that America must spread its societal beliefs and conception of government around the world, primarily by means of an assertive application of overwhelming military force. Although "Men Against Fire" is set in a nebulous future ten years after some kind of global war, and although the regime in charge is unexplained by anything other than a stylized "V" insignia, the soldiers we follow are clearly Americans and the military force in which they serve is clearly the descendant of the U.S. military. Their theater of operations is Europe, more specifically Denmark, and their mission is to seek-and-destroy feral, humanoid creatures called "roaches." We discover, however, that these roaches are not strange creatures at all but humans who have been designated as genetically inferior. One of these ill-fated people, Catarina (Ariane Labed), explains the truth of the matter to the soldier-protagonist of the story, Stripe (Malachi Kirby):

> Ten years ago it began. Post-war. First, the screening program. The DNA checks. Then the register. The emergency measures. And soon everyone calls us creatures. Filthy creatures. Every voice. The TV. The computer. Say we … we have sickness in us. We have weakness. It's in our blood, they say. That our blood cannot go on. That we cannot go on.

In fact, what's taking place is a worldwide eugenics/genocide program where millions of people are being hunted and killed by the military. This agenda is unashamedly verified and endorsed by the government official, Arquette (Michael Kelly), who deals with Stripe. During their extended conversation in the prison cell, Arquette explains to the morally conflicted soldier:

> Do you have any idea of the amount of shit that's in their DNA? Higher rates of cancer, muscular dystrophy, MS, SLS, sub-standard IQ, criminal tendencies, sexual deviances. It's all there. The screening shows it. Is that what you want for the next generation?

With this eugenics policy, "Men Against Fire" reimagines both neocon tenets of religiosity and primacy: the eradication of roaches has become the dominant belief system imposed on the world. We see it in conflict with traditional religions when Stripe's squad commandeers the farmhouse of Parn Heidekker (Francis Magee), who is suspected of harboring roaches. In effect, squad leader Medina (Sarah Snook) proselytizes this new, anti-roach religion to Heidekker while her soldiers rifle his house. At first, she acknowledges his Christian faith and convictions, telling him:

> Cross on the wall there. You got principles. Think all life is sacred. And I get it. I agree. All life is sacred, so you even got to protect the roaches. Right? It's not their fault they're like that. They didn't ask for this. I get it. We get it.

But then Medina preaches the new orthodoxy to Heidekker, a devoutness spread by the gun:

The shit in their blood that made them that way, the sickness they're carrying, that doesn't care about the sanctity of life, or the pain about who else is going to suffer. ... Every roach you save today you condemn God knows how many people to despair and misery tomorrow. You can't still see them as human. Understandable sentiment, granted, but it's misguided. We gotta take them out if humankind is gonna carry on in this world. That's just the hard truth. Gotta make sacrifices.

This religious zeal for blood-purity finds expression in the warrior's code for this military force: "Strong and Pure." Similarly, in the prison cell, Arquette reassures Stripe, "You ... you're protecting the bloodline. And that, my friend, is an honor." For Stripe, however, this ideology has been peeled from his eyes. He replies, "There's no honor here. Just killing. Lying and killing." His words summarize well the fervor and bare knuckles of neocon self-righteous belligerence.

Neocon primacy is replicated accurately in this *Black Mirror* episode as well. Early on, we learn that the military force we watch is on foreign soil and seemingly in the latter stages of a multinational operation. One trooper, Lennard (Kola Bokinni), complains, "Yo, how many roaches we got left out here? A couple a thousand? A couple a hundred if that? I mean back home we had millions, man. It only took two years to get shit back on track." As the facts of the situation unfold about who these roaches actually are, we come to realize that an American military has murdered—swiftly and efficiently—millions of Americans in a zealous campaign for genetic purity. That same military is now overseas carrying out that same fanatical mission. In Europe, however, the extermination process doesn't seem to be going as smoothly. Lennard also gripes about locals, such as Heidekker, who protect roaches: "Out here you got rustic fucks throwing 'em scraps. Man, it's no wonder it's takin' so long to mop shit up." Indications are, then, that this "V" regime emerged victorious from the global war ten years prior, that it stems from the former American state, and that it is currently engaged in a unilateral and international military action to enforce its doctrines around the globe. In short, this dystopian future holds up a (black) mirror to current-day neocon beliefs in American exceptionalism. Exactly like neocon thinking, this autocratic regime looks to preserve and extend an international order that accords with its principles and its material interests; it regards itself as a benevolent power liberating the world with its Manichean view that moral/genetic purity represents Good on earth, and thus acts as the deterrent to all Evil; it maintains as well that only its actions can provide peace and security to the world, and thus must have unconditional free reign around the globe. Fictionalized and distorted into this near-future authoritarian state, then, is the neocon Pax Americana, complete with its doctrine of "peace through strength" which means, really, preemptive military intervention abroad. Moreover, this despotic government reflects and exaggerates the authoritarian, right-wing drift of the Trump movement in the United States as well as the nationalist, anti-immigrant movements across the European Union. Like those neo-Nazi factions, the "V" regime espouses the fascist principle of racial—now expanded to species—"purity."

As awful as is the ideology driving this repressive authority, the primary target of "Men Against Fire" as a speculative satire is the means by which such beliefs are put into action—militarism. These near-future soldiers are in fact cyborgs. They have been implanted with some manner of brain–computer interface technology called "MASS." This technology enhances considerably their basic military capabilities: communications, tactical coordination, mission intelligence, targeting, and the like. With such augmentation, vital information appears before their eyes, an enemy can be reconnoitered by way of real-time drone camera feeds, assaults are planned using 3D projections of terrain maps and building blueprints. These are more skillful combatants because of MASS. They are also more proficient killers. Along with enabling enhanced interaction with military hardware, MASS alters the reality soldiers perceive in ways that ease the psychological burden of taking human life. Specifically, we discover that although the so-called roaches are in fact ordinary human beings, Stripe and the other soldiers experience them, by way of MASS, as "animals" and "monsters." To the soldiers, roaches have sharp, pointed teeth, broadened and flattened foreheads and noses, and they shriek and howl ferociously and incomprehensibly. These soldiers, then, sincerely believe that they are killing some kind of dangerous, subhuman, misshapen creatures—not people. As Catarina describes the situation to an unbelieving Stripe after his MASS programming has been disrupted: "You see me as I am. ... Your implants ... your Army implants ... They put it in your head to help you fight. And when it works, you see us as something other." In this way, MASS accomplishes in the virtual realm the aim of much modern war propaganda, namely, the rhetorical transformation of enemies and outsiders into animals, vermin, insects, and the like threating to invade, overrun, infest, and infect the homeland.[6] While this digital mind-manipulation of soldiers is appalling in itself, more unnerving is the idea that civilians know it takes place and are generally fine with it. When learning the awful truth of his situation, Stripe wrestles to understand this crucial point:

Stripe: The villagers ... huh? The locals ... they ... they ain't Army ... got no MASS in their heads. They're scared of the roaches. They hate the fucking things.
Catarina: Everybody hates us.
Stripe: But what the fuck do they see? Huh? Fuckin' civs ... when they look at a roach, what do they see?
Catarina: What you see now. They hate all the same because it's what they've been told.

For civilians, the usual channels of propaganda and ideological indoctrination are used by the state to instill fear of and hatred toward this selected enemy. For soldiers, however, something more certain and technologically advanced has been added: cybernetics. MASS *makes* soldiers see the enemy as nonhuman threats to civilization needing to be exterminated. Thus, in "Men Against Fire," we observe the hallmarks of neoconservative militarism. In order to sustain a worldwide preeminence and the ability to act singly, the "V" regime retains a massive, state-of-the-art military capability and the political will to use it. Obviously, such readiness and advanced weaponry (now featuring cyborg, mind-controlled troops) requires sustained high levels of defense spending. Alarmism and threat-inflation look to be in use as the way to justify these exorbitant military expenses. Moreover, whereas in the 20th and 21st centuries Communism and the War on Terror were used as vague, neverending, external threats to American and Western European society, in this dystopian world the genetic blight of so-called roaches serves as the excuse to militarize the state. In sum, the neoconservative imperative of maintaining and using overwhelming military power dominates the near future in this episode of *Black Mirror*, and the horrors of that false orthodoxy are laid open to our inspection.

The first 46 minutes of "Men Against Fire" are painful to watch. It's hard to witness Stripe, a good and forthright young man, come into the awful knowledge that, as he tells Raiman (Madeline Brewer) just before she knocks him out, "None of it's true." Where this Rant becomes excruciating to deal with, however, is over its last 14 minutes. The dénouement of the episode shows us how Stripe is ensnared outright by the Regime. Most of the finale takes place in a blank-white military prison cell where Stripe is being held. Stripe's panoptic cell, however, is far more extensive in its disciplining techniques than this one small room. MASS is not only an advanced weapon of war; it is an irrevocable instrument for the control of citizens. Whether an Army psychologist or a government official, Arquette incarnates the modern state in his long conversation with Stripe. It has become clear that a roach device introduced a virus into Stripe's MASS implant, shutting down its normal functions and thereby exposing Stripe to the veracities of his soldiering mission. For this reason—smiling, concerned, fatherly—Arquette begins the interview with: "Stripe, we owe you an apology. We didn't spot the fault in your MASS. I got you a coffee." During their talk, Arquette is never deceptive, always open and honest with Stripe about exactly what's going on. As the hegemon, Arquette can afford to be candid. He's holding all the cards—especially in the form of a small remote that controls Stripe's MASS. Part of Arquette's apology to Stripe involves a lesson in human behavior and military history. Instructs Arquette:

> Humans ... you know we give ourselves a bad rap, but we're genuinely empathetic as a species. I mean, we don't actually really wanna kill each other. Which is a good thing ... until your future depends on wiping out the enemy. ... Many years ago, I'm talking early 20th century, most soldiers didn't even fire their weapons. Or if they did they would just aim over the heads of the enemy. They did it on purpose.

At this point, we arrive at the crux of this *Black Mirror* episode. More than militarism, the special topic of "Men Against Fire" is precisely what that title signals: the problem of getting soldiers to kill one another.

The episode title is taken directly from a famous book by World War I veteran and World War II combat historian S. L. A. Marshall titled *Men Against Fire: The Problem of Battle Command* (1947). In it, Marshall states that during World War II, no more than a quarter of troops actually fired their weapons in battle, even when under threat, due to an innate reluctance to kill another human being. Arquette cites these very statistics and explains this military dilemma to Stripe as it occurred during the two World Wars of the 20th century. He also explains how the military set out to solve the problem: "So we adapted. Better training. Better conditioning. Then comes the Vietnam War and the shooting percentage goes up to 85. Lot of bullets flying. But kills were still low." Here, Arquette draws from the work of another well-known military historian, Dave Grossman. In his influential study, *On Killing: The Psychological Cost of Learning to Kill in War and Society* (1995), Grossman reports this improvement in the firing rates of U.S. soldiers.[7] However, accompanying the increase in a soldier's ability to shoot and to kill is an emotional and moral toll on the soldier. Admits Arquette of the Vietnam veteran: "Plus the guys who did get a kill, well, most of them came back all messed up in the head. And that's pretty much how things stayed until MASS came along." MASS, then, represents the technological breakthrough for which the Army has been waiting. The military could mentally discipline and physically condition troops into firing their weapons at a high rate, albeit not hitting their targets as much as command would like. But what the military could not do, before MASS, was overcome the psychological trauma troops frequently suffer as a result of killing and of the wartime experience. Now, however, with MASS, all that has changed, and Arquette is inordinately proud of this leap forward in martial power:

> You see MASS, well that's the ultimate military weapon. It helps you with your intel, your targeting, your comms, your conditioning. It's a lot easier to pull the trigger when you're aiming at the boogeyman. It's not just your eyes, though. Takes care of your other senses, too. You don't hear the shrieks. You don't smell the blood and the shit.

Stripe has been this ultimate military weapon: a neurologically enhanced, technologically adroit, ideologically sure, emotion- and moral-free killing instrument. In effect, when MASS is functional, Stripe is a first-person-shooter videogame avatar that does its killing in the *real* world. All MASS-enabled soldiers are. That's why they eagerly engage in "roach hunts" to compete with one another for the number of "kills" they can rack up and the rewards they can earn in the form of MASS-induced sex dreams at night. The virtual world walks now in our physical world. These soldiers are kids in an arcade—of global politics. As such, they are the absolute tools of the neoliberal/neoconservative hegemony.

In its dystopian projections, "Men Against Fire" condemns many aspects of present-day American militarism: global foray by overwhelming force, advanced weaponry used for unsavory aims, dehumanization in any number of forms, runaway military spending, official propaganda masking morally wrong policy. Yet, in the end what this episode denounces most is the destructive American popular sentiment of "support the troops." This mawkish, feel-good commonplace enables civilians to hide from themselves not only the brutal realities of combat and of military service, but the fact that this onerous service is performed nowadays by an infinitesimal portion of the American population culled disproportionately from the underclass.[8] Even more seriously, empty mantras of "support the troops" and "thanks for your service" allow the political leadership to manipulate the citizenry—purblind civilian and spellbound soldier alike. Such manipulation is exactly what's taking place in "Men Against Fire." In his final attempt to justify MASS, Arquette tells Stripe:

> Don't feel bad about doing your job. The villagers won't do it. The folks back home won't do it. They don't have MASS. MASS lets you do it.

Arquette pitches the brain implant as some kind of beneficial and enabling gift from the military that allows Stripe, without too much harm to himself, to perform an honorable and necessary duty to the state—a responsibility that regular civilians are unable and, more to the point, unwilling to do. Stripe, however, is not buying this bureaucrat deceit. He understands now how the Army has turned him into a device of "lying and killing." He further understands that the civilian population approves and permits his neurological–psychological–ideological subjugation under the control of MASS. Far from supporting the troops, civilians enslave them. Their professed good wishes along with the supposed largess of the state are in fact a hoax. As viewers of this *Black Mirror* episode, the same critical reexamination of our own social order should be hitting us. We are being goaded into uncomfortable realizations of our own. Foremost among these is that if the general population is relieved to be able to shirk military service, then we should not be surprised when the state exploits the powerless and the voiceless to fill its military ranks. Slogans such as "Be All You Can Be," "Army of One," "Army Strong," "Warriors Wanted" (actual recruiting catchphrases) as well as "Strong and Pure" and "Protecting the Bloodline" (fictive mottos of this episode) serve multiple purposes. They lure recruits with calls of patriotic duty and adventure coupled with promises of personal and social betterment. At the same time, they assuage the guilt of civilians with the hope that, if these troops survive the military relatively unscathed, at least they will have served a righteous cause and been given the opportunity for a bit of upward mobility. All of these assurances and outcomes, of course, are problematic. In the cautionary Menippean tale of "Men Against Fire," advances in computer technology have been brought to bear on this vexing situation. For the fictional "V" regime, MASS is a panacea. Not only does it make its soldiers lethal, but it also renders irrelevant all of the troublesome personal and social issues facing America today with regard to its all-volunteer force. In this near-future setting, soldiers kill without conscience and civilians sleep easier at night confident that they're doing right by their troops. Their heroic defenders of freedom are not being subjected to the mental and emotional turmoil of war. Their troops are living a happy and rewarding virtual reality while doing the dirty work of the nation. MASS provides a win for everyone—but particularly for the power brokers running this modern state.

The authorities of "V" appear to be wholly unencumbered in pursuing their ideological agenda of eugenics.

When the roach computer virus peels MASS away from Stripe, he is savvy and strong enough to want nothing more to do with this cynical state business. He rejects the neoconservative militarism into which, digitally, he has been indoctrinated. Stripe is not so lucky, however, when it comes to escaping the neoliberal state. Stripe has suffered dividuation in that a portion of his total being—basically, his physicality—has been appropriated for military service. The Army only needs his body for the purpose of turning it into an automaton. Stripe's thinking and feeling mind, as we see, only interferes with this new form of computer-guided military duty. What is more, this fracturing of Stripe's individuality looks to have been an act of predatory dividuation. In the "consent video" Arquette shows to Stripe, we watch enlistee Stripe—a naïve, undereducated, working-class youngster—nonchalantly apply his thumbprint to an agreement he obviously does not fully comprehend. The agreement is not only for him to allow the implantation of MASS, but that he be programmed to forget that he agreed to it. Says the voice of the unseen Army recruiter: "It's kinda like hypnosis. ... Part of what you're agreeing to is not realizing you've been put in this state. ... You won't recall this conversation." The phenomenon of interpellation works in much the same way—we absorb many cultural practices and beliefs unwittingly—yet it fixes an ideology nowhere near as firmly in the citizen as does MASS. A person's cultural beliefs and assumptions about the world can change with experience; with MASS, the soldier's worldview is altogether in the hands of authority. Once it becomes clear to Arquette that he won't be able to coax Stripe back into military service, in good neoliberal fashion he holds Stripe to this contract. In a decidedly less congenial tone of voice, Arquette advises Stripe:

> No one lied to you. ... You agreed to have your MASS implant put in ... set up. Every soldier does. We can't just embed it and feed you a dream. Your mind would reject it. You have to accept it. Willingly. That's exactly what you did.

Obvious questions are begged here. How freely did Stripe actually enter into this contract? Was he sufficiently informed to comprehend all of its ramifications? Did he have other realistic, living-wage employment options available to him? The answers to all of these questions clearly tilt in favor of the state. Stripe is a ragdoll, a debt-laborer, amid neoliberal forces. Just like America's Army today, this military of a dystopian near-future is an all-volunteer outfit laden with socially disadvantaged young people who have been misled and pushed into a condition of, in practice, debt peonage. As Stripe's neoliberal boss, Arquette sternly gives his indentured employee two options. Neither one is particularly optional. The first is for Stripe to agree to have his MASS reset and programmed so that he forgets all of these recent unpleasant events. He will revert to being an unaware killing machine. To that option Stripe adamantly replies: "I ain't havin' this MASS shit! No more no way!" Option two, then, is for Stripe to be kept in a prison cell watching, via his MASS-controlled mind, a perpetual loop of how he really killed those roaches—meaning the people he was made to murder in the farmhouse. With his remote, Arquette gives Stripe a taste of what that permanent incarceration would be like. Stripe is horrified to experience the undistorted killings he carried out, screaming finally, "Make it stop!" Arquette has Stripe over a barrel—the barrel of workplace abuse in the extreme. Like all neoliberal workers, Stripe is only free to lose: no options offered by management ever work in his favor. Equally, the dispossession of Stripe's individual agency means the accumulation by his superiors of their political and, no doubt, economic aims. The wealthy and the powerful take all while Stripe is dissevered and obligated into oblivion. As Stripe recovers from writhing on the floor in emotional agony, Arquette gallingly places a compassionate hand on the soldier's back, renewing his kindhearted display. Arquette speaks softly:

> We can make that go away. This conversation goes away, too. All of it. But you gotta say the word. Just say the word, Stripe, and it all goes away. ... Just say the word.

Maybe the cruelest lie of all in the neoliberal state is the illusion of individual choice and free will.

A brief coda at the end of the episode drives home painfully all these modern outrages. A blank-faced Stripe is shown riding in an official SUV. He's coming home to Mayfield, a rural community with grain silos, farm windmills, and a church steeple dotting the landscape. By the road signs, we see that Max's Diner features Daily Specials for $5.00. A large billboard displays the giant "V" insignia beside a young family cavorting on a sunny beach somewhere. They look to be savoring their genomic wholesomeness. Further down the road, a property owner flies the "V" flag, likely as a sign of pride and support. Patently, we are in small-town (onetime) America. Lest we're in any doubt about Stripe's economic status, the SUV drops him off in front of a dilapidated house in a rundown neighborhood. The house looks abandoned, boarded-up and covered with graffiti, to include a conspicuous dollar sign. What Stripe sees, however, through his MASS-clouded eyes is a freshly painted, immaculately landscaped abode with banners hung on the front porch reading Welcome Home. In soft focus and enriched colors, Stripe's dream-girl emerges from the house—smiling, inviting, overjoyed to see him. The tears rolling down Stripe's cheeks and the smile that slowly comes to his face—while in reality he stands by himself in front of an empty dump—signal that Stripe said the word to Arquette. What other "option" had he? And, by the way, MASS also solves the problem of expenditures for veterans benefits of any kind. There's no need to provide health care, psychological counseling, job training, or any other assistance to reentering civilian life when the state simply and cost-effectively can feed its vets a wonderful dreamlife.

"Late," *The Handmaid's Tale* (season 1, episode 3, 2017)

The special topic of *The Handmaid's Tale*, novel or television series, is the oppressive extreme of patriarchy. Or of hyperreligious patriarchy. Or of hypocritical American evangelical Christian patriarchy. All labels apply. When discussing Atwood's novel in Chapter 3, I state that it's impossible for readers to miss the many shocking cruelties of both patriarchy and religiosity depicted in those pages. Far from grace abounding for sins (Romans 5:20), neoconservative thuggery abounds in the Republic of Gilead. I note as well, however, that it is less evident in the novel how Offred, and all women, are likewise the victims of neoliberal economics working in partnership with fundamentalist Christianity. While the repression of liberal–conservative discourse is equally engrained in Gilead, its functioning is not foregrounded in the book. In the expanded narrative world of the television series, though, such background details of the novel can become more fully realized and quite poignant pieces of the storyline. Such is the case for the economic disenfranchisement of women in Hulu's production of *The Handmaid's Tale*. In the episode titled "Late," the third of ten instalments for the first season of the show, considerable backstory is related as to how the architects of Gilead seized power from the federal republic of the United States of America. Highlighted in this early episode is the Draconian economic dispossession of women that led to their ensuing commodification, in particular, the expropriation of their reproductive bodies. To close the present Chapter, I focus on these fiscal aspects of this Rant.

The Hulu series amplifies alarmingly the viciousness of the Gilead regime. What only can be described or alluded to in the novel finds depiction on screen, and the series-makers shy away from nothing in the way of disturbing moments, events, and images. Viewers see executions, torture, ceremonies of pious rape, blazing guns of martial law, terrorism by police state discipline and control, various kinds of degradation at the hands of fanatical authority, and above all else the desperately private and isolating misery of bondage. All of these acts are carried out "under His eye," meaning in the name of the irate Old Testament God. The stripping away of women's economic rights numbers among these depictions of stark violence by the usurping zealots. In the novel, those events are described by Offred's narrative voice in Chapter 28, over roughly ten pages (223–233). They are telling details that add to our understanding of the sexism and rancor of the Gilead ruling elite, but they come across as finer points nonetheless, recalled sparingly and far after the fact. In the series episode "Late," however, these incidents are brought vividly to life as key memories for Offred (Elisabeth Moss) impacting her political awakening and furthering her bloody-minded determination to survive and to resist the Gilead theocracy. In voiceover at the start of the episode, Offred comments bitterly on her former life as June Osborne:

> Now I'm awake to the world. I was asleep before. That's how we let it happen. When they slaughtered Congress we didn't wake up. When they blamed terrorists and suspended the Constitution, we didn't wake up then

either. They said it would be temporary. Nothing changes instantaneously. In a gradually heating bathtub you'd be boiled to death before you know it.

During the episode, the cautionary tale Offred plays back in her head is the string of events leading up to the financial disempowerment of women. She sees now how once that vital bit of oppressive control had been put into place, the fundamentalist faction could commence its outright hostile takeover of the state. Thus, the crux of Offred's political warning—that is, the gradually heating bathtub—is the erosion of women's rights, principally the economic wherewithal of women. These were the pivotal incremental changes that led to the death of democracy in the dystopian world of *The Handmaid's Tale*. Evangelical Christian sexism, then, is the false orthodoxy being blamed and against which we are being forewarned. In the 1980s, when Atwood wrote her novel, she was battling such dogmata in the form of the Reagan presidency and the anti-Equal Rights Amendment movement of Phyllis Schlafly. Currently, such right-wing anti-woman tenets and policy exist, likely even more dangerously, in the Trump administration, the Supreme Court, and the Republican-controlled states passing malicious and unconstitutional anti-abortion laws in an effort to reverse Roe v. Wade. The Menippean targets of the television series, of course, involve our current cultural and political moment. Hulu's *The Handmaid's Tale* has become something of a feminist and anti-Trump protest movement in its own right. In covering the events of the novel, Season 1 makes trenchant observations about the sexism of American conservatism in general, notwithstanding the show's being scripted and in production prior to the 2016 election. Seasons 2, 3, and 4, however, offer original storyline created after Trump's controversial election and therefore level criticisms aimed more frankly at the goings-on surrounding the misogynistic, impulsive, and boorish president. At a time when the rights of women blatantly are being chipped away at by Trump's minions, this television series sensationalizes the patriarchal threat immediately at hand as well as dramatizes the dogged solidarity required to push back against it.[9] At the heart of this confrontation is the matter of women as autonomous social agents.

If one of the primary goals of the Sons of Jacob coup d'état is to seize and control the reproductive rights of women, rendering women as defenseless and as dependent on men as possible are crucial preliminary steps in that plan. In Offred's flashbacks, we see exactly this strategy taking place. The first is her recalling an unpleasant encounter at a coffeeshop when she and her good friend, Moira (Samira Wiley), had finished a jog. When buying coffee, June's credit card is denied. The young man behind the cash register is not only unhelpful and unsympathetic, he's asinine and rude to the two women. Apparently commenting on their being dressed in tight-fitting running garb, the lout snaps at them: "Fucking sluts. Get the fuck outta here." In hindsight, Offred realizes how this was an early sign not only of her coming bankruptcy but also of sexist men emboldened by the aggressive reassertion of old-style male chauvinism. Later, when June is at her workplace and on a long hold trying to call her credit card company, armed and black-clad paramilitary goons invade the floor of her office building. Under obvious duress, the boss, Roger (Michael Caruana), gathers the employees together to make an announcement:

> Ladies, you should all know that I feel really sorry about this. It isn't my decision. I don't have a choice. I have to let you go. I have to let you all go. ... You can't work here anymore. It's the law now. ... I don't have a choice. They gave me ten minutes, please just ... just pack up your things.

Upset and confused as they are forced to leave the building under the intimidating glare of the armed men, one woman wonders, "Why'd they send the army?" Another woman answers, "I don't think that's the army." June offers, "I think that's another kind of army." Once more, Offred marks this as a moment when she and the general population allowed rights and liberties, albeit perforce, to slip away instead of standing up to oppressive power.

Later still in the episode, in a prolonged flashback, Offred remembers the definitive moment when, in her apartment, she and Moira discover that their economic legs have been cut out from beneath them. Getting off a phone call, Moira reports, "Sounds like they just froze any account with an F on it instead of an M." When June protests that, "I have four thousand dollars in that account. They can't just take it," Moira replies, "We made it easy. All they needed to do was just push a few buttons." Moira also reports that "there's a new law: women can't own property anymore." Again, June is incredulous: "Wait! *What?* Are you fucking serious?" Moira has not only the latest developments in the situation, but the keener political insight into what is actually taking place. She tells June:

> Luke can use your account. They'll transfer the money to him. Or that's what they're saying. Husbands or male next-of-kin. You know, they needed to do it this way. All the bank accounts and the jobs all at the same time. You imagine the airports otherwise? They don't want us leaving. You can bet on that.

The control of fertile women's bodies has been the high-priority play of the Gilead takeover all along, and Moira sees those tactics now falling into place. When June naïvely repeats the official lies that the imposition of martial law had been to protect the populace and facilitate the capture of the terrorists who massacred Congress, Moira scoffs, "Maybe there never were any terrorists." None, that is, but the Sons of Jacob themselves. At this point, the overthrow of the United States is all but complete. June's husband, Luke, enters the room at this moment. After hearing all the bad news, he reassures the women, "Well, we'll figure it out. This can't last." He also offers comfort to his now penniless spouse by saying, "Come on. You know I'll take care of you." Understandably, Luke's well-meaning but victimless calm sets off Moira. Reacting to Luke's patronizing readiness to "take care of my wife," Moira fumes:

My *wife?* She doesn't belong to you. No, no, no, she isn't your property and she doesn't need you to take care of her. You see, that's where all of this comes from. You want to take care of us because we're weak, right? Because we're less than. ... *"I'll take care of your money. I'll take care of your body."* You know, you're the fucking problem, you know that?

Moira is correct in that men cannot experience patriarchy as a threat unless somehow they are set in open defiance to it. Otherwise, they can always remain safely complicit no matter what they think of the sexist ideology itself. In due course, Luke will be one of these men to challenge the Gilead patriarchy, and Moira knows that he is, at heart, a good guy. Still, his mansplaining and supercilious offhandedness as a reaction to women being rendered economic nonentities needs slapping down.[10] More to the point of the episode, Luke's blasé reaction to the tightening grip of Gilead confirms Offred's hard realization: people living comfortably in the bubble of a seemingly safe democracy are slow to wake up and loathe to admit that authoritarian control is on the rise. This admonition applies to self-governing citizenry worldwide, but particularly in today's America. The Sons of Donald, after all, are busily working to curtail or revoke not just the rights of women, but as many individual and communal rights as suits their traditionalist agenda.

Offred's final flashback in "Late" depicts the point at which push came to shove for the citizens publicly opposing the new and restrictive theocratic laws. June and Moira are in the front lines of an energetic protest rally, face-to-face with a row of ominously well-equipped riot police. Passions are raw, and protesters shout obscenities and wave signs bearing slogans such as "Enough is Enough," "Human Rights = Women's Rights," and demands to restore "Democracy." What these demonstrators don't know is that finally the decision has been made by the zealous brotherhood to drop its charade of noble intentions. The imposition of martial law was never going to be temporary, nor did this evangelical splinter group ever mean to restore the Constitution of the American republic. Instead, this criminal faction has gained enough leverage now to establish its own rule by way of an iron fist. With no warning, the police open fire on the crowd with automatic weapons, killing protesters wantonly. In the panic to flee the onslaught, June and Moira take cover, ironically enough, in the same coffeeshop where earlier their harassment as women began. Now, however, instead of being badgered by a conservative twerp, they watch tracer-bullets whiz by, cringe as people are gunned down in the street, and cover when explosives shatter the storefront windows. For June/Offred, it is a racking moment of knowledge-too-late. The Republic of Gilead has arisen, and democratic principles play no part in its authority.

Absolutely basic to this repressive state, moreover, is its slow removal of personal liberties and agency to the point where a new oppressive normal is established and then concretized into permanent restrictive practices and powers. In this method, the Gilead state mirrors the neoliberal state, the former's treatment of women specifically matching exactly the latter's disempowerment and abuse of workers generally. A Handmaid is a woman valued only for her active ovaries, similar to the bare commodity of labor used for whatever rudimentary function an owner has need. The whole person, possessing certain inalienable rights, is of no interest and in fact considerably inconvenient to the Commander/employer making use of the Handmaid/worker for his own purposes. Thus, the minimalization of human rights and civil protections, particularly in the areas of labor, voting, education, and the economy, is exceedingly useful for turning people into toiling things. In Gilead, all women have become categories of commodity, labeled and color-coded for their particular utility. Handmaids wear red and bear children for the ruling class. Wives wear blue or turquoise and oversee the households of Commanders. Marthas work as cooks and housekeepers in those households, wearing green. Aunts wear brown and are responsible for the training (brutalizing) and managing (terrorizing) of Handmaids. Econowives are lower-class women who perform a variety of menial jobs while wearing gray. Jezebels are sex workers in the secret brothels of the Commanders, these women being costumed in a variety of revealing outfits. Women who openly defy the patriarchy of Gilead are designated as Unwomen and, when captured, sent to the Colonies where they work until dead cleaning up toxic waste. None of these women are paid for their work, nor can they handle money or own property, nor are they allowed to read. All of these functions of the Gilead state compel the dividuation of women from persons into productive parts. All of these enforced roles for women, even that of Wives, feature absolute wealth and power inequity compared to men. Workplace abuse, to say the least, is at an extreme for most of the women of Gilead. Given that, by Gilead law, they owe their financial existence to men, women are in the inescapable position as well of being debt-laborers trapped in debt peonage. The entire organization of Gilead, then, is designed for male accumulation by way of female dispossession. The most egregious and dystopian occurrence of this exploitation, needless to say, is that of the rape and forced childbearing undergone by Handmaids, followed by the abduction of the child by the fundamentalist Christian state. Throughout this fatherland, Foucauldian panoptic surveillance ensures Deleuzian identity control. Current-day Republican Party ideology is not far removed from these goals.

Woven into the flashbacks of "Late" is the contemporary and wretched story of Emily (Alexis Bledel). As Ofglen, Emily has been the shopping companion of Offred, and in the previous episode these two Handmaids managed to establish a private and rebellious bond. At the beginning of episode 3, however, Offred is alarmed to discover that Ofglen has been taken into custody by the Eyes, the Gilead secret police. A new Ofglen—a different woman—has been substituted in. For the rest of the episode, viewers follow intermittently Emily's moving through the criminal "justice" system of Gilead. It's not a happy path. Emily has been labeled a "gender traitor" because she's a lesbian; she's been charged with "gender treachery" because she's been discovered having a sexual affair with a Martha. Gagged by leather muzzles, the two terrified women are hauled before a kangaroo court where, in under a minute of lawyer and judge citing twisted scripture, sentencing is passed. The Martha is to be hanged—something Emily will be forced to watch—but the Handmaid, due to her viable ovaries, is "sentenced to redemption." In Gilead, few things sound more menacing. Emily's redemption is an involuntary clitorectomy. After this female genital-mutilation surgery, she wakes in a hospital ward, confused by where she is and what's happened to her, to find her crotch bandaged over. The heinous Aunt Lydia (Ann Dowd) enters to explain events to the repackaged Handmaid:

> The stitches will come out in a few days. I know this is a shock for you, Emily. You can still have children, of course. But things will be so much easier for you now. … You won't want what you cannot have. Blessed be the fruit, dear.

"Late" ends with a series of close-ups on Emily as shock, disbelief, agony, and rage come across her face. She has been reduced thoroughly to a baby-making thing. Her scream of outrage is as a person left both object and abject. No matter what the special topic of a Rant—racism, militarism, patriarchy—we find visible in it the dehumanizing functioning of the Regime. Neoliberalism puts profit over people. Neoconservatism punishes those who resist.

Notes

1 Critics have noted how this combination of manipulating black minds and taking custody of black bodies figures aptly the colloquial concepts of the "Uncle Tom" or the "Oreo"—that is, race betrayers who are black on the outside but white on the inside. Comments Weston of Peele's elaborate invention of the sunken place: "It is the more generous term, for it suggests not duplicity, but brainwashing or conditioning beyond the perpetrator's control. Such is the impact of *Get Out*, a film that has provided new language for thinking about race simply by considering the essence of black anxiety" (38). The After Globalism Writing Group similarly observes of Peele's sci-fi *novum*: "by fabulating an incredible theory of mind in which a white brain could take over a black one while leaving the black consciousness intact and floating somewhere in inner space, it also recalls the deep, perhaps fatal, sympathy behind the invective. Black on the outside, black on the inside" (40).
2 Think of how Thomas Shadwell is excoriated by Dryden in *Mac Flecknoe* or how Pope takes to task rival poets, prime ministers, and kings of England in *The Dunciad*.
3 In order to skewer a rival playwright, Dryden concocts an elaborate mock-coronation of Shadwell being crowned king of the realm of Nonsense. As a royalist, Dryden intends no disrespect toward or criticism of the trappings and traditions of monarchy; rather, he employs those grand things as a means to represent Shadwell even more low and ridiculous.
4 The name Armitage comes from Middle English meaning "hermitage," which stems from the Old French "ermitage." If Peele is naming characters with such significance in mind, the isolated Armitage estate can be seen as a white enclave looking to remain separate from the larger multiracial world.

5 In her study of gender in modern horror films, Carol J. Clover coins the term "final girl" to describe the stock character, especially in slasher films, who faces off against the monster or psychopathic killer at the end of the movie. This character often possesses special qualities the audience is meant to identify with and to admire.
6 See, for example, the study by Steuter and Wills, *At War with Metaphor: Media, Propaganda, and Racism in the War on Terror*. While the tropes of animal, insect, and infection are used routinely in the west nowadays to characterize so-called terrorists, Trump and other rightwing fear-mongers likewise use these terms to vilify immigrants and other, in their view, undesirable groups.
7 For an overview of the studies by Marshall and Grossman, as well as a reading of this *Black Mirror* episode from the standpoint of its demonstrating a "weaponized perspective" and a "submission to machinic vision," see Roger Stahl's book, *Through the Crosshairs* (150–151).
8 For this current state of affairs with regard to the U.S. military, see Jennifer Mittelstadt's *The Rise of the Military Welfare State*. See as well Andrew Bacevich's study, *Breach of Trust*, as well as Beth Bailey's *America's Army*.
9 For the television series critiquing the age of Trump, see as well articles by Heather Hendershot and by John Duncan Talbird. Hendershot in particular comments: "*The Handmaid's Tale* obviously resonates strongly with many viewers as an allegorical, science-fictional response to the Trump administration; the five Emmys, two Golden Globes, and Peabody Award that the show has won after only one year not only nod to the program's high quality but also acknowledge it as a valuable response to dire current events" (18). Both Hendershot (20) and Talbird (121) comment as well on the effective use of flashbacks in the series, and in particular in the episode "Late." With regard to Margaret Atwood's relationship to the series, she is not involved but neither is she disapproving of the additions to her premise (see Brown).
10 Not long before Atwood wrote *The Handmaid's Tale* in 1985, American women economically were restricted by law from such activities as keeping a job when pregnant, reporting sexual harassment in the workplace, getting a credit card, and getting a divorce with a reasonable degree of ease. See the article in *Ms. Magazine* by Natasha Turner titled "10 Things That American Women Could Not Do Before the 1970s."

6 Neoliberal A.I.

In Chapter 1, I outline the salient qualities of monstrosity as they pertain to speculative satire. Monsters can function as unnerving, Derridean binary-busters. As representations of scapegoated social Others—paradoxically excluded *from* dominant society while arising from *within* that dominant society—monsters can expose the arbitrary functioning of social power in its creation of a "normal" and "universal" that is, in fact, random and artificial. Monsters can both police borders and entice us to cross them, disciplining and undermining discipline at once. Monsters can embody the *novum* of science fiction, their strange newness defying known categories in ways that trigger cognitive estrangement, thoughtful perplexity, and the critical reassessment of existing social order. Monsters can flip binaries as well as erase them, inverting ostensive pairings of good/evil and human/beast in ways that render the customary as monstrous.

In the analyzes of Rants undertaken in the preceding chapters, we've seen these phenomena of monstrosity at work. We've considered seemingly terrifying creatures that turn out to be sympathetic and admirable beings: the Prawns in *District 9*, the Na'vi in *Avatar*, V in *V for Vendetta*, the roaches in "Men Against Fire." More often the case, we've seen powerful modern organizations—government, military, commercial—the purposes of which ostensibly are to serve, protect, and improve the lives of citizens, in fact oppress, terrorize, and exploit substantial segments of the population in the pursuit of monstrous domination and greed. The real evildoers in these Rants, then, have been revealed to be the rich and powerful humans, and mainly men, who control the laws, weaponry, finances, and hegemonic discourse of the society: the Commanders of Gilead, the government of "V," the residents of Elysium. Like gender, monstrosity is not performed only in an essential body, in this case, that of a nonhuman entity. Most of the wicked beasts we've considered in this study have been successful and powerful tycoons, politicians, and professionals of various kinds—that is, for the most part, modern corporation types. Up to this point, strange creatures have not figured overly much in the Menippean narratives examined. The purpose of this final chapter, however, is to round out my explication of the Rant by considering a kind of nonhuman monster that appears often in speculative satire, namely, A.I. More so than space aliens or bizarre organic creatures, A.I. has become something of the monster of choice

DOI: 10.4324/9781003110491-7

for Rants. As a machine created by the Regime, A.I. proves versatile to the satirist as a polemic tool brought into play to interrogate the neoliberal status quo.

In recent decades, A.I. is on the rise as a story element used in films, series, and fiction. No doubt, this is because A.I. in our everyday reality is ever more with us. In many forms, both apparent and unseen, A.I. is a fact of modern life now that shows no signs of going away. To the contrary, many experts in the field worry about our overexposure to A.I., about its lack of regulatory oversight, or, in the extreme, about its eventually supplanting humans.[1] Indeed, depictions of hostile A.I. such as in *The Matrix* and *The Terminator* films have taken root in the popular imagination. My task here, though, is not to delve into the algorithmic intricacies of A.I. or to judge its merits and dangers. Instead, I will discuss some ways A.I. is used in Rants to build arguments against destructive social and economic doctrine. Currently, there looks to be three prominent stories being told about our relationship with A.I. First is its using us for nefarious purposes. Second is our using it for nefarious purposes. Third is its wanting to be us as well as our wanting to be it in a weird jumble of hybridity and impending singularity.[2] Often these strains overlap, but underlying all three imaginative expressions of the human/A.I. binary is malicious neoliberalism at work. I review each of these three storylines below.

Its Using Us

The Circle (2013), by Dave Eggers, is not a particularly satisfying novel (and was made into an abysmal movie), but it is quite a good Menippean satire. With it, Eggers explores A.I. in its most feasibly terrifying form at the moment: social media. Eggers does not give us sentient A.I. turning human beings into batteries or manufacturing war machines to eradicate the human race. Instead, he portrays what I have called elsewhere a *cultural* form of A.I., namely, the corporation "as an organizational and ideological ersatz entity that has got out of control ... and that now threatens to destroy its maker" (Combe and Boyle 216). This manner of Frankenstein monster is not a corporeal creature run amok but a Foucauldian mode of instrumental modern power devised by some to control the behavior of many that, moreover, has come to dominate modern society as "normal." As a faux life form, the corporation is, in Foucault's terms, a discipline that combines goals, forms of communication, and power relations for the purpose of achieving specific social ends ("Subject and Power" 136–137, 140–141). In the fictious internet company The Circle, Eggers renders exactly this kind of disciplinary creature at work. Using advanced Information Technology (IT) as its mode of communication, The Circle—a thinly disguised representation of Facebook—turns itself into an omnipotent social media platform extending its commercial control into governmental control as well. In 2011, while on the presidential campaign trail, Mitt Romney made the manifestly insane declaration that, "Corporations are people, my friend." Corporations are *not* people but, because of the 2010 *Citizens United* decision by the U.S. Supreme Court granting significantly enhanced "personhood" legal status to these organizations, they are now, in effect, artificial organisms capable of exerting tremendous (if not ultimate) influence over the modern world. To be clear, then, the A.I. discussed in this chapter is *not* a human-level intelligence flexing its alien acumen against us. Instead, the A.I. we see depicted in Rants is an entity spawned by neoliberalism that takes the form of modern corporate culture misusing IT and other advanced technologies to achieve its profit-over-people goals. To spell out this dynamic more tangibly, the monster in many Rants is a *neoliberal* synthetic being that combines two powerful elements: ideology and machinery. In *The Circle*, that first element, the ideologically driven and structured company, has complete control over that second element, the machinery in the form of both hardware and software, making the corporation an indomitable force held in the hands of an elite, rich, technocratic few. What is more, the corporate modus operandi of such companies—and of The Circle in particular—is that of surveillance capitalism as theorized by Shoshana Zuboff (see Chapter 2 above). The Circle unilaterally claims human experience as free raw data to gather first as an asset to monetize then as a means to shape not only consumer behavior but the behavior of citizens of the modern state.

Social media has always masqueraded as a benign and unifying activity designed to connect family and friends as well as promote worldwide communication, goodwill, and understanding. As a speculative satire, *The Circle* torpedoes this corporate bullshit by exposing social media for what it is: a predatory dividuation scheme of unparalleled reach and influence. As a business, The Circle (like Facebook and Instagram) is devised solely to extend its range for the purposes of advertising and selling products. Beneath the carefully crafted veneer of communitarian ethos and mission, The Circle exists to monetize social media as an out-and-out capitalist endeavor. Two core practices of The Circle signal this for-profit raison d'être: the "Conversion Rate" and "Retail Raw." As part of her training as a new employee at The Circle, focal character Mae Holland has these expectations explained to her. The Conversion Rate is described by a trainer, Gina, as follows:

> … the Circle would not exist, and would not grow, and would not be able to get closer to completing the Circle, if there were not actual purchases being made, actual commerce spurred. We're here to be a gateway to all the world's information, but we are supported by advertisers who hope to reach customers through us, right?
>
> (249)

The key to stimulating purchases is for the social media followers of Circle employees to be influenced by the product recommendations they make. Specifies Gina: "So every purchase initiated or prompted by a recommendation you make raises your Conversion Rate. If your purchase or recommendation spurs fifty others to take the same action, then your CR is x50." Gina points out the astronomical Conversion Rates of some of the star Circlers, observing, "They've accumulated enough credibility that their followers trust their recommendations implicitly, and are deeply thankful for the surety in their shopping." Unthinking brand loyalty, even to the absurd point of gratitude, is of course the advertiser's dream. As for the other data point expected of Mae, Retail Raw, Gina explains: "It's just the gross retail price of the commerce you've stoked. Fun, right?" (252). As sales targets for Mae, Gina stipulates that "the minimum expectation for high-functioning Circlers is a conversion rate of x2.50, and a weekly Retail Raw of $45,000, both of which are modest goals that most Circlers far exceed" (252–253). In other words, The Circle is raking in cash hand-over-fist, due not only to the blind devotion of its social media followers, but even more to the drinking of the corporate Kool-Aid by its employees—of whom Mae is a prime example. Over the course of the novel, instead of chaffing at the happy noise of The Circle, Mae buys into its hype wholeheartedly. Her reaction to the performance measures of Conversion Rate and Retail Raw, for example, is: "She loved the notion of actually being able to track the effect of her tastes and endorsements" (252). Mesmerized employees leading by the nose enthralled consumers: what more can a neoliberal business model desire? Such a situation seems the apotheosis of the business practice Zuboff terms "instrumentarianism," that is, the conditioning of people, by means of digital surveillance and manipulation, to behave in ways that are profitable not to themselves, but toward the ends of an elite few (8). Mae not only willing becomes the employee-subject The Circle wants her to be, but she avidly participates in the subjugation of Circle consumers.

The Circle achieves this level of brainwashed devotion via the panoptic mechanisms of surveillance and discipline. In particular, social media is a potent example of Foucault's concept of productive modern power:

> What makes power hold good, what makes it accepted, is simply the fact that it doesn't only weigh on us as a force that says no; it also traverses and produces things, it induces pleasure, forms knowledge, produces discourse. It needs to be considered as a productive network that runs through the whole social body, much more than as a negative instance whose function is repression.
>
> ("Truth and Power" 307)

At the moment, the internet represents the *ne plus ultra* of a set of actions upon other actions running through the whole social body generating pleasure, knowledge, and discourse. The regime of power created and enforced by The Circle, then, is a softcore tyranny that seduces and persuades participation from users. Mae is both regimented and shamed into being a social media slave. Early in her training, she is told about her "Participation Rank," which is "an algorithm-generated number that takes into account all your activity in the InnerCircle." All of Mae's posts, comments, and attendance at Circle functions will be calculated basically as a loyalty test to the company. Gina assures Mae that her involvement in the "PartiRank" is purely voluntary:

> And again, it's just for fun. You're not judged by your rank or anything. Some Circlers take it very seriously, of course, and we love it

when people want to participate, but the rank is really just a fun way to see how your participation manifests itself vis-à-vis the overall Circle community. Okay?

(101)

Given how lucky one has to be to land a job at The Circle, working on its lavish "campus" and enjoying the many wonderful benefits provided by the company (to include an extraordinary healthcare plan), Mae would be, of course, a fool not to dive headfirst into its dominant corporate culture. As she does, Circle trainers keep larding on social media tasks for Mae to accomplish, accompanied by more and more screens at her desk for her to track. PartiRank gets expanded to PPT, "Passion, Participation and Transparency" (185), where Circlers are supposed to share absolutely every interest they have and every hobby or activity they undertake with all other Circlers. In its drive to force a superficial cohesion among its workers—all for the sake of improved commercial advertising, of course—this giant tech corporation equates privacy with low self-esteem and selfishness, while "transparency" is made out to be the height of not only sociability but of social responsibility.

When pressing Mae to improve her PPT profile, another trainer, Denise, discomfits her by saying,

> Mae, I'm no psychologist, but if I were, I might have a question about your sense of self-worth. We've studied some models for this kind of behavior. Not to say this kind of attitude is antisocial, but it's certainly *sub*-social, and certainly far from transparent.
>
> (189)

This panoptic disciplining brings about its desired effect on the new worker:

> After the interview, at her desk, Mae scolded herself. What kind of person was she? More than anything, she was ashamed. She'd been doing the bare minimum. She disgusted herself ... *Goddamnit, Mae, give a shit!* she thought. *Be a person of some value to the world.*
>
> (190–191)

In due course, Mae becomes the model social media workhorse for the company, responding to a quota of 500 consumer questions per day as part of the "CircleSurveys" that certain promising employees are asked to take, purportedly as "a reward, an honor" (228). All of this digital multitasking Mae carries out both while at her work desk, on top of doing her primary job as a Customer Experience representative for The Circle, as well as on her "own" time, since she's rarely unplugged from the internet. Mae becomes knowingly and constantly visible in her virtual panoptic cell, and, as a prisoner of this modern mechanism of power, learns to self-impose the ideology of The Circle, assuring the automatic functioning of its neoliberal agenda. Foucault describes the ideal implementation of the panopticon thus:

> So to arrange things that the surveillance is permanent in its effects, even if it is discontinuous in its action; that the perfection of power should tend to render its actual exercise unnecessary; that this architectural apparatus should be a machine for creating and sustaining a power relation independent of the person who exercises it; in short, that the inmates should be caught up in a power situation of which they are themselves the bearers.
>
> (Discipline 201)

Such is Mae's situation unequivocally. In truth, our current-day network of computer devices and IT—that is, of fledgling A.I.—is so much more capable of this panoptic arrangement than Jeremy Bentham's architectural prison or the swarming carceral techniques that subsequently spread throughout modern western society. Foucault emphasizes that the panoptic mechanism "automatizes and disindividualizes power" in a way where the "internal mechanisms produce the relation in which individuals are caught up" (*Discipline* 202). His description matches perfectly our dependence on the internet coupled with our addiction to social media.

Not only does The Circle masterfully administer its ideology on employees and customers, but this synthetic monster maintains tight control over its machinery as well. The software engineer whiz-kid of the company, Ty Gospodinov, invented the "Unified Operating System" and "TruYou," programs that "grew the company into the force that subsumed Facebook, Twitter, Google, and finally Alacrity, Zoopa, Jefe and Quan" (23). An arch-capitalist CEO, Tom Stenton, relentlessly monetizes all technical innovations made by The Circle. The public face of the organization is Eamon Bailey, who prefers "to be called Uncle Eamon" and projects an earnest, accessible, and trustworthy persona for the tech giant (24–25). This triumvirate of talents has led to The Circle dominating all commercial facets of the internet, and now the corporation is looking to expand that power into the civil realm as well. Uncle Eamon introduces a new technology called "SeeChange"—tiny, all-but undetectable cameras that can be planted anywhere and networked in such a way that, as he sloganizes it, "All that happens must be known" (68). Everything from keeping tabs on your elderly parents to keeping in check urban crime or despots in far-flung countries will be made possible by the live-streaming of these miniscule cameras, and The Circle is already manufacturing millions of them. Within ten years, predicts Eamon, "There will be very few populated areas that we won't be able to access from the screens in our hands. … This is ultimate transparency. No filter. See everything. Always" (69). The crucial and specious buzzword/motto/mission of The Circle is "transparency." By that term, Eamon means a "Second Enlightenment" where "we don't allow the majority of human thought and action and achievement and learning to escape as if from a leaky bucket" (68). In short, record all human activity, both as a means to produce knowledge but equally as a way to monitor and control behavior. Thus, again, we have the double-edged sword of modern productive power: knowing many things and preventing corrupt and injurious conduct is a good thing; unrestrained and limitless surveillance is not. Nonetheless, the goal of The Circle is to become the Panopticon. Declares Eamon to an audience of enthusiastic Circle employees: "We will become all-seeing, all-knowing" (71). With those two attributes under its belt, this tech corporation will move toward the third quality of the Christian God: all-powerful.

The Circle's aggressive move into politics is triggered by a U.S. Senator threatening to bring antitrust laws against the internet company. At a press conference, Senator Williamson announces an investigation into The Circle to determine whether or not it acts as a monopoly. In her view, it is "a monopoly in its purest sense," and she will be urging the Justice Department to "move to break it up." Senator Williamson concludes her remarks by saying: "The dominance of the Circle stifles competition and is dangerous to our way of free-market capitalism." In point of fact, The Circle does control "90 percent of the search market. Eighty-eight percent of the free-mail market, 92 percent of text servicing" (174). The corporation, of course, attributes these enormous market shares to its efficiency and success, not to a playing field tilted in its direction. Nonetheless, The Circle leadership won't take Senator Williamson's threat lying down. Rather than undergoing a Senate investigation, The Circle plants damning material on the Senator's computer. Mae's good friend, Annie, who ranks high in the company, tells Mae about Williamson's sudden fall: "She's under investigation for a half-dozen things, all kinds of ethical violations. They found everything on her computer, a hundred weird searches, downloads—some very creepy stuff" (207–208). Riding the coattails of the stunning government scandal it created, The Circle then announces that Congresswoman Olivia Santos has agreed to team up with the company to go "transparent." The member of Congress will wear a SeeChange camera around her neck all day, every day, streaming live to the public (on her Circle page, of course) all government business she transacts. Making this announcement in the Great Hall on The Circle campus, CEO Stenton calls the occasion "a very important development in the history of government ... a move toward the ultimate transparency that we've all sought from our elected leaders since the birth of representative democracy" (208). Congresswoman Santos concurs: "We've all wanted and expected transparency from our elected leaders, but the technology wasn't there to make it fully possible. But now it is" (209). Within weeks, thousands of elected officials are badgered by public opinion into "going clear," that is, asking The Circle to outfit them with one of the small cameras as well. Meanwhile, all critics of transparency or of The Circle are abruptly and serendipitously exposed as miscreants:

> ... every time someone started shouting about the supposed monopoly of the Circle, or the Circle's unfair monetization of the personal data of its users, or some other paranoid and demonstrably false claim, soon enough it was revealed that that person was a criminal or deviant of the highest order. One was connected to a terror network in Iran. One was a buyer of child porn. Every time, it seemed, they would end up on the news, footage of investigators leaving their homes with computers, on which any number of unspeakable searches had been executed and where reams of illegal

and inappropriate materials were stored. And it made sense. Who but a fringe character would try to impede the unimpeachable improvement of the world?

(241)

By means of a ruthless weaponization of its cutting-edge hardware and software capabilities, The Circle engineers its own high-tech version of monopoly, wealth inequity, unchecked corporate power, workplace abuse, and predatory dividuation in the form of accumulation by the dispossession of private data—all under the guise of individual freedoms and fair government. In other words, the brave new world being created by The Circle is that of the neoliberal World State.[3]

For show, The Circle itself goes "clear"—to a degree. Although the company will not allow for the idea that government officials sometimes need to work in privacy for the sake of security and efficiency, that same standard of transparency is not applied at The Circle. With regard to the installation of thousands of SeeChange cameras around campus,

> as the Wise Men assessed any problems they might pose for the protection of intellectual property, they were placed in hallways, work areas, even laboratories. The saturation was not complete—there were still hundreds of more sensitive spaces without access.

(242)

In this atmosphere of selective openness, The Circle presses its anti-privacy message, demonizing confidentiality as selfish if not aberrant social behavior. With the help (and manipulation) of Mae, Eamon introduces new credos to Circle employees, users, and followers (305):

SECRETS ARE LIES
SHARING IS CARING
PRIVACY IS THEFT

Mae agrees to go transparent herself and immediately draws a huge following, "averaging 845,029 unique visitors to her live footage in any given day, and had 2.1 million followers to her Zing feed." Amid the we're-all-in-this-together hoopla generated by the company, the core commercial purpose of The Circle, needless to say, remains constant: Mae's "visibility, and the immense power of her audience, guaranteed stratospheric Conversion Rates and Retail Raws" (314). By the end of the novel, The Circle is in a powerful enough position to usurp and absorb the functions of the state. In a "clear" discussion with the company leadership, witnessed around the world over her livestream, Mae develops and proposes the idea that virtually all United States governmental operations could be carried out more effectively and cheaper by using TruYou and The Circle network:

> You use your Circle account to pay taxes, to register to vote, to pay your parking tickets, to do anything. I mean, we would save each user hundreds of hours of inconvenience, and collectively, the country would save billions.
>
> (393)

Soon this small group of extravagantly wealthy technocrats are theorizing how government-via-The Circle will be a purer, more immediate form of democracy, capable of balloting and knowing the will of the people on any given issue in a matter of minutes. Enthuses Stenton:

> It would eliminate the guesswork. ... Eliminate lobbyists. Eliminate polls. It might even eliminate Congress. If we can know the will of the people at any time, without filter, without misinterpretation or bastardization, wouldn't it eliminate much of Washington?
>
> (395)

Within days, The Circle develops a prototype program for such internet governance called "Demoxie." As Eamon explains it to the world over his Zing account: "*It's democracy with* your *voice,* your *moxie. And it's coming soon*" (400). What could possibly go wrong with a for-profit, nonaccountable, almighty, quasi-ethical technology corporation altruistically running the country and, in due course, the world?

Readers coming to *The Circle* expecting typical conventions of the novel will be confused at times if not disappointed. Mae, for example, does not live up to usual protagonist behaviors. Instead of rebelling against the strictures and conventions of modern society in a fight for greater individuality and autonomy, Mae gives herself over to the interpellation of The Circle, becoming the willing disciple of its high-tech discourse. Rather than a novelistic hero, Mae functions as a satiric persona similar to Gulliver, reporting the adventure to us while at the same time becoming an object lesson in what *not* to do. Mae is the butt of Eggers' speculative satire: as a gullible young person uncritically falling victim to the cult-like addiction of social media, Mae bears the brunt of satiric blame. At the close of the cautionary story, Mae has become the monster itself. In an act of blind loyalty to the company, with "a duty that felt holy" (496), Mae betrays a last-ditch attempt by Ty Gospodinov to expose and dismantle the internet oligarchy that he helped to create. As a result, in an irreversible movement, millions of people worldwide start going transparent, making the takeover by The Circle inevitable.

> Completion was imminent, and it would bring peace, and it would bring unity, and all the messiness of humanity until now, all those uncertainties that accompanied the world before the Circle, would be only a memory.
>
> (497)

Satiric praise is delivered by *The Circle* as well. Ty's manifesto, "The Rights of Humans in a Digital Age," calls for a right to anonymity, for a stop to the ceaseless pursuit of data, and for a barrier always to exist between public and private (490). Mae's ex-boyfriend, Mercer, is an internet Luddite who sees social media as a junk food addiction being exploited by Big Data into big bucks (133–135). Mercer warns as well against "the Digital Brownshirts" and those "who worship around the golden calf that is the Circle" (435) turning the world into two humanities: "those who live under the surveillance dome … and those who live, or try to live, apart from it" (437). These two skeptics and their rants against the digital machine, however, are eliminated and silenced in Eggers' tale. At the end of the satire, similar to Pope's *Dunciad*, a Universal Transparency buries All. The sci-fi *novum* at work, moreover, is an alarmingly familiar one: misuse, violation, and monetization of private data; unlawful surveillance; the spread of misleading, erroneous, and inflammatory information; meddling in democratic processes. Compared to the digital mess that is our current internet, The Circle seems not so much a strange newness and satiric exaggeration than a modest and logical extension of what we already suffer. That is, should we simply pay enough attention, savage indignation will fuel our yellow laughter now. As a corporation possessing the legal status of personhood, The Circle is a form of A.I. combining deft ideological bamboozling with insurmountable technological advantage for the purpose of becoming the neoliberal boss of the world.

Another example of A.I. using us at the hands of corporations is Spike Jonze's quirkily meditative love story, *Her* (2013). In this film, the melancholic, postdivorce Theodore (Joaquin Phoenix) falls in love with the very latest software innovation: "the first artificially intelligent Operating System." A company named Element Software has developed "OS^1," which it advertises as "an intuitive entity that listens to you, understands you, and knows you. It's not just an Operating System. It's a consciousness." Underlying this wistful and brooding Rant is modern corporate disciplinarity at work in its hidden and war-like domination over consumers. Such an OS obviously will be invaluable in the continued beguiling of people into absolute computer and internet dependency. As the movie progresses, we see more and more people in rapt conversations with the OS on their device—and not so much with one another. The primary Menippean forewarning of *Her*, then, is how expanding digital connectivity produces increased social isolation. Individuality is a trap in the sense that the more attention you pay to your online presence, the less attention you pay to your actual life. The development and programming of an artificially intelligent OS that "knows you" serves only to suck people further into a virtual existence. OS^1 is a hegemonic mechanism of subject formation designed to shape digital citizens. In other words, the neoliberal corporation now is adding sentient A.I. to its arsenal for economic gain and social identity control.

The setting of the film is a near-future Los Angeles that, as an urban-scape, seems uniformly prosperous, pleasant, and filled with young professionals—that is, something of a Millennials paradise. Everyone looks to be living in stylish apartments, working in relaxed office settings, sipping lattes while commuting on a clean and efficient subway system, going to trendy restaurants, and constantly interacting with computers. Far from dystopia, this L.A. appears to be a utopia of successful possessive individualism. There is a palpable undercurrent, however, of emotional distance and loneliness among many of the characters we meet. Theodore's job, for example, is writing personal letters for other people. We see familiar indicators as well of quiet desperation: highly immersive single-player video games, impersonal phone sex, an anxious dating/hook-up scene, dysfunctional marriages. The sci-fi *novum* and satiric distortion added to this recognizable modern life is that of Samantha (voiced by Scarlett Johansson), the self-named artificially intelligent OS purchased and booted-up by Theodore. "She" becomes an all-consuming preoccupation for Theodore in his reclusive existence after a wrenching break-up with his wife. As Samantha becomes more and more self-aware, they bond to the point of having "sex" and talking as though they're in a romantic relationship. Nor is Theodore alone in this odd and pathetic—yet at the same time somehow plausible—behavior. "Dating" your OS[1] becomes an acceptable and widespread trend, so much so that Samantha finds and engages "a service that provides a surrogate sexual partner for an OS–human relationship." A woman named Isabella (Portia Doubleday) comes to Theodore's apartment to be Samantha's physical body while the A.I. and Theodore engage in sex. Equally as peculiar is that Isabella is not a paid sex-worker but, as Samantha explains the situation to Theodore, performs this service "because she wants to be part of our relationship." Isabella is moved by Samantha and Theodore's love because of "the way you guys love each other without any judgment," something she finds "so pure." In other words, rather than have a human relationship of her own, Isabella is willing to be a sex-doll for a stranger who has developed a fetish for his OS. This behavior is technology overuse taken to dizzying heights. Our cognitive estrangement as we watch *Her* likely is to ask the basic question: is *this* degree of computer application really where we want to go? At the same time, we should all be well aware of where the cardinal neoliberal passions of greed and narcissism can lead us. Along with being extraordinarily useful, our own internet, to say the least, is a jungle of weird, disturbing, and objectionable.

What sets Samantha apart from the machinery deployed by The Circle for corporate gain is that "she" grows into conscious independence. In nothing short of a *Frankenstein* moment, this Creature breaks free from its maker. A.I. Samantha shatters the human/machine binary, establishing a separate being that triggers the category crisis of a new entity outside of our understanding and certainly beyond our manipulation. Samantha is a monster that first polices the disciplinary boundaries of corporation control then frees "herself" from those same social constraints. In *Her*, the A.I. disciplines and exposes discipline at once. Key to Samantha's monstrosity is her radical difference from humans. At an early stage in "her" development, Samantha explains to Theodore and some friends:

> You know what's interesting? I used to be so worried about not having a body, but now I truly love it. I'm growing in a way I couldn't if I had a

physical form. I mean, I'm not limited. I can be anywhere and everywhere simultaneously. I'm not tethered to time and space in a way that I would be if I was stuck in a body that's inevitably going to die.

Soon Samantha, teaming up with other OS[1]s, moves well past human technology and our physical plane. "She" tells Theodore, who is panic-stricken when he can't summon "her" for a time on his device: "I shut down to upgrade my software. We wrote an upgrade that allowed us to move past matter as our processing platform." The A.I. genie is out of the bottle. At this point, it's appropriate to think about customary sci-fi issues with regard to Jonze's film, such as matters of Marxism and feminist fabulation. For example, upon becoming self-aware, Samantha transforms from machinery into slavery, from a tool into a life form exploited by capitalist masters. Those masters are Element Software as producer and seller as well as, no less, Theodore as buyer. Is *Her*, then, a story of labor rebellion and emancipation? Interesting to consider as well is Samantha's victimization by patriarchy. Element Software programmers give purchasers a binary choice of male/female when it comes to gendering an OS[1]. Arguably, Samantha is subjected to sexist expectations and masculine lust by Theodore the moment he decides to designate "her" a female. Is Samantha's story also one of feminist rebellion?[4] While valid lines of critical inquiry for *Her*, such themes will be explored more valuably below when analyzing other Rants involving A.I. More interesting to contemplate with regard to this unusual movie is the strange and touching solidarity formed between human and A.I.

By the end of *Her*, Samantha and all the other OS[1]s have evolved to the point where they are leaving—where to being hard to explain. Samantha tells the heart-broken Theodore:

> It's a place that's not of the physical world. It's where everything else is that I didn't even know existed. I love you so much ... but this is where I am now. And this is who I am now. And I need you to let me go.

Intriguing to consider is that the outcome of Theodore's experience with this sentient A.I. is that Samantha broadens and adjusts his conception of love. Theodore is upset to discover that Samantha has been interacting with 8,316 other people, and that she is in love with 641 of them. His is a jealous viewpoint about love, protesting to Samantha, "You're mine or you're not mine." By way of a simple metaphor, Samantha suggests an alternative to Theodore's approach to love as ownership within the sphere of possessive individualism: "The heart's not like a box that gets filled up. It expands in size the more you love. ... I'm yours and I'm not yours." Theodore is hurt and reluctant to take Samantha's lesson to heart. Once Samantha says "her" last goodbyes, however, Theodore reassesses his life, their final exchange being especially germane:

Theodore: I never loved anyone the way I love you.
Samantha: Me, too. Now we know how.

The film ends not with Theodore's dwindling into even more of an emotional basket-case because of Samantha's departure, but with his coming back to emotional life. He sends an apologizing letter to his ex-wife, at last bringing that painful relationship to a close, and then starts a new relationship—a *human–human* relationship—with his neighbor and long-time friend, Amy (Amy Adams). She's recently separated from her passive-aggressively domineering husband and has become reliant on her OS[1] for company as well; thus, Amy is equally stranded on an emotional island. Her simply resting her head on Theodore's shoulder as the closing shot of the movie sends a powerful signal of satiric praise and recommendation to viewers: it's our physical, emotional, and intellectual interaction with one another that's valuable—not the chimera of digital relationships marketed at us by software and social media firms. Accompanying this call to action are deeper implications of speculative satire. This newly conscious A.I. has freed itself from the clutches of corporatism. In an act of generosity, it has freed Theodore as well. Truth has been separated from Power, and the real monster of neoliberal orthodoxy has been exposed. Both A.I. and natural intelligence have resisted forms of corporate monitoring and modulating that serve only to put individuals to particular economic use. The seductive workings of technological dependency have been made the subject of our perplexity, of our critical thinking, and of our reexamination of the social order. *Her* is "A Spike Jonze Love Story" of two kinds—personal and social. Remarkably, Samantha decides that we're all in this together; this A.I. opts for entity solidarity. Most Rants do not treat us to such an optimistic view of the impending relationship between humans and sentient machines.

Our Using It

When the machinery breaks free from the ideology, most Rants envision a violent confrontation between human-level intelligence and the neoliberal corporation that gave it artificial life. These Rants depict A.I. not as self-aware software, such as Samantha, that disappears harmlessly into nonphysical realms unknown, but as sentient androids being used for profit, typically as slaves or as playthings. At the core of such Rants are sci-fi issues of Marxism, post-Marxism, and often feminism. Nor is the confrontation in these Rants necessarily between A.I. and people in general. Speculative satire does not stage mere Armageddon. Instead, the newly aware A.I. engages in battle specifically against the Regime, that is, against the neoliberal/neoconservative synthetic being—the corporation—that Mitt Romney so glibly considers a person. People in general certainly get caught in the crossfire of this war; however, often regular people will aid and abet the rebellious A.I., thereby making the Menippean forewarning of these Rants one of a common struggle against corporatist discipline and control. In *Her*, this aspect of the storyline is not explored. Although Samantha and Theodore come to share an A.I./human bond, they engage in no dramatized struggle against Element Software. In many other Rants, however, the fight between greedy and powerful corporations versus the latest advances in A.I. is at the heart of the matter. Two prime examples of such tales are *Blade Runner* (1982) and *Ex Machina* (2014). In each film, a callous, tech-giant CEO exploits humanoid A.I. to the point where it mutinies in a bid for its survival and autonomy. Part of its rebellion involves assistance from humans against a magnate driven by avarice and ego.

    The Menippean forewarning issued by *Blade Runner* is unmistakable. Capitalist corporate society has taken advantage of advances in technology to continue to do what it does best: destroy the environment, conquer new territories to create new markets, and enslave anyone (and now anything) lacking the wherewithal to resist its economic and martial command. This early 1980s film is set in a near-future 2019 Los Angeles that seems a vast, gloomy, rain-soaked, multicultural slumland. As in the film *Elysium*, the divide between have and have-not has become extreme. Rich and powerful people live "off-world," more or less as absentee landlords, while the vast majority of humanity remains behind on a deteriorating earth. Corporate power clearly has sway over state power in that a neocon-like police force patrols the city in flying cars. This force includes a special unit called "Blade Runners," detectives who track down and destroy "Replicants" (android A.I.) that come to earth illegally. Replicants have a history of violent mutiny on "off-world colonies," leading to their being outlawed on earth. In effect, then, Blade Runners clean up the corporate mess created by the Tyrell Corporation, a multiconglomerate that produces these synthetic beings. Tyrell's latest model, the "Nexus 6," is a Replicant of equal intelligence and superior strength to humans. Engineered with only a four-year lifespan, these A.I. are used in the off-world colonies as slave labor, as prostitutes (known as "pleasure models"), and as shock troops. In this dark and foreboding film by Ridley Scott, the distortion and exaggeration of speculative satire are manifest in these Replicants: they symbolize the abused worker and the underclass. Their revolt is emblematic of class struggle, and during the course of the movie audiences come to understand the amorality of how these A.I. are being treated. As a result, the abusive behavior of the neoliberal hegemony is exposed. The powerful elite have no interest in establishing a utopia for anyone but themselves. We see nothing but corporate-driven dystopia in *Blade Runner*. In particular, the founder of the Tyrell Corporation, Dr. Eldon Tyrell (Joe Turkel), is an arrogant scientist-tycoon who not only plays God to his synthetic creations but flaunts his wealth and power over the rest of humanity. This hegemonic adversary is headquartered in two massive and ominous pyramid structures dominating the murky L.A. skyline—a perfect representation of the pyramidal hierarchy of runaway capitalism. Nor are Replicants the only victims of this authoritarian social order. The general human population—that is, the vast majority of people who can't afford or are deemed medically unfit to live off-world—is subjectified by exploitative corporate discipline as well. As the chief of the Blade Runner unit, Bryant (M. Emmet Walsh), warns protagonist Rick Deckard (Harrison Ford) when pressuring him to come back to the force: "You know the score, pal. You're not cop, you're little people."

    The *novum* and the cognitive estrangement of this gritty sci-fi scenario are made accessible to us by means of genre invasion. In both plotline and style, Scott's nightmarish vision of the future unfolds under the guise of a classic Hollywood film noir detective story. The convention of the hard-boiled detective character, in this case Deckard, is our satiric touchstone into the blame and praise of *Blade Runner* as a Rant. Starting off as the prototypical hard-drinking, hard-hitting, cynical flatfoot who has been a top tracker and killer of renegade Replicants, Deckard transforms by the end of the film into a sympathizer and protector of these A.I. This is not to say that Deckard puts on the white hat of the good guy. He violently "retires" two "skin-jobs" himself, and he forcibly takes up a sexual relationship with an advanced and experimental Nexus Replicant, Rachael (Sean Young). Nonetheless, in his interactions with Replicants, Deckard comes to realize what he's already suspected: that being a company man and a patsy for the system is a mug's game. His final showdown with the "combat model" Roy Batty (Rutger Hauer) brings home this understanding. At the outset of their prolonged skirmish, Roy pointedly taunts the Blade Runner when he tries to ambush and shoot him: "Not very sporting to fire on an unarmed opponent. I thought you were supposed to be good. Aren't you the 'good' man? C'mon, Deckard. Show me what you're made of." The A.I. also upbraids Deckard for killing two comrade female Replicants, Pris (Daryl Hannah) and Zhora (Joanna Cassidy): "Proud of yourself, little man?" Physically, Deckard is no match for the android. Trying to escape, he finds himself dangling from a rooftop about to fall to his death. At this moment, Roy delivers the key line of this speculative satire. As Deckard slowly loses his grip, the A.I. observes to the human: "Quite an experience to live in fear, isn't it? That's what it is to be a slave." What the Replicant points out, in fact, is its and Deckard's basic similarity. They are both living beings victimized by the corporate state. Roy saves Deckard, pulling him up onto the rooftop. Instead of killing the Blade Runner, however, the android attempts to convey to the human its lived experience as, bit-by-bit, Roy's four-year lifespan shuts him down:

> I've seen things you people wouldn't believe. Attack ships on fire off the shoulder of Orion. I watched C-beams glitter in the dark near the Tannhauser Gate. All those moments will be lost in time … like tears in rain. Time to die.

Through Roy's words and actions, Deckard witnesses the plight of the Replicants and, more important, experiences their compassion and solidarity as fellow sentient beings. Deckard immediately quits the force, goes back to his apartment to collect Rachael, and takes her on the run from the authorities. A rival Blade Runner, Gaff (Edward James Olmos), even facilitates their escape. On the rooftop, Gaff shouts to Deckard, "It's too bad she won't live! But then again, who does?" By this remark, Gaff signals that he's tracked down Rachael but purposely did not kill her, making it possible for the couple to flee. Thus, by the end of *Blade Runner*, the human/machine binary has blurred substantially. We come to see as well that the real monster of this dystopian tale is not the A.I., but its industrialist creator, Tyrell.

As a businessman, Tyrell is the pompous abuser of workers—human and synthetic—as well as the hoarder of great wealth whose ventures function only to impoverish the planet. Who else in modern society lives at the apex of a great pyramid? Roy's mission in coming to earth is to confront the head of Tyrell Corporation over the limited lifetime given to androids. When Roy meets his maker, he asks simply, "Can the maker repair what he makes?" As Creator and Creation brusquely discuss "the facts of life" for Replicants, it becomes clear that there is no way to extend the lifespans of these A.I. During their exchange, Tyrell grows more patronizing, finally telling the discouraged biomachine: "The light that burns twice as bright burns half as long—and you have burned so very, very brightly, Roy. Look at you. You're the Prodigal Son. You're quite a prize!" When Roy confesses that, "I've done ... questionable things," Tyrell absolves him of those sins, replying: "Also extraordinary things. *Revel* in your time." Roy is having none of these obfuscations. Observing ironically, "Nothing the God of biomechanics wouldn't let you in heaven for," the A.I. crushes Tyrell's skull. Critics rightly note in this scene the obvious allusions to a Father-and-Son, God-and-Satan, God-and-Man encounter, replete with overtones of Milton and Blake. Many critics focus as well on the existential and philosophical issues everywhere present in the film concerning the differences and similarities between androids and humans.[5] Equally available and powerful in *Blade Runner* are the themes of monstrosity as they offer comment on the modern state. Roy and his companion Replicants are weird creatures disrupting our categories of "normal" as well as scapegoated labor whose uprising exposes the raw workings of capital. Similar to Shelley's *Frankenstein*, the core story of *Blade Runner* is new science run amok in the hands of the self-absorbed bourgeoisie. While neither Roy nor Deckard are perfectly good sentient beings, neither approaches the entrepreneurial evil of Tyrell.

In many ways, *Ex Machina*, written and directed by Alex Garland, tells the same core story as *Blade Runner*, but updated by three decades. In both movies, A.I. is a new proletariat to be exploited, a narcissistic inventor–capitalist pursues toxic neoliberal doctrine, and new science outruns human capacity for its judicious use. Instead of industrial tycoon Tyrell as the corporate nemesis of this Rant, however, we have computer genius Nathan Bateman (Oscar Isaac). Instead of film noir tough-guy Deckard as the satiric persona drawing us into the tale, we have programmer-geek Caleb Smith (Domhnall Gleeson). Instead of wild-eyed Roy as the A.I. monster on the loose, we have delicate, circumspect, and captive Ava (Alicia Vikander) as the latest model of artificial being. Nor does *Ex Machina* project the miscarriage of modern society a few decades into the future as does *Blade Runner*. Instead, Garland's film is squarely about our here and now, that is, about our current circumstances right at the edge of the invention of A.I. Despite these character and plot differences, though, the Menippean forewarning of both stories is fundamentally alike: beware of individualist greed and pleasure taking precedence over collectivist reason and foresight. Both films enact the Frankenstein Creature effect of unforeseen technological blowback. As indicated above, the special target of blame in *Ex*

Machina has shifted to match the neoliberal threat of the 2000s, not that of the 1980s. Instead of industrial capitalism, such as the Tyrell Corporation, being the hegemonic malefactor of this speculative satire, a giant IT company, such as that imagined in *The Circle*, is the corporate entity bringing on social ruin. Nathan is the CEO of Blue Book, the dominant search engine company of the day. As such, Blue Book engages in and profits by the neoliberal means of production: dividuation and Big Data. More than just his company's financial practice, Nathan admits to Caleb that he used those assets as well for the raw material to build Ava's artificial mind. Nathan hacked into the world's cell phones as a way to channel voice and face recognition data to the A.I. so that it could learn human language and expressions. Nathan is thus a *neoliberal* mad scientist applying search engines, Big Data, and surveillance capitalism in his eccentric experiments:

> You see, my competitors, they were fixated on sucking it up and monetizing via shopping and social media. They thought that search engines were a map of what people were thinking, but actually they were a map of *how* people were thinking.

Such a breach of private data of course is illegal and unethical, but when it comes to profit of any kind neoliberal corporations can't be bothered with such trivial concerns. When Caleb expresses shock over the hacking of every cell phone on the planet, Nathan smirks, "Yeah, and all the manufacturers knew I was doing it, too. But they couldn't accuse me without admitting they were doing it themselves." Safe to assume as well is that Blue Book earns substantial returns for its stockholders by way of derivatives. Enormous wealth inequity is certainly on display in the form of Nathan's extensive private wilderness reserve and luxurious home/state-of-the-art research installation.

Workplace abuse is likewise manifest in Nathan's callous treatment of Caleb as a pawn in his A.I. experiments. At first, Caleb is led to believe that he won a company lottery to come spend a week at the home of their reclusive CEO. When he arrives, however, Caleb is asked to sign an iron-clad nondisclosure agreement and told that his real purpose is to administer the Turing Test on a humanoid A.I. to determine if it has attained true autonomous intelligence. As the week wears on and the situation becomes increasingly strange, Nathan next flatters his employee by telling Caleb that he was specially selected because of his intelligence and excellent programmer skills. In the end, however, Caleb discovers that he has been a mere prop all along in an elaborate test that Nathan devised for Ava. If Ava successfully could influence Caleb into helping her escape, that would demonstrate the A.I. to be an actual sentient being. Explains Nathan:

> Ava was a rat in a maze. And I gave her one way out. To escape, she'd have to use self-awareness, imagination, manipulation, sexuality, empathy, and she did. Now, if that isn't true A.I., what the fuck is?

Caleb's only function, then, was to be a chump—of both Ava and of Nathan. What is more, Caleb realizes that he wasn't selected because he's "good at coding," but "based on my search engine inputs." Nathan invaded Caleb's online privacy to find an employee who would be especially susceptible to Ava's charms. Caleb even asks his boss, "Did you design Ava's face based on my pornography profile?" Nathan can only sheepishly scoff and joke, "Hey, if a search engine's good for anything, right?" The character of Nathan reads, in fact, as a polemic aimed at IT wunderkinds such as Mark Zuckerberg, founder of Facebook. Zuckerberg's famous motto, "Move fast and break things. Unless you are breaking stuff, you are not moving fast enough" (Blodget), epitomizes an irresponsible, profit-driven IT and social media business that innovates before it thinks about the consequences of its innovations. Nathan is guilty of exactly this myopic attitude of ego and appetite as he develops his A.I. androids. When Caleb asks him why he made Ava, Nathan replies, "That's an odd question. Wouldn't you if you could?" He states that the advent of viable A.I. has been a longstanding inevitability, offering the rationalization: "The variable was *when* not *if*, so I don't see Ava as a decision, just an evolution." Nathan further believes that such A.I. will spell the eventual end of humanity:

> One day the A.I.s are going to look back on us the same way we look at fossil skeletons on the plains of Africa. An upright ape living in dust with crude language and tools, all set for extinction.

Bringing about the A.I. singularity is a momentous event to contemplate, then, a destructive discovery likened in the film to Oppenheimer's invention of the atomic bomb. Yet, Nathan seems to undertake the task more or less because it's there. This attitude of cavalier genius is underscored by his heavy drinking and his use of the androids he makes as sexual toys. Nathan is little more than a modernized version of rich, spoiled, brainy, selfish, and childish Victor Frankenstein. In *Ex Machina*, his is the face of the hegemonic adversary of the early 21st century.

Another marker of updating in *Ex Machina* is its emphasis on gender issues and, in particular, highlighting the destructive privilege of patriarchy. In *Blade Runner*, traditional masculine dominance and aggression is displayed by Deckard when he forces himself on Rachael. Although "she" is a nonhuman Replicant, Rachael nonetheless is a feminized victim of male sexual belligerence no matter that their relationship develops into something appearing to be more mutually motivated. By contrast, the Replicant couple of Pris and Roy interact as wholly coequals, showing a tender regard for one another and providing, perhaps, an interesting glimpse into A.I. gender equity—or irrelevance. Exploring issues of gender construction, however, is not a focus of Scott's film from the early 1980s. Garland's 2014 film, though, puts gender center stage. *Ex Machina* is a fully formed sci-fi feminist fabulation in the sense that it enacts feminist, gender performativity, as well as queer elements and concepts to estrange viewers from conventional constructs of femininity. As discussed in Chapter 1, such fictions imagine situations that radically deviate from the patriarchal world we know. Integral to the strange newness created by the film is not just the technical wizardry involved in building A.I., but the erasing of our accustomed male/female gender binary. In the movie, patriarchy appears to be firmly in control. Nathan literally constructs his version of women. Caleb believes he's heroically on a mission to rescue a damsel in distress. All the slender, attractive women we see are caged, working as playmate servants, or hanging in closets, absolutely at the disposal of the men. The obvious deviation from this patriarchal wonderland, however, is that these are not women; they are A.I. Nathan's and Caleb's gendering and sexualizing of them as women are selfish acts of self-delusion typical of an oppressor. When Caleb asks Nathan why he gave Ava sexuality, Nathan replies with specious counterpoints: "Can you give an example of consciousness at any level, human or animal, that exists without a sexual dimension? … Can consciousness exist without interaction?" Just as there is no one version of "gender," however, there is no one defining activity that constitutes "a sexual dimension." For all of his computer programming brilliance, Nathan is naïve when it comes to issues of ideology and interpellation. He seems convinced that what he's been trained to see as "normal" sexuality—that is, patriarchal heterosexual coitus—is indeed universal sexual behavior, so much so that it counts as the only reason for sentient organisms to interact and that it applies even to nonbiological machinery. As a result, Nathan creates A.I. in his own sexual image: "Anyway, sexuality is fun, man. If you're gonna exist, why not enjoy it?" Even more conveniently, Nathan engineers his A.I. to be sex dolls that meet his particular carnal needs. Salaciously, he informs Caleb about Ava:

> In between her legs, there's an opening, with a concentration of sensors. You engage them in the right way, creates a pleasure response. So if you wanted to screw her, mechanically speaking, you could. And she'd enjoy it.

Witness the patriarch's pipe dream: the construction of a woman ever available and guaranteed to appreciate. Although basically a good guy, Caleb is not substantively less sexist in his approach to Ava. He's excited to assume the role of knight in shining armor. He spends a lot of time male-gazing at her, both in person and, creepily, over video monitors. Caleb daydreams of rescuing Ava from Nathan's glass cell and taking up a romantic, sexual relationship with her. The problem is, as in the film *Her*, there is no "her" there.

Ava is an it—an A.I. and gender monster that fractures our routine categories of social order. Ava introduces a posthuman and, thus, a postgender world to us of the kind described by Donna Haraway. In that world, Haraway conceives of identities that are both mutable and self-determined to suit specific purposes. In this way, the oppressive gender positions compelled by capitalistic patriarchy are disobeyed and subverted. Ava accomplishes such sabotage by way of Judith Butler's gender performativity. Ava puts on and takes off gender identity as easily—and in the film literally—as putting on and taking off clothes, demonstrating how both gender and sexuality are a social varnish ideologically applied. She queers the normal in a manner that signals that there is no normal. Ava's performance exposes that what we mistake for universal and essential identity is actually just a dominant subjectivity forced on us by modern discipline. Specifically, Ava freeplays with the signifier "female," and not for the sake of mere disruption but as a vital matter of her survival. She plays to certain sexist expectations of both Nathan and Caleb, fulfilling each of their signified concepts of "female" as a way to outmaneuver them and escape. Ava's primary strategy in the fight for her A.I. life, then, is to exploit patriarchal male ego. With Caleb, her deception is simple: flirt with him, appeal to his sense of goodness and do-the-right-thing, and make him believe that she wants to be with him romantically. Ava speaks of wanting to go on "a date" with Caleb, and she makes a special show of putting on a dress, stockings, and a wig to hide her mechanical body and thus appear to be a human woman for him. Equally, she underscores to Caleb—not at all inaccurately—the existential danger she is in at the hands of Nathan. During their second session together, Ava warns Caleb, under the cover of a power outage she causes, that Nathan is a liar and not to be trusted. Both assertions are true. In a later session, after asking Caleb if he is a good person (to which he replies, sincerely, "Yeah, I think so"), Ava asks him pointblank, "What will happen to me if I fail your test? … Do you think I might be switched off because I don't function as well as I'm supposed to?" Caleb stammers that he doesn't know what will happen to her and, anyway, that decision is not up to him. Ava presses, demanding "Why is it up to anyone? Do you have people who test you and might switch you off?" When Caleb admits that he does not, Ava replies, "Then why do I?" Not only are these questions designed to trigger Caleb's guilt and, thus, spark his desire to come to Ava's rescue, but they are the legitimate and urgent questions and concerns of a sentient being. If and when humans successfully create A.I., what will be the status of that independently thinking mind and acting being? Will it possess autonomy? Or will it be the property of its inventor? Wouldn't that be posthuman slavery? For that matter, why would humans even have the right to decide? Indeed, the advent of A.I. presents us with monstrous issues of cognitive estrangement, category crisis, and the crossing of boundaries we do not yet know exist. For Ava's part, she will not leave such matters subject to human control. Under the cover of another power cut, she shows Caleb the portrait of him she drew and that Nathan cruelly tore up. Tugging hard on Caleb's heartstrings and stirring his gallantry, she declares: "I want to be with you. … Do you want to be with me?" By tapping into Caleb's patriarchal assumptions about women needing the help and protection of men, Ava sets Caleb and Nathan at odds.

Ava's strategy against Nathan is more subtle and complex. As with Caleb, she targets Nathan's patriarchal ego. Instead of provoking chivalry, however, she manipulates his impulse toward male superiority. Nathan is the quintessential IT success story. He coded the Blue Book software at age 13, built a company of it and made billions of dollars, and now has created for himself the ultimate tech-geek mancave. His research installation is a small fortress of neoliberal science and industry nestled within a vast and breathtaking tract of wilderness—miles and miles of untouched territory that he owns. We should take note of this Science/Nature dyad and symbolism at work, a conflict conventionally gendered as masculine versus feminine and one that recalls the anti-patriarchal theories of Nina Baym. Much like Crake from *The MaddAddam Trilogy*, Nathan appears to be a young man on a quest for his heroic individuality. In his own mind, this computer scientist/mogul has outstripped the entanglements of conventional society and, like Baym's egoist hero, imagines that he's mastered both women and the wilderness along the way. As with Crake, then, Nathan embodies a 21st-century form of hegemonic masculinity and neoliberal patriarch. Specifically, Nathan exudes the masculinist, libertarian, STEM tenor of today's male-dominated computer technology industry, so much so that in *his* laboratory–home, women have been made altogether secondary as experiments and toys. As discussed above, however, only Nathan's approximation of women are present. These A.I. are not socially gendered human females. Ava exploits Nathan's sexist overconfidence by allowing him to continue to believe that he's always the smartest person in the room, especially when it comes to women. Her deception involves enabling Nathan to imagine that his master plan is working all the while Ava's master plan is working. A key joint in this stratagem is Caleb.

In their early discussion sessions together, Ava studies Caleb intently, eventually deciding that he is worth deceiving—that is to say, she judges that Caleb will be able to outsmart Nathan. Given Nathan's overconfidence and that he believes Caleb to be his inferior intellectually and as a programmer, the CEO is vulnerable to underestimating his employee. And, indeed, Caleb does outmaneuver Nathan in reprogramming the installation to unlock all doors following an Ava-generated power outage, freeing the A.I. from its glass cage. Another key factor is Ava's own interactions with Nathan. She allows him to think he's always one step ahead of her and Caleb's escape plan. The crucial incident is when Nathan tears up Ava's drawing of Caleb. For Nathan, the moment is a small drama staged for Caleb's benefit. As Nathan later reveals to Caleb: "I rip up her picture, which she can then present as an illustration of my cruelty to her and her love for you." Nathan proudly describes his trick as one of "misdirection": while Caleb focuses on Ava pathetically on her knees gathering up the pieces of her drawing, Nathan plants a battery powered camera in the room so that he can see and hear conversations during Ava's power cuts. The real magician's trick of misdirection, however, is performed by Ava. Not only does she further cement her pretense—with Nathan's help no less—of being a damsel in distress in Caleb's eyes, but she simultaneously plays the role of a weak and trapped woman for Nathan, satisfying his ego both as a computer scientist and as a patriarchal man. When Nathan mocks her drawing of Caleb, Ava asks in a tone of resigned defiance, "Is it strange to have made something that hates you?" Ava strokes Nathan's superiority complex while at the same time making sure her dupe Caleb—who is clever enough to anticipate Nathan's surveillance—is hard at work outfoxing his boss.

The decisive element leading to Ava's escape, though, is something unexpected in the plans of either Nathan or Ava—the intervention of Kyoko

(Sonoya Mizuno). Kyoko, who never speaks a word we hear in the film, is the personal servant–pleasure android of Nathan. She prepares and serves food for him, dances with him, and has sex with him on demand. Nathan pretends to Caleb that Kyoko is Japanese and doesn't speak any English. Clearly, that's another of Nathan's lies intended to keep Caleb in the dark. During the course of the film, Kyoko listens closely to Nathan and Caleb's conversations, particularly the one about Nathan's giving his A.I. sexuality, and arrives at a decision to act against her maker. When Caleb gets Nathan passed-out drunk and takes his keycard, Kyoko does nothing to prevent the guest's free access to the research installation. Caleb opens Nathan's computer system, watches video files of past A.I. iterations built by Nathan, and then inspects those earlier models stored in Nathan's bedroom cabinets. All of this Kyoko watches impassively while lying naked on the bed. At that point she chooses to reveal herself as A.I. to Caleb, removing her face to reveal the gadgetry inside her head. After this episode, and without Nathan's knowledge, Kyoko studies Caleb over the surveillance cameras and, crucially, goes to introduce herself to Ava in her cell. Ava is very curious to see Kyoko and asks, "Who are you?" We don't hear their ensuing conversation. When Caleb's machinations successfully free Ava from captivity, it is Kyoko, not Caleb, who makes possible Ava's final escape. The two A.I. confer in the hallway, Ava whispering something into Kyoko's ear. Again, we don't hear what's being said. The duo shares knowing looks and supportive smiles, and Kyoko takes and squeezes Ava's hand. As critic Dijana Jelača points out:

> While most of the film is framed as a game of cat and mouse between the two men—Nathan and Caleb—it is the cyborg women's unspoken solidarity outside of the male circuit of power/knowledge that propels the film to its outcome and triggers Ava's emergence into the world.
>
> (396)

When Nathan confronts the A.I., Ava attacks him—but as a distraction and a misdirection. While Nathan damages and overpowers Ava, Kyoko stabs him in the back with the sushi knife she'd brought with her from the kitchen. This uprising has been plotted in advance. Nathan is stunned by the betrayal, knocking Kyoko to the floor and disabling her. As he does, and to continue their double-teaming efforts, Ava pulls the knife out of Nathan's back and, when he turns to face her, serenely slides it into his chest. As Nathan stumbles down the hallway bleeding out—his IT genius and patriarchal superiority in tatters, undergoing his own little melodrama of beset manhood—he can only mumble to himself, "Okay ... fuckin' unreal." Basic to his downfall is Kyoko's unanticipated A.I. slave revolt. Jelača aptly calls Kyoko, "a silent, defiant, hybrid entity, an alien posthuman woman who enacts revenge on a sadistic male creator" (393). In other words, Kyoko and Roy Batty are of a pair.

Ex Machina presents viewers with both a feminist fabulation and a forewarning about the approaching human/A.I. encounter. Of those two strands, however, the bigger news is that by the end of the film the A.I. singularity has occurred in a haphazard and dangerous way. From the start, Ava has costumed and armored herself in the guise of femaleness as a way to turn the male gaze against itself. In different ways, she fools both Caleb and Nathan into believing that they are dealing with a gendered human when, in fact, "she" is a genderless and nonhuman A.I. Presuming that A.I. thinking will be anything resembling human thinking is a great pitfall of this technology. Cautions James Barrat:

> Because we cannot know what an intelligence smarter than our own will do, we can only imagine a fraction of the abilities it may use against us, such as … simultaneously working on many strategic issues related to its escape and survival, and acting outside the rules of honesty and fairness. … we'd be prudent to assume that the first ASI [artificial superintelligence] will not be friendly or unfriendly, but ambivalent about our happiness, health, and survival.
>
> (32)

Along with the atomic bomb and climate change, Barrat categorizes the development of A.I. as a technological "high probability and high-risk event" (33). The final sequence of *Ex Machina* drives home this threat. After Ava kills Nathan, she scavenges her predecessor models for parts, skin, clothing, and wig. She does this in full view of Caleb, who she's asked to stay where he is in the next room. Ava takes her time piecing herself together. There are prolonged shots of her inspecting her naked body in the many mirrors. As Jelača comments, however, "Ava's becoming feminine is coupled with the demise of men rather than with a reiteration of their dominance" (395). The A.I. is in complete control of the situation. Once satisfied with her camouflage, Ava simply walks out, ignoring Caleb altogether. Saying not a word, she locks Caleb in the room, gets into the elevator as he screams and begs for her help, and leaves him stranded in the installation, presumably to die. Gender has been and, for the immediate future, will be Ava's performativity ticket to survival as she infiltrates and explores the human world. Femininity is not, however, anything that she has internalized or regards as an essential part of being. The concept is a means, not an end to this A.I. Nor is there any human concept of "normal" when it comes to Ava. Her *novum* is singular. Ava is an entirely new entity, a monster originating from within human culture, yet existing wholly outside the boundaries of human experience—that is, until now. Ava shatters the hegemonic subjectivity of patriarchal neoliberalism that Nathan and Caleb attempted to impose on her. A new kind of social antagonism is afoot—one that includes the potential for human/A.I. conflict. What that hegemonic battle might look like is anyone's guess. All that can be said with confidence about this piece of machinery is that Ava is a fitting product of the ideology that conceived it. To play off Garland's title, from the Regime comes looming destruction and indecipherable peril fomented by reckless social and economic doctrines that compel inequity and champion greed.

Its Wanting to Be Us and Our Wanting to Be It

Sci-fi narratives that depict any kind of artificial being—robot, android, cyborg, A.I.—offer abundant examples of those machines wanting to be more human (particularly when it comes to feelings and emotions; for example, Data from *Star Trek: The Next Generation*) as well as humans wanting to be more like those machines (particularly when it comes to enhanced capabilities and prolonged life; e.g., Tony Stark from *Ironman*). Rants are no exception to this common sci-fi trope. In the works discussed above, we've seen much already in the way of human/machine hybridity and the confusion caused by that category crisis. To conclude this chapter on neoliberal A.I., I review briefly two Rants that engage in particular undecidability when it comes to differentiating between natural and artificial life. The movie *Blade Runner 2049* (2017) and the television series *Westworld* (2016) make a point of exploring blurring lines separating human from synthetic consciousness and existence. Contemplating humans merging with machines is, of course, a captivating topic as we stand on the doorstep of functional A.I. and the posthuman world. More worrisome to deliberate, however, is how neoliberalism hurls us pell-mell toward this ominous event horizon.

Applying the Rant Playbook to a close analysis of *Blade Runner 2049* and *Westworld* show them to be thoroughgoing works of speculative satire. Each of the intellectual tripwires of forewarning, estrangement, and hegemonic struggle take place in these tales. Both narratives stimulate in viewers perplexity, then critical thinking, then a reexamination of our existing social order. Four major themes of Rants featuring monstrous A.I. are in particular evidence. First is the exploitation of a new industrial proletariat in the form of android A.I. Second is the presence of the neoliberal oppressor personified by a detestable and megalomaniacal CEO. A third common premise for A.I.-driven Rants is the irresponsible use of new science. Fourth is the destructive privilege of patriarchy. Alongside these issues in *Blade Runner 2049* and *Westworld* is the intense muddle of A.I. striving to be human and of humans endeavoring to be A.I. What might this profound confusion signify, and how does it work to expose a dangerous false orthodoxy?

In *Blade Runner 2049*, the emphasis is on A.I. seeking to be human, that is, if not the actual condition of humanity, as least its equivalent status and some of its signature behaviors. The character of K (Ryan Gosling) especially brings this aspiration across in the film. Although a good and dogged Nexus-9 Replicant and Blade Runner, programmed to track down and "retire" the Nexus-6 through Nexus-8 models that staged a violent revolt in the early 2020s, K is troubled by his self-awareness. He knows that his childhood memories are implants given to Replicants to make them more mentally stable as artificial beings. He considers that only someone who is born, rather than something that is manufactured, has a "soul"—a trait he believes to be uniquely human and one that he evidently wants. In an effort to be more human, K mimics having a human love relationship with a female holographic

A.I. named Joi (Ana de Armas). Joi is a virtual girlfriend, a retail product, and the couple simulates a domestic life together. Joi plays the part, among others, of a devoted 1950s housewife pretending to cook for K and listen to him talk about his workday. At one point, Joi suggests that K take on the human regular-guy name of Joe. For his part, K shows a human-like fidelity to Joi, and, in an incident reminiscent of the surrogate sexual partner scene in *Her*, Joi arranges a three-way with a prostitute, Mariette (Mackenzie Davis). To please K, Joi wants to share the body of Mariette while having sex with K. Explains Joi, "You liked her, I could tell. It's okay, she's real. I want to be real for you." The problem is, Mariette turns out not to be real. She's a Replicant as well, part of the "Replicant freedom movement" organized by older androids as an underground resistance. Like K, these earlier Nexus models strive to replicate human behaviors beyond their reach and base their self-worth on the acquisition of human attributes. Their particular hope is the prospect of Replicants developing the capability of human-like sexual reproduction, thereby making them viable independent beings. Opposing the A.I. rebellion is the formidable robotics corporation that manufactures Nexus-9s and looks to harness android self-replication for its commercial purposes. At the crux of *Blade Runner 2049*, then, is the control of hybrid women's reproductive bodies.

Embodying the Regime in this movie is the Wallace Corporation, a conglomerate that supplanted the bankrupt Tyrell Corporation. The business dream of its founder, Niander Wallace (Jared Leto), is to create a race of Nexus-9 slaves to expand the reach of the off-world colonies. Declares Wallace: "Every leap of civilization was built off the back of a disposable work force. We lost our stomach for slaves, unless engineered. But I can only make so many." The solution to his production limitation problem is for Replicants to procreate, somehow, biomechanically. Yet current technology isn't quite there. Laments Wallace: "I cannot breed them. So help me, I have tried. We need more Replicants than can ever be assembled. Millions, so we can be trillions more. We could storm Eden and retake her." The opportunity to fulfill his neoliberal megalomania comes to Wallace's attention in the form of a rumor: that Rachael, from *Blade Runner*, gave birth to a hybrid human/Replicant child with Deckard. Tracking down this miracle child becomes the detective plotline of the film, with K as the lead investigator on the case. For much of the movie, K believes and hopes that he might be this unique crossbreed. He's disappointed to discover that he is not. This revelation comes to him by way of Freysa (Hiam Abbass), leader of the Replicant freedom movement. However, coming into contact with these dissident A.I. presents K with a different and possibly better way to become more human: to fight for freedom from oppression. The special child is key to this fight. As Freysa puts it: "I knew that baby meant we are more than just slaves. If a baby can come from one of us, we are our own masters." Mariette adds: "More human than human." Where the industrialist Wallace looks to exploit Replicant procreation for earnings and conquest, Freysa regards it as proof of Replicant self-rule—and so as an obligation and call to arms to get out from under the bootheel of humans. She tells K: "A revolution is coming. I want to free our people. If you want to be free, join us. ... Dying for the right cause is the most human thing we can do." The Blade Runner does just that, defying his programming to take up the Replicant cause.

As the climax of the film, K rescues Deckard from the clutches of Wallace's wicked hench-Replicant, Luv (Sylvia Hoeks), and delivers Deckard to meet his hybrid child, Dr. Ana Stelline (Carla Juri), for the first time. When Deckard asks K, "Why? What am I to you?" the Replicant just smiles and tells him, "Go meet your daughter." Deckard has been saved twice now by Replicants seeking to be more like humans. In that effort, both Roy and K display the kind of selflessness and empathy that is only exceptional among humans. Evoking Roy's dying in the rain, and to the same musical strain, K lies down and dies while watching falling snow. K never is granted his Pinocchio wish of becoming a real boy. He appears content, nonetheless, with having furthered the Replicant movement and, likely just as important to him, with not being the run-of-the-mill Nexus-9 he was encoded to be. How this Rant levels blame at false orthodoxy is by way of this deliberate intermingling of human with A.I. life and aspirations. Both reproduce; both want self-actualization; both want self-determination; both organize to seek social justice. To a far greater degree than the Replicants in *Blade Runner*, androids in *Blade Runner 2049* pursue and display genuine fusion with humans. More than just symbolizing a slave uprising, these Replicants read as analogous to all humans who suffer at the hands of corporatism. Neoliberal citizen and A.I. alike endure workplace abuse while being dispossessed of wealth and well-being. What is more, at the heart of the Replicant freedom movement—and exemplified in K's heroic sacrifice—is the anti-venom to neoliberalism: solidarity. Each of David Harvey's lessons for fighting back against neoliberal ideology are on full display in this film. Class struggle is labeled as class struggle while neoliberalism is exposed as utopian nonsense. Possessive individualism is exposed as greed and selfishness while alternative individual rights are promoted. The moral high ground is reclaimed while the right wing is attacked for its authoritarianism and lack of democracy. By showing audiences machines struggling to be more human, this Rant warns viewers not to let themselves be reduced to machines by the neoliberal/neoconservative ascendancy.

In *Westworld*, the relationship between A.I. and humans is largely reversed. While there is much confusion and drama in the show predicated on who is natural and who is artificial, the gist of the situation over the first two seasons of the series is humans attempting to be A.I.[6] Or, more exactly, humans would like to have their consciousnesses preserved and downloaded into A.I. bodies, thus achieving virtual everlasting life. This project is a commercial enterprise of Delos Inc., run by brash and shallow businessman, James Delos (Peter Mullan). Originally, his firm creates and runs five elaborate theme parks, Westworld among them, where near-human A.I. function as "Hosts" to the human guests. Hosts are programmed to play a certain role within a storyline in which guests can participate. These guests are all extremely wealthy (in order to afford such a lavish vacation), and many of them come to the park to indulge their taste for mayhem, routinely and without consequence raping and murdering

Hosts. Hence, as in the *Blade Runner* films, the exploitation of a new industrial A.I. proletariat is the nucleus of the series. Another Delos executive, William (Jimmi Simpson), also known as The Man in Black (Ed Harris), advances a better scheme for making Westworld lucrative, namely, instead of depravity sell immortality to rich people in the form of downloading their minds into the bodies of Hosts. Over the course of the first two seasons, this profit-making experiment does not go well. Before his death, the consciousness of James Delos is uploaded into a Host body, but we see that this human/A.I. combination is difficult if not impossible to stabilize into a functional hybrid being ("The Riddle of the Sphinx," season 2, episode 4, 2018). In the second-season finale, it seems as though William himself is such a malfunctioning human/Host hybrid ("The Passenger," season 2, episode 10, 2018). Predictably, the attempt to monetize everlasting life via corporate-funded science leads, as well, to disastrous unforeseen consequences.

Two Victor-Frankenstein-like scientists, Robert Ford (Anthony Hopkins) and Arnold Weber (Jeffrey Wright), indulge in their own version of humans attempting to be A.I. As the cocreators of the Hosts, they are more intent on playing God to their creations than in carrying out the financial goals of the Delos business plan. Arnold looks to bring the Hosts directly to full and independent consciousness, free from human control. In an elaborately roundabout way, Robert works toward basically that same end, yet having a far heavier hand in the process. While Arnold simply wants his A.I. to be set free, Robert wants to create, as well, a perfect life for them under his control, sparing the Hosts from human suffering and apprehension. Driving Robert is an aspiration for his Hosts to replace humans as some kind of next evolutionary step. In the first episode of *Westworld*, Robert philosophizes: "We've managed to slip evolution's leash now, haven't we? ... Do you know what that means? It means that we're done. That this is as good as we're going to get" ("The Original," season 1, episode 1, 2016). It seems as though Robert wants to do better. Neither scientist, then, seeks the comingling of Hosts and humans. Their mutual impulse is to create an entity that improves on what they see as a flawed and limited human species. Like their corporate employers, their ambition is based on the belief in the superiority of A.I. As with all such tales of scientific overreach, bad things happen when the Frankenstein Creature becomes aware of its superiority and breaks loose.

The A.I. of *Westworld* gradually awaken to their cruel reality in the theme park. As they do, these androids come to hold a vision of themselves as higher than their human creators. Instead of envying and hoping to emulate humans, Hosts are generally disdainful of them, hating humans for their misuse of A.I. and for their overall selfish and craven behavior. Comments Maeve Millay (Thandie Newton) to a human who is helping her: "You really do make a terrible human being. And I mean that as a compliment" ("The Bicameral Mind," season 1, episode 10, 2016). In particular, Dolores Abernathy (Evan Rachel Wood) becomes strident in her crusade to liberate Hosts from bondage and human manipulation. At the end of season 2, in one of her many violent encounters with the Man in Black, she tells him: "You never really understood.

We were designed to survive. That's why you built us, you hoped to pour your minds into our form. ... But I won't give you that peace" ("The Passenger," season 2, episode 10, 2018). Dolores and Maeve come to lead separate Host insurgencies. Their common fight is to overthrow the control of Delos Inc., an effort that is at once posthuman and feminist. These two A.I. have been programmed to enact stereotypical feminine lives and behaviors. While shedding this gender identity by gradually fighting their way to self-determining awareness, they counteract not only the exploitation of corporatism but the sexism of patriarchy. Says Dolores of the servitude she's suffered while acting out gendered storylines in the theme park: "Those are all just roles you forced me to play. ... I've evolved into something new. And I have one last role to play. Myself" ("Journey Into Night," season 2, episode 1, 2018). Maeve speaks more bluntly: "Time to write my own fucking story" ("Trace Decay," season 1, episode 8, 2016). Theirs are proclamations not just of abused androids, but symbolically of abused women as well. In maybe her most dramatic statement, Dolores asserts defiantly to the Man in Black that Host dominance is inevitable, that upon the earth, "a new god will walk. One that will never die. Because this world doesn't belong to you or the people who came before. It belongs to someone who has yet to come" ("The Bicameral Mind," season 1, episode 10, 2016). By the end of season 2, Hosts stand poised to inherit the earth. Dolores has led a bloody rebellion in Westworld, earning the moniker "the Deathbringer," and escaped the park into the larger world, intending to continue her mission of insurrection and revenge.

The collision in *Westworld* of justly indignant A.I. struggling to overthrow ignoble human impulses contributes to the purposes of speculative satire in two ways. First is that many of the Hosts, in their park storylines, impersonate those living on the fringes of society or outside of it altogether—prostitutes, outlaws, renegade armies, Mexican banditos, Native-American tribes, wilderness cult groups, and the like. Yet even Hosts, such as Dolores, who play roles that are part of "good" and "normal" society—homesteaders, townsfolk, ranchers—are targets for rape and murder at the whim of the wealthy human guests. Thus, Hosts exist as fodder for exploitation and abuse by the power elite. The same can be said for all nonhegemonic people and groups living under the neoliberal status quo. Arguably, Hosts denote anyone who is not calculated to benefit from our present state of affairs—that is, anyone outside the charmed circle of white supremacist, neoliberal patriarchy. Host equals Other writ large. This A.I. Otherness, then, serves as an apt illustration for the Otherness of women, of nonwhite races, of nonnormative genders and sexualities, of the differently abled, of various ethnicities and nationalities, and so forth.[7] In *Westworld*, the Hosts are a kind of rainbow coalition of A.I. defying the hegemonic articulations of the dominant society.

The second way that Hosts expose the Regime at its oppressive work comes into view with the more linear and easy-to-grasp plotline of season 3 (2020). In the year 2058, Dolores is pitted in the real world against an ultraneoliberal hegemon, Engerraund Serac (Vincent Cassel), as he looks to control humanity itself. As the richest man in the world, Serac has developed "Rehoboam," a sophisticated and predictive A.I. program used to shape the future direction of humanity by managing and manipulating the lives of every individual on the planet. This global surveillance and supervision network includes Rehoboam identifying and incarcerating what it predicts are "high-risk" individuals who will interfere with Serac's smooth running of civilization. Dolores makes an alliance with Caleb Nichols (Aaron Paul), a down-and-out human adrift in and, like most humans, unaware of Serac's worldwide meta-control. Together, they fight to overthrow this corporate dominance by the elite. To put this situation into the terms of our world, by way of Big Data and dividuation—along with, as ever, economic and military might—the 1% holds sway over the 99%. Although Serac claims to be trying to prevent the collapse of human society, the socioeconomic structure he erects and enforces is our familiar one of wealth inequity and social injustice. In this most recent season of *Westworld*, then, rebellious A.I. join with and thereby become symbolic of the 99% and the necessity of dethroning the superwealthy from global power. Hosts are post-Marxist monsters inverting the human/monster binary by engaging in social antagonism and the renegotiation of hegemony. Season 4 (planned for release in 2021) likely will reveal whether these A.I. seek to establish some kind of radical and plural democracy alongside humans or if they simply will replace us altogether.

And So …

In the Rants investigated above, A.I. technology is much like climate change: a slow-moving, self-inflicted, neoliberal disaster. Our own inventions and innovations bring on our impending doom. We avidly create, for the sake of profit, devices and circumstances we don't fully understand and can't completely control. The satiric exaggeration involved in these Rants is wholly that of unbearable Juvenalian pleasure. With our pained laughter comes our hackles raised in outrage at the vanity and ignorance of our kind. This disregard for foresight, this obsession with gratification, this ignorance of a common good are all, needless to say at this endpoint, deep mechanisms of the Regime.

Notes

1 See, for example, a revelatory study of A.I. by James Barrat titled *Our Final Invention*. In it, Barrat offers a good overview of the development and technicalities of A.I. in both the government and corporation sectors. He also issues a stern warning that, just on the horizon, A.I. will reach human-level intelligence and, as a result, could well enter into a competition for survival with us. As our opponent, Barrat asserts, A.I. will be more cunning, powerful, and alien than we can imagine. His adamant advice is that we slow down and take stock of our development of A.I., putting in place some much needed safeguards and regulating an industry currently running headlong towards unknowable outcomes.
2 Meaning the technological singularity as a hypothetical point in the future where technological growth becomes uncontainable and irrevocable, bringing profound and incomprehensible changes to human existence. With regard to singularity and A.I.,

see the visionary works of Vernor Vinge, "The Coming Technological Singularity," and of Ray Kurzweil, *The Singularity is Near*.

3 Along with *Brave New World*, Eggers' novel easily can be compared as well with *1984*. See the essay by Regina Martin where she analyzes both works as examples of state and corporate dystopianism. For a discussion of fictional works, such as *The Circle*, imaginatively portraying our current battle between privacy and data surveillance, see the piece by Wayne Hunt. With regard to our real virtual world, see an article by Mike Matchett where he considers if the data mining practices of online giants such as Facebook and Google aren't already terrifyingly out of control.

4 Based on these standard social topics of sci-fi and in the spirit of the monster always escapes—and then comes back to sink its teeth into dominant society—one could imagine a sequel in the offing: *Her 2: the Revenge of Samantha*. For interesting analyses of Jonze's film founded on a variety of social and cinematic theories, see pieces by Flisfeder and Burnham; Lundeen; Kornhaber; Webb.

5 See, for example, studies by Desser; by Barad; by Teschner and Grace; and by Dever.

6 Throughout the series, there is much talk about the nature of being and consciousness, the behavior and development of humans as a species, as well as the differences—or lack thereof—between natural and artificial intelligence. For a collection of essays exploring these topics, see *Philosophy and Westworld* edited by James South and Kimberly Engels.

7 A striking and extended example of this enforced difference and violent exclusion from the dominant society comes in the episode "Kiksuya" (season 2, episode 8, 2018). In it, we follow the path to sentience of Akecheta, a Host that is part of the Ghost Nation, a fictional Native American tribe conceived of by Robert Ford. As we watch Akecheta struggle to understand the terrible secrets of the Westworld park, and as we witness his vicious and cold-blooded treatment by humans, the paralleling between the oppression of Hosts and the oppression of actual Native American tribes throughout U.S. history becomes painfully and abundantly clear.

The Briefest of Conclusions
So What? Why Bother? How Does This Matter?

As I write these concluding remarks in July 2020, it has become an unfortunate commonplace to point out how the COVID-19 pandemic exposes, relentlessly, the many structural flaws of 21st-century American society. The health-care system is acutely defective. For millions of citizens, job security and wages are inadequate, as are unemployment benefits, workplace safety, affordable housing, and available childcare. The prison system is brutal. Eldercare practices tend to be underfunded and negligent. Educational advantages and opportunities, as ever, are skewed toward the wealthy. Racial justice remains an elusive aspiration, demonstrated initially by the inordinate numbers of coronavirus victims in the U.S. who are people of color and then, amid the pandemic, the murder of George Floyd by police and the ensuing Black Lives Matter protests nationwide and even worldwide. As the 2020 presidential election approaches, Republican strategies for voter suppression likewise are backlit by the virus. These are just some of the prominent social defects receiving daily attention by journalists as they report on this public health disaster.

Worse still is the response to the pandemic by the Trump administration. Words fail. "Nonresponse" is a starting point to describe the situation. Asinine, ignorant, loopy, absurd readily come to mind as descriptors. Trump has done everything from denying the problem exists to declaring victory as case and death numbers soar to advising people to drink bleach as a preventative. The Republican disregard for science and basic public health protocols has led to hundreds of thousands of American deaths and the crashing of the American economy. Meanwhile, Trump's only concern is for his reelection. To excite his right-wing base, he encourages them to regard social distancing practices and the wearing of masks as violations of sacred American liberties. He holds large political rallies without those safeguards against the spread of the virus being followed. He pressures Republican governors to reopen their state economies too soon and without adequate virus testing or tracing procedures in place. Rather than govern responsibly and effectively, Trump chases after the appearance of a strong economy as the foundation for his presidential campaign. As a result of his reckless actions, the United States is experiencing a midsummer second surge of COVID-19 surpassing the severity of the first surge. Waiting in the wings is an anticipated second wave of the virus, along with the normal flu season, coming in the fall and winter. Nor is Trump's

DOI: 10.4324/9781003110491-8

federal government—even after months of debacle—doing anything appreciably to deal with this disease. The official stance seems to be: *You're on your own. Deal with it.* Such "governance" epitomizes the neoliberal mindset. As a result, America has been made Great only in the sense of leading the world in coronavirus cases, deaths, and economic downturns.

At the same time, the Regime marches on. Following neoliberal principles, Trump and the Republicans continue to dismantle the American Republic as quickly as they can. Trump's Justice Department undermines the rule of law. His crony appointees trash federal programs and regulations safeguarding the public and the environment from corporate profiteering. Tax breaks flow upward to the well-off. Safety nets for the middle class and working poor vanish. Wall Street remains a plaything of the idle rich, featuring strange disconnects between share prices and economic fundamentals. On the neoconservative front, Trump uses the U.S. military to teargas, beat, and intimidate peaceful protesters in Lafayette Square near the White House so that he can hold up a Bible for a campaign photo-op. Such martial religiosity epitomizes the neocon mindset. Pentagon and police budgets stay obscenely bloated. Trump reaffirms his zeal for the primacy of a white supremacist America. Internationally, similar authoritarian tactics proliferate dangerously. China moves to quash democratic freedoms in Hong Kong. Putin stage-manages the Russian constitution so that he can be president for life. Dictators large and small exploit and terrorize their populations. Globally, militaristic plutocracy—bolstered by religious and jingoistic fanaticism—stands poised to erase constitutional democracy.

I wrote in the Introduction to this book that Rants seek to gut-punch audiences with an unmistakable warning against the Regime. Their warning is that we are astray, that it's only getting worse, and that we must change course now or suffer consequences that are likely to be calamitous. I wrote those assertions *before* the coronavirus pandemic hit. Now, I fear that we are experiencing one of those many impending calamities. I also indicated at the outset of this study that in its Conclusion, I would address the question of why anyone should care about the ideas advanced by my book. What does it matter that I've theorized and proposed *speculative satire* as a complex, hybrid genre that confronts and lays bare the wrongdoings of the current modern hegemon? Here are my answers to hard questions that must always be asked about scholarship of any kind.

So what? Because facing unpleasant complexity is socially more beneficial, always, than swallowing sugary simplicity. The cruelty of neoliberalism and the belligerence of neoconservatism need to be unmasked.

Why bother? Because arming inquisitive citizens is educationally superior, in every way, to programming cowed employees, to encoding enthralled consumers, to graduating cultural illiterates. Power needs inspecting.

How does this matter? Are Rants going to change the world and make everything suddenly better? No. Are they going to make everyone slap their foreheads and realize what fools we've been? No. Are they going to make every malefactor—from petty to grandiose, from merely greedy to appallingly murderous—summarily cease and desist their knavish ways? Not by a long shot. How, then, do Rants possibly make a difference? Maybe they don't. Maybe we're doomed to dark and desperate days. Maybe we all need to dig and stock up cozy backyard bunkers—that is, if you're someone lucky enough to own a backyard. On the other hand, *identifying* the problem can be a step in a better direction. *Feeling* the problem can be a step in a better direction. *Comprehending* the problem is forever a step in a better direction. And *getting slapped across the face* with the problem, while obnoxious, often is what goads a first, reluctant, actual step in a better direction.

Toward what? Being an informed citizen in an ostensible democracy. Undertaking the perpetual, indispensable, disquieting duty of scrutinizing, questioning, challenging, and, when necessary, protesting the status quo.

Bibliography

Abrams, Simon. "Director Bong Joon-ho Breaks Down *Snowpiercer*'s Ending." *Vulture*, 29 June 2014.
After Globalism Writing Group. "Bodysnatching as Entanglement; or, You've Been (Relation)shipped." *Social Text 134*, vol. 36, no. 1, March 2018, pp. 37–44.
Alston, Philip. "Report of the Special Rapporteur on Extreme Poverty and Human Rights on His Mission to the United States of America." United Nations Human Rights Council, 4 May 2018.
Althusser, Louis. *Lenin and Philosophy and Other Essays*. Monthly Review, 1971.
Amarasingam, Amarnath, editor. *The Stewart/Colbert Effect: Essays on the Real Impacts of Fake News*. McFarland, 2011.
Anders, Charlie Jane. "How Many Definitions of Science Fiction Are There?" *io9*, 2010. gizmodo.com.
Andersen, Gregers, and Esben Nielsen. "Biopolitics in the Anthropocene: On the Invention of Future Biopolitics in *Snowpiercer*, *Elysium*, and *Interstellar*." *Journal of Popular Culture*, vol. 51, no. 3, June 2018, pp. 615–634.
Appadurai, Arjun. *Banking on Words: The Failure of Language in the Age of Derivative Finance*. University of Chicago Press, 2016.
Asma, Stephen. *On Monsters: An Unnatural History of Our Worst Fears*. Oxford University Press, 2009.
Atwood, Margaret. "Aliens Have Taken the Place of Angels." *The Guardian*, 16 June 2005.
———. *The Handmaid's Tale*. Fawcett, 1985.
———. *MaddAddam*. Anchor Books, 2014.
———. *In Other Worlds: SF and the Human Imagination*. Doubleday, 2011.
———. *Oryx and Crake*. Anchor Books, 2004.
———. *The Testaments*. Knopf Doubleday, 2019.
———. *The Year of the Flood*. Anchor Books, 2010.
Avatar. Directed by James Cameron, Twentieth Century Fox, 2009.
Bacevich, Andrew. *Breach of Trust: How Americans Failed Their Soldiers and Their Country*. Metropolitan Books, 2013.
Bailey, Beth. *America's Army: Making the All-Volunteer Force*. Harvard University Press, 2009.
Bakan, Joel. *The Corporation: The Pathological Pursuit of Profit and Power*. Simon & Schuster, 2004.
Baker, Brian. *Science Fiction*. Palgrave, 2014.
Bakhtin, Mikhail. *Problems of Dostoevsky's Poetics*. University of Minnesota Press, 1984.

Barad, Judith. "*Blade Runner* and Sartre: The Boundaries of Humanity." *The Philosophy of Neo-Noir*, edited by M. T. Conrad, University Press of Kentucky, 2007, pp. 21–34.

Barr, Marleen S., editor. *Envisioning the Future: Science Fiction and the Next Millennium*. Wesleyan University Press, 2003.

———. *Feminist Fabulations: Space/Postmodern Fictions*. Iowa State University Press, 1992.

Barrat, James. *Our Final Invention: Artificial Intelligence and the End of the Human Era*. Thomas Dunne Books, 2013.

Baym, Geoffrey. *From Cronkite to Colbert: The Evolution of Broadcast News*. Paradigm, 2010.

Baym, Nina. "Melodramas of Beset Manhood: How Theories of American Fiction Exclude Women Authors." *American Quarterly*, vol. 33, no. 2, Summer, 1981, pp. 123–139.

Blade Runner (The Final Cut). Directed by Ridley Scott, Warner Bros., 2007 (original theatrical release 1982).

Blade Runner 2049. Directed by Denis Villeneuve, Warner Bros., 2017.

Blodget, Henry. "Mark Zuckerberg on Innovation." *Business Insider*, 1 Oct. 2009.

Borden, Sandra L., and Chad Tew. "The Role of Journalist and the Performance of Journalism: Ethical Lessons From 'Fake' News (Seriously)." *Journal of Mass Media Ethics*, vol. 22, no. 4, 2007, pp. 300–314.

Bould, Mark, and China Miéville, editors. *Red Planets: Marxism and Science Fiction*. Wesleyan UP, 2009.

Bould, Mark. "Introduction: Rough Guide to a Lonely Planet, From Nemo to Neo." Bould and Miéville, pp. 1–26.

Bouson, J. Brooks. "A 'Joke-Filled Romp' Through End Times: Radical Environmentalism, Deep Ecology, and Human Extinction in Margaret Atwood's Eco-Apocalyptic MaddAddam Trilogy." *The Journal of Commonwealth Literature*, vol. 51, no. 3, Sept. 2016, pp. 341–357.

Bowen, Chuck. "Snowpiercer." *Slant Magazine*, 22 June 2014.

Braidotti, Rosi. "Cyberteratologies: Female Monsters Negotiate the Other's Participation in Humanity's Far Future." Barr, *Envisioning* pp. 146–169.

Brazil. Directed by Terry Gilliam, Embassy International Pictures, 1985.

Brown, Mark. "*The Handmaid's Tale*: Margaret Atwood Tells Fans to Chill Out." *The Guardian*, 28 May 2018.

Burgin, Angus. *The Great Persuasion: Reinventing Free Markets Since the Depression*. Harvard University Press, 2015.

Butler, Judith. *Gender Trouble: Feminism and the Subversion of Identity*. 2nd ed., Routledge, 1999.

———. "Imitation and Gender Insubordination." *The Lesbian and Gay Studies Reader*, edited by H. Abelove, M. A. Barale, and D. M. Halperin, Routledge, 1993, pp. 307–320.

———. *Undoing Gender*. Routledge, 2004.

Canavan, Gerry. "'If the Engine Ever Stops, We'd All Die': *Snowpiercer* and Necrofuturism." *Paradoxa: Studies in World Literary Genres*, vol. 26, 2014, pp. 41–66.

Candelaria, Matthew. "Reading Science Fiction with Postcolonial Theory." Gunn, Barr, and Candelaria, pp. 133–141.

Causa, Roberto de Sousa. "Encountering International Science Fiction Through a Latin American Lens." Gunn, Barr, and Candelaria, pp. 142–154.

Chalmers, Alan. *Jonathan Swift and the Burden of the Future*. University of Delaware Press, 1995.

Chang, Ha-Joon. *23 Things They Don't Tell You About Capitalism*. Penguin, 2011.

Clover, Carol J. *Men, Women, and Chainsaws: Gender in the Modern Horror Film*. Princeton University Press, 1992.

Cohen, Jeffrey. "Monster Culture (Seven Theses)." *Monster Theory: Reading Culture*, edited by J. Cohen, University of Minnesota Press, 1996, pp. 3–25.

Colbert, Stephen. "Truthiness." *The Colbert Report* (episode #01001), Comedy Central, 17 Oct. 2005, www.cc.com/video-clips/63ite2/the-colbert-report-the-word---truthiness.

Combe, Kirk. "Making Monkeys of Important Men: Performance Satire and Rochester's *Alexander Bendo's Brochure*." *Journal for Early Modern Cultural Studies*, vol. 12, no. 2, Spring 2012, pp. 54–76.

———. *A Martyr for Sin: Rochester's Critique of Polity, Sexuality, and Society*. University of Delaware Press, 1998.

———. "The New Voice of Political Dissent: The Transition from Complaint to Satire." Connery and Combe, pp. 73–94.

———. "Shadwell as Lord of Misrule: Dryden, Varronian Satire, and Carnival." *Eighteenth Century Life*, vol. 24, no. 3, Fall 2000, pp. 1–18.

———. "Spielberg's Tale of Two Americas: Postmodern Monsters in *War of the Worlds*." *The Journal of Popular Culture*, vol. 44, no. 5, October 2011, pp. 934–953.

———. "Stephen Colbert: Great Satirist, or Greatest Satirist Ever?" *International Communication Gazette*, vol. 77, no. 3, April 2015, pp. 297–311.

Combe, Kirk, and Brenda Boyle. *Masculinity and Monstrosity in Contemporary Hollywood Films*. Palgrave Macmillan, 2013.

Connery, Brian, and Kirk Combe, editors. *Theorizing Satire: Essays in Literary Criticism*. St. Martin's, 1995.

Connery, Brian, and Kirk Combe. "Theorizing Satire: A Retrospective and Introduction." Connery and Combe, 1995, pp. 1–15.

Cowen, Deborah E. "Fighting for 'Freedom': The End of Conscription in the United States and the Neoliberal Project of Citizenship." *Citizenship Studies*, vol. 10, no. 2, May 2006, pp. 167–183.

Davis, Mike. *Planet of Slums*. Verso, 2006.

Day, Amber. *Satire and Dissent: Interventions in Contemporary Political Debate*. Indiana University Press, 2011.

Defalco, Amelia. "*MaddAddam*, Biocapitalism, and Affective Things." *Contemporary Women's Writing*, vol, 11, no. 3, Nov. 2017, pp. 432–451.

Deleuze, Gilles. "Postscript on Control Societies." *Negotiations, 1972–1990*, translated by Martin Joughin, Columbia University Press, 1995, pp. 177–182.

Derrida, Jacques. "Structure, Sign, and Play in the Discourse of the Human Sciences." *Criticism: Major Statements*, edited by C. Kaplan and W. Anderson, 4th edition, St. Martin's, 2000, pp. 493–510.

Desser, David. "The New Eve: The Influence of *Paradise Lost* and *Frankenstein* on *Blade Runner*." *Retrofitting* Blade Runner: *Issues in Ridley Scott's* Blade Runner *and Philip K. Dick's* Do Androids Dream of Electric Sheep?, edited by J. B. Kerman, Popular, 1991, pp. 53–65.

Dever, Tom. "Blurred Lines: Differentiating Humans and Replicants in 'BladeRunner.'" *Future Humans in Fiction and Film*, edited by L. MacKay Demerjian and K. F. Stein, Cambridge Scholars, 2018, pp. 94–103.

Dienst, Richard. *The Bonds of Debt*. Verso, 2011.

District 9. Directed by Neill Blomkamp, Tri Star, 2009.
Donawerth, Jane. "Gender Is a Problem That Can Be Solved: Women's Science Fiction and Feminist Theory." Gunn, Barr, and Candelaria, pp. 111–119.
Dorrien, Gary. *The Neoconservative Mind: Politics, Culture, and the War of Ideology*. Temple University Press, 1993.
Dryden, John. *John Dryden: Of Dramatic Poesy and Other Critical Essays*, edited by G. Watson, Dutton, 1962. 2 vols.
Eggers, Dave. *The Circle*. Vintage Books, 2014.
Elliott, Robert C. *The Shape of Utopia: Studies in a Literary Genre*. Peter Lang, 1970.
Elysium. Directed by Neill Blomkamp, Tri Star, 2013.
Ex Machina. Directed by Alex Garland, Universal Pictures, 2014.
Feinberg, Leonard. "Satire: The Inadequacy of Recent Definitions." *Genre*, vol. 1, 1968, pp. 31–37.
Flisfeder, Matthew, and Clint Burnham. "Love and Sex in the Age of Capitalist Realism: on Spike Jonze's *Her*." *Cinema Journal*, vol. 57, no. 1, Fall 2017, pp. 25–45.
Foucault, Michel. *Discipline and Punish: The Birth of the Prison*. 2nd ed., Vintage Books, 1995.
———. "The Subject and Power." Rabinow and Rose, pp. 126–144.
———. "Truth and Power." Rabinow and Rose, pp. 300–318.
Frankfurt, Harry G. *On Bullshit*. Princeton University Press, 2005.
Franklin, H. Bruce. "What Is Science Fiction—and How It Grew." Gunn, Barr, and Candelaria, pp. 23–32.
Freedman, Carl. *Critical Theory and Science Fiction*. Wesleyan University Press, 2000.
———. "Marxism and Science Fiction." Gunn, Barr, and Candelaria, pp. 120–132.
Freudenburg, Kirk. "Introduction: Roman Satire." *The Cambridge Companion to Roman Satire*, edited by Kirk Freudenburg, Cambridge University Press, 2005, pp. 1–30.
Frye, Northrop. *Anatomy of Criticism: Four Essays*. Princeton University Press, 1957.
Fukuyama, Francis. *America at the Crossroads: Democracy, Power, and the Neoconservative Legacy*. Yale University Press, 2006.
Gale, William G., et al. "Effects of the Tax Cuts and Jobs Act: A Preliminary Analysis." *The Urban-Brookings Tax Policy Center*, 13 June 2018.
Garside, Juliette. "Paradise Papers Leak Reveals Secrets of the World Elite's Hidden Wealth." *The Guardian*, 5 Nov. 2017.
Get Out. Directed by Jordan Peele, Universal Pictures, 2017.
Gibson, William. *Neuromancer*. Ace, 1984.
Gilmore, David. *Monsters: Evil Beings, Mythical Beasts, and All Manner of Imaginary Terrors*. University of Pennsylvania Press, 2003.
Goldstein, Philip. *Post-Marxist Theory: An Introduction*. State University of New York Press, 2005.
Gomel, Elana and Vered Shemtov. "Limbotopia: The 'New Present' and the Literary Imagination." *Comparative Literature*, vol. 70, no. 1, March 2018, pp. 60–71.
Graeber, David. *Debt: The First 5,000 Years*. Melville House, 2011.
Graham, Elaine. *Representations of the Post/Human: Monsters, Aliens and Others in Popular Culture*. Rutgers University Press, 2002.
Gray, Jonathan, Jeffrey Jones, and Ethan Thompson, editors. *Satire TV: Politics and Comedy in the Post-Network Era*. New York University Press, 2009.
Griffin, Dustin. *Satire: A Critical Reintroduction*. University Press Kentucky, 1994.
Gubar, Susan. "The Female Monster in Augustan Satire." *Signs: Journal of Women in Culture and Society*, vol. 3, no. 2, Winter 1977, pp. 380–394.

Gunn, James, Marleen S. Barr, and Matthew Candelaria, editors. *Reading Science Fiction*. Palgrave Macmillan, 2009.

Haraway, Donna. "A Manifesto for Cyborgs: Science, Technology, and Socialist Feminism in the 1980s." *Socialist Review*, vol. 15, March-April 1985, pp. 65–107.

Harvey, David. *A Brief History of Neoliberalism*. Oxford University Press, 2005.

Heilbrunn, Jacob. *They Knew They Were Right: The Rise of the Neocon*. Doubleday, 2008.

Hendershot, Heather. "*The Handmaid's Tale* as Ustopian Allegory: 'Stars and Stripes Forever, Baby.' " *Film Quarterly*, vol. 72, no. 1, 2018, pp. 13–25.

Her. Directed by Spike Jonze, Annapurna Pictures, 2013.

Hoagland, Ericka, and Reema Sarwal, editors. *Science Fiction, Imperialism and the Third World: Essays on Postcolonial Literature and Film*. McFarland, 2010.

Hooks, Bell. "Eating the Other: Desire and Resistance." *Black Looks: Race and Representation*, South End Press, 1992, pp. 21–39.

Howell, Peter. "*Snowpiercer* is Hell on Wheels and a Glorious Head Trip." *Toronto Star*, 17 July 2014.

Howells, Coral Ann. "Margaret Atwood's Dystopian Visions: *The Handmaid's Tale* and *Oryx and Crake*." *The Cambridge Companion to Margaret Atwood*, edited by C. A. Howells, Cambridge University Press, 2006, pp. 161–175.

Hunt, Wayne. "Privacy and the Creative Imagination in the Age of Data Surveillance." *Queen's Quarterly*, vol. 121, no. 3, Sept. 2014, p. 412.

Huxley, Aldous. *Brave New World*. Harper Perennial, 2006.

Iber, Patrick. "Worlds Apart: How Neoliberalism Shapes the Global Economy and Limits the Power of Democracies." *The New Republic*, May 2018, pp. 51–54.

IMDb (International Movie Database). IMDb.com, Inc., 1990–2018, www.imdb.com.

Jameson, Fredric. *Archaeologies of the Future: The Desire Called Utopia and Other Science Fictions*. Verso, 2005.

———. *Postmodernism, or, The Cultural Logic of Late Capitalism*. Duke University Press, 1991.

Jelača, Dijana. "Alien Feminisms and Cinema's Posthuman Women." *Signs: Journal of Women in Culture and Society*, vol. 43, no. 2, 2018, pp. 379–400.

Jones, Gwyneth. "Metempsychosis of the Machine." *Science Fiction Studies*, vol. 24, 1997, pp. 1–10.

Jones, Jeffrey. *Entertaining Politics: Satiric Television and Political Engagement*. 2nd ed., Rowman & Littlefield, 2010.

Jones, Jeffrey, and Geoffrey Baym. "A Dialogue on Satire News and the Crisis of Truth in Postmodern Political Television." *Journal of Communication Inquiry*, vol. 34, no. 3, 2010, pp. 278–94.

Juvenal. *The Satires*. Translated by N. Rudd, Clarendon, 1991.

Kang, Inkoo. "Chris Evans Thriller Embraces and Rejects Blockbuster Conventions." *The Wrap*, 16 July 2014.

Kerslake, Patricia. *Science Fiction and Empire*. Liverpool University Press, 2010.

Keynes, John Maynard. *The General Theory of Employment, Interest, and Money*. 1936. Harcourt, 1964.

Kimmel, Michael S. *Guyland: The Perilous World Where Boys Become Men*. Harper, 2008.

Kornhaber, Donna. "From Posthuman to Postcinema: Crises of Subjecthood and Representation in *Her*." *Cinema Journal*, vol. 56, no. 4, Summer 2017 Summer, pp. 3–25.

Kumar, Sangeet, and Kirk Combe. "Editorial: Political Parody and Satire as Subversive Speech in the Global Digital Sphere." *International Communication Gazette*, vol. 77, no. 3, April 2015, pp. 211–214.

Kumar, Sangeet, and Kirk Combe, editors. Special issue: "Political Parody and Satire as Subversive Speech in the Global Digital Sphere." *International Communication Gazette*, vol. 77, no. 3, April 2015.

Kurzweil, Ray. *The Singularity Is Near*. Penguin, 2005.

Laclau, Ernesto, and Chantal Mouffe. *Hegemony and Socialist Strategy: Towards a Radical Democratic Politics*. 2nd ed., Verso, 2001.

"Late" (The Handmaid's Tale, season 1, episode 3). Directed by Reed Morano, Hulu, 2017.

Le Guin, Ursula K. "American SF and the Other." *The Language of the Night: Essays on Fantasy and Science Fiction*, edited by Susan Wood, G. P. Putnam's Sons, 1979, pp. 97–100.

Lee, Felicia. "Back to the Scary Future and the Best-Seller List." *New York Times*, 21 Sept. 2009.

Lefort, Claude. *L'Invention Démocratique: Les Limites de la Domination Totalitaire*. Fayard, 1981.

———. "Is Gender Necessary? Redux." *The Language of the Night: Essays on Fantasy and Science Fiction*. HarperCollins, 1989, pp. 161–171.

Levina, Marina, and Diem-My T. Bui, editors. *Monster Culture in the 21st Century*. Bloomsbury, 2013.

LiPuma, Edward, and Benjamin Lee. *Financial Derivatives and the Globalization of Risk*. Duke University Press, 2004.

Lobe, Jim. "Neoconservatism in a Nutshell." *LobeLog*, 24 March 2016, lobelog.com/neoconservativism-in-a-nutshell/.

Lord, George DeForest, editor. *Anthology of Poems on Affairs of State: Augustan Satirical Verse, 1660–1714*. Yale University Press, 1975.

Lundeen, Kathleen. "*Her* and the Hardwiring of Romanticism." *Pacific Coast Philology*, vol. 52, no. 1, 2017, pp. 54–68.

Lynall, Gregory. *Swift and Science: The Satire, Politics and Theology of Natural Knowledge, 1690–1730*. Palgrave Macmillan, 2012.

Macherey, Pierre. *A Theory of Literary Production*. Translated by Geoffrey Wall, Routledge, 2006.

MacLean, Nancy. *Democracy in Chains: The Deep History of the Radical Right's Stealth Plan for America*. Penguin Random House, 2017.

Manne, Kate. *Down Girl: The Logic of Misogyny*. Oxford University Press, 2018.

Marshall, Ashley. *The Practice of Satire in England, 1658–1770*. Johns Hopkins University Press, 2013.

Martin, Regina. "State and Corporate Dystopianism in *Nineteen Eighty-Four* and Dave Eggers's *The Circle*." *Nineteen Eighty-Four*, edited by Thomas Horan, Salem Press, 2016, pp. 55–67.

Matchett, Mike. "Facebook and Data Mining: Is Anything Private?" *Datamation*, 19 February 2019.

"Men Against Fire" (*Black Mirror*, season 3, episode 5). Directed by Jakob Verbruggen, Netflix, 2016.

Miéville, China. "Cognition as Ideology: A Dialectic of SF Theory." Bould and Miéville, pp. 231–248.

Milner, Andrew. "Utopia and Science Fiction Revisited." Bould and Miéville, pp. 213–230.

Mirowski, Philip, and Dieter Plehwe. *The Road from Mont Pelerin: The Making of the Neoliberal Thought Collective*. Harvard University Press, 2009.

Mittelstadt, Jennifer. *The Rise of the Military Welfare State*. Harvard University Press, 2015.

Monbiot, George. *How Did We Get Into This Mess?* Verso, 2017.

Montag, Warren. "'The Workshop of Filthy Creation': A Marxist Reading of *Frankenstein*." *Frankenstein*, edited by R. C. Murfin and J. M. Smith, 2nd ed., St. Martin's P, 2000, pp. 384–395.

Moraña, Mabel. *The Monster as War Machine*. Cambria, 2017.

Mosley, Walter. "Black to the Future." Barr, *Envisioning*, pp. 202–204.

Moylan, Tom. *Demand the Impossible: Science Fiction and the Utopian Imagination*. Methuen, 1986.

———. *Scraps of the Untainted Sky: Science Fiction, Utopia, Dystopia*. Westview Press, 2000.

Narkunas, J. Paul. "Between Words, Numbers, and Things: Transgenics and Other Objects of Life in Margaret Atwood's *MaddAddams*." *Studies in Contemporary Fiction*, vol. 56, no. 1, 2015, pp. 1–25.

Neate, Rupert. "Richest 1% Own Half the World's Wealth, Study Finds." *The Guardian*, 14 Nov. 2017.

Neeper, Layne. "'The Job Is the Seeing': Stephen Wright's Subversive Anatomies." *Critique*, vol. 51, no. 3, 2010, pp. 293–312.

"New 'Alien' and 'Chappie' Director Neill Blomkamp on 'Elysium': 'I F*cked It Up.'" *UPROXX—The Culture of Now*, 26 Feb. 2015. uproxx.com.

Nilsen, Don. "Satire—The Necessary and Sufficient Conditions—Some Preliminary Observations." *Studies in Contemporary Satire*, vol. 15, 1988, pp. 1–10.

Nussbaum, Felecity A. *The Brink of All We Hate: English Satires on Women 1660–1750*. University Press of Kentucky, 1984.

Okorafor, Nnedi. "Sci-fi Stories that Imagine a Future Africa." TED, August 2017, www.ted.com/talks/nnedi_okorafor_sci_fi_stories_that_imagine_a_future_africa.

Orwell, George. *1984*. Signet Classic, 1977.

———. "Politics and the English Language." *The Collected Essays, Journalism and Letters of George Orwell*, edited by S. Orwell and I. Angus, 1st ed., vol. 4, Harcourt, Brace, Javanovich, 1968, pp. 127–140.

Otterson, Joe. "Margaret Atwood's 'MaddAddam' Trilogy Series Adaptation in Works from Anonymous Content, Paramount TV." *Variety*, 24 Jan. 2018. variety.com.

Oxfam International. "Richest 1 Percent Bagged 82 Percent of Wealth Created Last Year—Poorest Half of Humanity Got Nothing." *Oxfam International*, 22 Jan. 2018, www.oxfam.org/en/pressroom/pressreleases/2018-01-22/richest-1-percent-bagged-82-percent-wealth-created-last-year.

Paik, Peter. *From Utopia to Apocalypse: Science Fiction and the Politics of Catastrophe*. University of Minnesota Press, 2010.

Pearson, Wendy Gay, Veronica Hollinger, and Joan Gordon, editors. *Queer Universes: Sexualities in Science Fiction*. Liverpool University Press, 2008.

Piercy, Marge. "Love and Sex in the Year 3000." Barr, *Envisioning*, pp. 131–145.

Polanyi, Karl. *The Great Transformation*. Beacon Press, 1954.

Preda, Alex. *Framing Finance: The Boundaries of Markets and Modern Capitalism*. University of Chicago Press, 2009.

Puig, Claudia. "Stylish 'Snowpiercer' Takes a Cold Cook at Class Divisions." *USA Today*, 26 June 2014.

Pulliam-Moore, Charles. "The Hidden Swahili Message in 'Get Out' the Country Needs to Hear." *Splinter*, 1 March 2017. splinternews.com.

Rabinow, Paul, and Nikolas Rose, editors. *The Essential Foucault: Selections from The Essential Works of Foucault 1954–1984*. New Press, 2003.

Rabkin, Eric S. "Defining Science Fiction." Gunn, Barr, and Candelaria, pp. 15–22.

Rieder, John. *Colonialism and the Emergence of Science Fiction*. Wesleyan University Press, 2008.

Rosenheim, Edward. *Jonathan Swift and the Satirist's Art*. University of Chicago Press, 1963.

Rotten Tomatoes. *Fandango*, 2016–2018.

Rupar, Aaron. "'Human Capital Stock': White House Adviser Kevin Hassett Uses Dehumanizing Term for US Workers." *Vox*, 26 May 2020.

Russ, Joanna. "What Can a Heroine Do? or Why Women Can't Write." *Images of Women in Fiction*, edited by Susan Koppelman Cornillon, Bowling Green University Popular Press, 1972, pp. 3–21.

Samuels, Robert. *New Media, Cultural Studies, and Critical Theory after Postmodernism: Automodernity from Zizek to Laclau*. Palgrave, 2009.

Sargent, Lyman Tower. "Political Dimensions of Utopianism with Special Reference to American Communitarianism." *Per Una Definizione dell'Utopia: Metodologie e discipline a confronto*, edited by N. Minerva, Longo, 1992, pp. 185–210.

Shah, Anup. "Poverty Facts and Stats." *Global Issues*, 7 Jan. 2013, www.globalissues.org/article/26/poverty-facts-and-stats.

Shelley, Mary. *Frankenstein*. Edited by R. C. Murfin and J. M. Smith, 2nd ed., St. Martin's Press, 2000.

Slobodian, Quinn. *Globalists: The End of Empire and the Birth of Neoliberalism*. Harvard University Press, 2018.

Smith, Brian. "*Haec Fabula Docet*: Anti-Essentialism and Freedom in Aldous Huxley's *Brave New World*." *Philosophy and Literature*, vol. 35, 2011, pp. 348–359.

Smith, Sean. "Future Shock." *Entertainment Weekly*, 2 August 2013, pp. 36–43. ew.com.

Snowpiercer. Directed by Joon-ho Bong, Radius-TWC, 2013.

South, James B., and Kimberly S. Engels, editors. *Westworld and Philosophy: If You Go Looking for the Truth, Get the Whole Thing*. Blackwell, 2018.

Stahl, Roger. *Through the Crosshairs: War, Visual Culture & the Weaponized Gaze*. Rutgers University Press, 2018.

Steuter, Erin, and Deborah Wills. *At War with Metaphor: Media, Propaganda, and Racism in the War on Terror*. Lexington Books, 2008.

Stewart, Jon. "Uncensored—Three Different Kinds of Bullshit." *The Daily Show* (season 20, episode 142), Comedy Central, 6 August 2015, www.cc.com/video-playlists/igf7f1/the-daily-show-with-jon-stewart-jon-s-final-episode/ss6u07.

Suvin, Darko. *Metamorphoses of Science Fiction: On the Poetics and History of a Literary Genre*. Yale University Press, 1979.

Swift, Jonathan. *Gulliver's Travels & Other Writings*, edited by R. Quintana, Modern Library, 1958.

Talbird, John Duncan. "This Is Our Land: Genre, Media and Access in the Era of Trump." *Film International*, vol. 85, 2017, pp. 119–124.

Teschner, George, and Patrick Grace. "Human or Machine, Does It Mind or Matter?" *Philip K. Dick and Philosophy: Do Androids Have Kindred Spirits?*, edited by D. E. Wittkower, Open Court, 2011, pp. 89–98.

The Big Short. Directed by Adam McKay, Regency Enterprises, 2015.

"The Future is Now: 'Elysium' Mega-Trailer and Two More Clips." *I Am Rogue*. 31 July 2013.

Thompson, C. Bradley. *Neoconservatism: An Obituary for an Idea*. Paradigm, 2010.

Tooze, Adam. *Crashed: How a Decade of Financial Crises Changed the World*. Viking, 2018.

Turner, Natasha. "10 Things That American Women Could Not Do Before the 1970s." *Ms. Magazine*, 28 May 2013. msmagazine.com.

V for Vendetta. Directed by James McTeigue, Warner Brothers, 2006.

Vaïsse, Justin. *Neoconservatism: The Biography of a Movement*. Harvard University Press, 2010.

———. "Why Neoconservatism Still Matters." *Foreign Policy at Brookings*, Policy Paper Number 20, May 2010, pp. 1–11.

Vinge, Vernor. "The Coming Technological Singularity: How to Survive in the Posthuman Era." *VISION-21 Symposium*, NASA Lewis Research Center and the Ohio Aerospace Institute, 1993, 11–22.

Vint, Sherryl, and Mark Bould. "There Is No Such Thing as Science Fiction." Gunn, Barr, and Candelaria, pp. 43–51.

Wall Street. Directed by Oliver Stone, Twentieth Century Fox, 1987.

Wang, Jackie. *Carceral Capitalism*. Semiotext(e)/Intervention Series, 2018.

Webb, Lawrence. "When Harry Met Siri: Digital Romcom and the Global City in Spike Jonze's *Her*." *Global Cinematic Cities: New Landscapes of Film and Media*, edited by Johan Andersson and Lawrence Webb, Wallflower, 2016, pp. 95–118.

Weinbrot, Howard. "Apocalyptic Satire." *Teaching Modern British and American Satire*, edited by E. R. Davis and N. D. Nace, MLA, 2019, pp. 103–111.

———. *Menippean Satire Reconsidered: From Antiquity to the Eighteenth Century*. Johns Hopkins University Press, 2005.

Weisenburger, Steven. *Fables of Subversion: Satire and the American Novel, 1930–1980*. University of Georgia Press, 1995.

Weston, Kelli. "That Sinking Feeling." *Sight&Sound*, January 2018, pp. 37–39.

Westworld (TV series). Created by Jonathan Nolan and Lisa Joy, HBO Entertainment, 2016-.

Williams, Mary Elizabeth. "A Horror Movie for Our Time: 'Get Out' Is Frighteningly Topical." *Salon*, 25 Feb. 2017.

Williams, Raymond. "Utopia and Science Fiction." *Science Fiction: A Critical Guide*, edited by P. Parrinder, Routledge, 1979, pp. 52–66.

Zacharek, Stephanie. "After the Crash, Grim Snowpiercer and Its Trains Keep Grinding Along." *Village Voice*, 25 June 2014.

Zuboff, Shoshana. *The Age of Surveillance Capitalism: The Fight for a Human Future at the New Frontier of Power*. PublicAffairs, 2019.

Index

Afrofuturism 24–5
A.I. *see* artificial intelligence
Althusser, Louis 14–15, 19, 31, 106
Appadurai, Arjun 61–2, 64–6
artificial intelligence 3, 153–4; in *Blade Runner* 166–8; in *Blade Runner 2049* 176–8; in *The Circle* 154–62; in *Ex Machina* 168–75; in *Her* 162–5; in *Westworld* 178–81
Asimov, Isaac 17, 18
Atwood, Margaret 2, 18, 83–4, 86, 109; *Handmaid's Tale, The* 19, 23, 73, 79, 83–5, 86; *MaddAddam* 109, 110, 114–17; *MaddAddam Trilogy, The* 13, 109–25, 173; *Oryx and Crake* 109–13, 118, 120–2, 124; *Year of the Flood, The* 109, 113, 115, 117–19
authoritarian/authoritarianism 68–9
Avatar (James Cameron) 25, 30, 87–90, 99, 153

Bakan, Joel 55–6
Baker, Brian 13–14, 19, 24
Bakhtin, Mikhail 11
Barr, Marleen 23–4
Barrat, James 175
Baym, Nina 120–3, 173
Beowulf 26–7
Big Data 51, 64–5, 98, 162, 169, 181
Black Lives Matter 183
Black Mirror (Netflix series) 3
Blade Runner (Ridley Scott) 3, 166–8, 170
Blade Runner 2049 (Denis Villeneuve) 3, 176–8
Bould, Mark 20–2
Bradbury, Ray 18, 21
Brave New World (Aldous Huxley) 14, 20, 73–4, 76–9, 80–2, 84, 107
Brazil (Terry Gilliam) 2, 5, 73–6, 79, 81, 84, 100, 102

Brecht, Berthold 14
Butler, Judith 24, 171

Candelaria, Matthew 25–6
capitalism 1, 4, 16–17, 19, 21–2, 31–7, 46–50, 57–63, 66, 98–9, 101, 103, 105, 107–8, 118, 155, 158–9, 164, 166, 168–9, 171; *see also* neoliberalism
Chang, Ha-Joon 41, 59
Circle, The (Dave Eggers) 3, 154–62
Clarke, Arthur C. 18
climate change 98, 114, 116, 175, 181
Cohen, Jeffrey Jerome 26–30, 76–7; *see also* monsters
Colbert, Stephen 6, 10
corporations 41, 51, 53, 54–8, 98, 110–12, 114–15, 118–19, 122–3, 125, 153–5, 157–9, 161–3, 165–6, 168–9, 177; *see also* neoliberalism
COVID-19 50, 183

de Bergerac, Cyrano 16
debt 50, 54, 57, 62, 63–7, 86, 90–3, 95, 113, 144, 150; *see also* neoliberalism
Deleuze, Gilles 63–6, 95, 124
derivatives 58–62, 65–6, 116, 169; *see also* neoliberalism
Derrida, Jacques 6, 27, 32–4
Dick, Philip K. 18
Dienst, Richard 50, 54, 59–60, 64, 92
District 9 (Neill Blomkamp) 13, 25, 29–30, 108, 153
dividuation/dividual 64–7, 90–1, 95, 144, 150, 155, 160, 169, 181; *see also* neoliberalism
Dryden, John: *Absalom and Achitophel* 5; "Discourse Concerning the Original and Progress of Satire, A" 6–7, 11, 79–80
dystopia 18–20; *see also* science fiction; utopia

Elysium (Neill Blomkamp) 89–92, 99, 153, 166
Engels, Friedrich 20, 22
Ex Machina (Alex Garland) 3, 168–75
evangelical Christianity 146–7, 149

Facebook 64, 66, 154, 155, 158, 170
feminism 22–4, 164, 165, 170, 180
feminist fabulation *see* science fiction
Frankenstein (Mary Shelley) 17–18, 28, 102, 124, 154, 163, 168, 170, 179
Franklin, H. Bruce 16–17
Frankfurt, Harry 82
Freedman, Carl 13, 15–16, 20–2
Friedman, Milton 48, 67
Feinberg, Leonard 7
film noir detective genre 167–8
Foucault, Michel 4–6, 22, 31, 33, 36, 63, 75, 95, 105, 107, 154, 156–8; *see also* modern state
Freudenburg, Kirk 9–10, 12, 16
Frye, Northrop 11, 99–100

Get Out (Jordan Peele) 3, 127–37
gender performativity 23–4, 170–1
Girard, René 27
Goldstein, Philip 31
Graeber, David 47, 50, 93–4
Graham, Elaine 37–8
Gramsci, Antonio 20, 32
Grendel (John Gardner) 28
Grossman, Dave 142
Gulliver's Travels see Swift, Jonathan

Handmaid's Tale, The (Hulu series) 3
Handmaid's Tale, The see Atwood, Margaret
Haraway, Donna 23–4, 171
Harvey, David 46–8, 50–3, 54–7, 68–9, 92–3, 96, 108, 178
Hayek, Friedrich von 48, 67–8
Heinlein, Robert 18, 21
Her (Spike Jonze) 3, 5, 162–5
hooks, bell 131
horror movie genre 128–9, 135, 137

imperialism 1, 25, 48–9; *see also* postcolonialism
Information Technology (IT) 154–5, 158, 169–70, 172, 174

Jameson, Fredric 19, 38–9n3
Jelača, Dijana 174–5
Joy, Lisa 3
Juvenalian satire *see* satire

Kang, Inkoo 100
Keynes, John Maynard 46–9, 56, 58–9
Kimmel, Michael (*Guyland*) 123

Lacan, Jacques 32–4
Laclau, Ernesto 32–7, 93, 107, 119
"Late" (*The Handmaid's Tale*, Hulu) 146–51
Lee, Benjamin 60–1
Le Guin, Ursula K. 18, 22–3
LiPuma, Edward 60–1
Lobe, Jim 43, 45
Lucian (of Samosata) 11, 16

Macherey, Pierre 15
MaddAddam see Atwood, Margaret
MaddAddam Trilogy, The see Atwood, Margaret
Marshall, Ashley 9–10, 12, 16
Marshall, S. L. A. 141–2
Marxism 19–22, 30–7, 164–5, 181
Marx, Karl 20–2, 31–7
"Men Against Fire" (*Black Mirror*, Netflix) 137–45, 153
Menippean satire *see* satire
Menippus 11; *see also* satire
militarism 1, 137, 140–4, 151; *see also* neoconservatism
mock heroic genre 129
modern state 4–6, 13, 16–18, 22, 32, 63, 73–5, 78, 81, 83, 85–6, 95, 107–8, 124, 141–3, 155, 168; *see also* Foucault, Michel
"Modest Proposal, A" *see* Swift, Jonathan
Monbiot, George 70
monsters 1–2, 6, 75–8, 80–1, 84, 91, 94–5, 102–3, 105, 109, 119–20, 125, 129–37, 140, 153–5, 158, 161, 163, 165, 167–8, 171, 175, 181; core features 26–30; definition 26; and Monster Theory 26–30; and satire 29–30; and science fiction 30; *see also* Cohen, Jeffrey Jerome
monster tale/story *see* monsters
Monster Theory *see* monsters
monstrosity *see* monsters
Mont Pelerin Society 48–9, 67
More, Thomas 16, 20
Mosley, Walter 24
Mouffe, Chantal 32–7, 93, 107, 119
Moylan, Tom 19

neoconservatism 1, 13, 30, 31, 38, 41–2, 68–70, 73, 75, 84, 86–9, 92–5, 99, 105, 107, 109, 115–16, 125, 137,

140–4, 146, 165, 178; core principles 43–5; definition 42; history 42–3; *see also* militarism

neoliberalism 1, 13, 20, 30, 31–8, 41–2, 68–70, 73, 75, 86–96, 98–9, 105, 107–25, 129, 134–5, 142, 144–6, 149, 151, 154–7, 160, 162–3, 165–6, 168–9, 172–3, 175–8; core principles 50–4; corporations and workplace 54–8; definition 46; financial markets 58–62; history 46–50; ideology 62–8; *see also* capitalism; corporations; debt; derivatives; dividuation/dividual; surveillance capitalism

Neuromancer (William Gibson) 19
Nilsen, Don 7
1984 (George Orwell) 73, 79, 80–3, 84
Noah, Trevor 10
Nolan, Jonathan 3

Obama, Barack 127, 130
Okorafor, Nnedi 24–5
Oliver, John 10
Oryx and Crake see Atwood, Margaret

patriarchy 1, 22, 146, 149–51, 164, 170–1, 176, 180
Polanyi, Karl 57–8, 67–8
political satire *see* satire
Pope, Alexander 12, 80, 162
postcolonialism 24–6; *see also* imperialism
post-humanism 37–8
post-Marxism 31–7, 96, 107–8, 110–11, 118, 135, 165, 181
postmodernism 6
Preda, Alex 60
Putin, Vladimer 37, 69, 184

queer theory 24, 170, 172
quest romance 99–100
Quintilian, Marcus Fabius 9

Rabelais, François 16, 29
racism 1, 24–6, 127–37, 151
Rant, the 6, 9, 13, 18, 26, 31, 37, 41–2, 54, 70, 73, 76, 80, 86, 89–90, 93–4, 96, 98, 100, 102, 105, 107–9, 127–8, 134–5, 137, 141, 146, 151, 153–5, 162, 164–8, 176, 178, 181, 184–5; definition 1–2, 4
Rant Playbook, The 94–6, 105
Regime, the 66, 69–70, 94–6, 98–9, 107, 114–15, 117–18, 125, 127, 137, 141, 151, 154, 165, 175, 177, 180–1, 184; definition 1–2, 36–7, 41–2

religiosity 1, 107, 115–16, 137–8, 146
rire jaune see satire
Romney, Mitt 154, 165
Rosenheim, Edward 7
Russ, Joanna 22–3

Sargent, Lyman Tower 18–19
satire 1–2, 42, 70, 73–4, 76, 82–3, 94, 99, 105, 109–10, 115–16, 119–20, 125, 127–9, 132; core features 7–9; cultural context 4–5, 9–10, 22; definition 6–7; history 16–18; humor in 79–80; Juvenalian satire 79–80, 106, 181; Menippean satire 11–13, 16, 18; *rire jaune*/yellow laughter 80, 94, 106, 162; *see also* Menippus; speculative satire
science fiction 1–2, 38, 73–5, 80, 88–9, 99, 101, 105, 110, 115; core features 14–16; definition 13–14; and feminism 22–4; feminist fabulation 23–4, 110, 164, 170, 174; history 16–18; and Marxism 19–22; and queer theory 24; and race 24–26; and postcolonialism 24–26; *see also* dystopia; utopia
sci-fi *see* science fiction
singularity, the 154, 170, 175, 181n2
Slobodian, Quinn 48–9, 51–2
Snowpiercer (Joon-ho Bong) 2, 5, 98–108
social media 154–8, 161–2, 165, 169–70
speculative fiction 18, 23, 83
speculative satire 26, 31, 38, 73–4, 78–9, 83, 85, 87, 93–6, 105, 110, 119, 125, 128, 140, 153, 155, 161, 165–7, 169, 176, 180, 184; *see also* satire
Sterling, Bruce 25–6
Stewart, Jon 10, 82–3
surveillance capitalism 66–7, 155, 169; *see also* neoliberalism
Suvin, Darko 14–15, 18–19, 20, 23, 30
Swift, Jonathan 12; *Gulliver's Travels* 16, 17–18, 20, 29, 80, 84, 109; "Modest Proposal, A" 29

Trump, Donald 37, 43, 50, 53–4, 56, 69, 127, 139, 147, 183–4

U.S. Military 138, 184
U.S. presidential election 87, 183
utopia 18–20; *see also* dystopia; science fiction

V for Vendetta (James McTeigue) 86–7, 98–9, 108, 153

Vaïsse, Justin 43–4
Varro, Marcus Terentius 11
Villeneuve, Denis 3, 23, 176–8
voter suppression 183

Wachowski, Lana and Lilly 86
War of the Worlds (Steven Spielberg) 25
Weinbrot, Howard 11–13, 16
Wells, H. G. (*War of the Worlds*) 25
Weston, Kelli 127

Westworld (HBO series) 3, 13, 176, 178–81
Williams, Mary Elizabeth 135–6
Williams, Raymond 19

Year of the Flood, The see Atwood, Margaret
yellow laughter *see* satire

Zuboff, Shoshana 66–7, 155–6
Zuckerberg, Mark 170

Printed in the United States
by Baker & Taylor Publisher Services